ETHIOPIA: THE ERA OF THE PRINCES

ETHIOPIA: THE ERA OF
THE PRINCES

The Challenge of Islam and
the Re-unification of the Christian Empire
1769–1855

———————*———————

MORDECHAI ABIR

Institute of Asian and African Studies
The Hebrew University of Jerusalem

LONGMANS

LONGMANS, GREEN AND CO LTD
London and Harlow
*Associated companies, branches and representatives
throughout the world*

© Longmans, Green and Co Ltd 1968

First published 1968

Made and printed in Great Britain by
William Clowes and Sons, Limited, London and Beccles

To my wife,
who shared the agonies –
and the pleasures –
of producing this book

Acknowledgements

I wish to thank 'The Friends of the Hebrew University of Jerusalem' (United Kingdom) for their financial aid throughout the period of research for this book. For the transliteration of names and words from Ethiopian languages I am indebted to my friend Dr Abraham Demoz (H.S.I.U.), who at the same time does not share responsibility for any mistakes. I am also indebted to Mr Shlomo Bachrach for reading the manuscript and correcting my English as far as he could. I wish also to mention my loyal secretary Mrs B. Katz, who struggled with my manuscript until it was finished. My colleagues in the history, sociology and geography departments of Haile Selassie I University (Addis Ababa) especially Professor S. Rubenson, should also be mentioned for the valuable advice which I have received from them. Last, but not least, I wish to thank my teachers and friends Professor Roland Oliver (S.O.A.S., London) for his encouragement and help, and Professor David Ayalon (Hebrew University, Jerusalem) for all he has done for me.

Note: Foreign terms and titles have been transcribed in a spelling that was felt to be adequate for the purpose, and foreign terms and titles, especially Ethiopian titles, have been italicized; the diacritical marks required for an exact phonetic rendition have been omitted in order to facilitate reading.

Four errors in the maps were observed too late for emendation in this edition: on page 28 DAMOT should be placed slightly more to the south; on page 45 for 'Derila' read 'Derita'; on page 74 for 'Sakko' read 'Sakka'; on page 145 for 'Muger R.' read 'Mugher R.'

Contents

Contents

Key to the lettering used on the maps

SHOWA .... Kingdoms

BOTOR .... Principalities

ENDERTA .... Provinces and districts

HABAB .... Tribes

xi

Illustrations

Maps

In those days there was no king in Israel:
every man did that which was right in his own eyes.

Book of Judges, chapter 21, verse 25, King James edition

who, in varying degrees, had mixed with earlier settlers. These Cushites then absorbed groups of Arabian immigrants who exerted upon them strong cultural and linguistic influences, but the resulting Axumite culture was far from being Semitic and had many specific Cushitic traits. However, the relationship between Semitic and Cushitic elements in the Axumite culture and the origins of the Axumite kingdom is still an open question.[1]

The only valid criterion for classification in Ethiopia may well be a linguistic one. With such a criterion in mind, and on the basis of the present linguistic pattern, one may say that the major recipients of Semitic influences were the people who are now called Tigrean and Amhara. These Semitized people, conscious and proud of their Semitic heritage, have been the ones who more or less dominated the history of the country (an important exception is the Zagwe period in the twelfth and thirteenth centuries, but even the Zagwe adopted much of the heritage of their predecessors) since the rise of Axum.

The physical nature of Ethiopia, added to the pride, individuality and independence of character of the population of the country, made the establishment of a political unit of any size or cohesion in any part of the country a major achievement. Prolonging the existence of such a unit against the natural tendencies towards fragmentation, which the physical characteristics of the country promote, was an even greater achievement.

The cultural and historical traditions and experience brought by Semitic immigrants, coupled with those which existed in the highlands, were an important factor in the achievement of unification. To some extent unification was also promoted by the lucrative trade of the highlands, which whetted the appetite of some groups for acquiring more revenue through state organization. Such was probably the case with the founders of the Axumite Empire. Once successful, they used their revenues and political organization to expand their territory. No less important for unity was the introduction of Christianity which, in itself and through its close connection with the rulers, tended to increase the cohesion of the people and their ties to their kings. The Solomonic myth, introduced with the decline of the Axumite Empire,

[1] Haberland, E., *Untersuchungen zum äthiopischen Konigtum*, Wiesbaden, 1965; Ullendorff, E., *The Ethiopians*, London, 1965.

when more cement was needed to patch up the cracking wall of unity, was an outstanding example of the importance of the Semitic heritage combined with Christianity. It is nevertheless a great wonder that in the later centuries, separated from the rest of Christianity and faced with the challenge of Islam, the Axumite Christian heritage continued to provide the unifying factor even when used by the Zagwe–Agaw dynasty.

While the Ethiopian plateau is generally fertile, well watered and has a pleasant climate, the coast of the Red Sea bordering on the plateau is to a large extent desert, exceedingly hot and unhealthy. In part it is volcanic country, broken, salty and with solidified lava streams; some parts are rocky and others are sandy. It is not surprising that the peoples living on the plateau always abhorred the coast and left it to nomadic pasturalists, who continuously fought among themselves for the meagre livelihood which such a country afforded. The comparatively lucrative trade of the highlands nevertheless attracted immigrant merchants, and Arab communities were to be found along the Ethiopian coast at the time of the emergence of Islam in Arabia; thus from the seventh century the Ethiopian coast underwent a relatively peaceful process of Islamization. Within a few centuries of the advent of Islam, a number of Muslim principalities emerged on the Ethiopian coast and, by-passing the Christian north, Islam started penetrating from the coast along the Harari plateau into Showa and the southern part of the highlands.

For a number of centuries Christian and Muslim principalities existed side by side in relative harmony. The Zagwe dynasty was hardly interested in the area beyond Lasta to the south, and on the other hand Christian Ethiopia had very little to fear from the weak and divided Muslim kingdoms. Only after the rise of the new Solomonic dynasty with Yekune Amlak in 1270 was a new policy of containing the Muslim principalities adopted. Still, the motivation for this policy was to a large extent political and commercial rather than religious. The wars of the thirteenth, fourteenth and even fifteenth centuries could be considered a struggle for authority, revenue and land between neighbouring political units.

The idea of a *Jihad* against Christian Ethiopia began to emerge only at the end of the fifteenth century, as a result of the overwhelming success of the wars carried out by the revived Solomonic dynasty against the Muslim principalities in the southern part of the highlands and on the coast. These wars, which may have started from purely political and commercial motives, quickly took on a religious character. The growing frustration and anger of the Muslims coupled with the appearance of the Ottomans in the Red Sea basin (1516) and the introduction of firearms into the area seriously aggravated the situation. Ahmad Grañ, a minor chief of the Adal kingdom, provided the needed leadership; and the masses of impoverished nomads, given an ideology and reinforced by a small number of Turks armed with firearms, united in a *Jihad* which threatened the existence of Christian Ethiopia in the second quarter of the sixteenth century. Probably only the timely intervention of the Portuguese, who landed a few hundred soldiers carrying firearms at Massawa, in 1541, saved Christian Ethiopia. But it was, ironically, the invasion of Ethiopia by the Galla in about the middle of the century which finally ended the Muslim threat. Having invaded the country, the Galla unintentionally came between the Christian and Muslim rivals, gave the Christians a much-needed breathing space, and broke the Muslim attack. Once the drive of the Muslims was broken and the chances for easy loot in the highlands faded away, the nomadic Muslim tribes of the coastal belt returned to their temporarily interrupted internal wars, and the Muslim front threatening Ethiopia disintegrated.

That Ahmad Grañ was temporarily successful in the conquest of Ethiopia is not at all surprising. The questions are why Grañ did not appear in the centuries after the rise of Islam, and why Islam (which had emerged triumphant in other mountain fortresses such as the Maghreb and Persia) failed to prevail in a country just across the Red Sea from its birthplace.

After the defeat of the Ottomans in Tigre, following their attempt to get a foothold in the highlands, and after the collapse of the Harar kingdom in the second half of the sixteenth century, a number of Muslim Amirates, Sultanates and principalities emerged along the coast and in some peripheral areas of the highlands. However, they were militarily and politically insignificant and constituted no major threat to Christian Ethiopia. In fact, most of them did not last very long, and only in places suitable to agriculture, or of commercial significance because of their connection with the highlands, did political units of limited importance continue to exist. The Somali returned to simple tribal organization, and the Afar Sultanates slowly shrank into loose tribal groupings with coastal villages, under chiefs carrying the proud but empty title of Sultan. Even Harar, at one time the centre of the Adal Empire, shrivelled into a small commercial city-state.

The Ottomans were driven out of the Yemen as early as the seventeenth century, and the Zaydi Imams, having conquered the coastal plains, also gained some authority on the northern Somali coast. The Pasha of Jedda was still the master of the *Pashalik* of *al Habasha*; but the latter consisted only of the islands of Massawa and Sawakin, and of a dubious claim to the whole coast of Ethiopia as far as Cape Guardafui. By the second half of the eighteenth century Ottoman authority in the Hijaz was so weak that the Ethiopian coast, having lost its commercial importance as a result of the decline of the Red Sea trade and the instability in Ethiopia, was left altogether to local rulers.

Once the Muslim threat was over, relations between Christian Ethiopia and the Muslim authorities on the coast improved. While the Gondarine Emperors reconciled themselves to their Muslim subjects, adjustment to the presence of Catholicism, in its Jesuit form as introduced by the Portuguese, was far more difficult. The orthodox Ethiopian Church, faced by the growth of Catholic influence in the beginning of the seventeenth century, considered this new threat to its existence at least as formidable as the Islamic threat, and again closed its ranks to fight for survival. Just when it seemed that Catholicism was about to emerge victorious in Ethiopia, Emperor Susenyos having become a Catholic, the tide was turned by the Ethiopian Church and in 1632 Susenyos was forced to abdicate in favour of his son Fasilidas. Fasilidas renewed the alliance between the ruling house and the Coptic Church and expelled all the Jesuits from Ethiopia. The Muslim coastal rulers willingly agreed to prevent *Ferenjoch* (Franks) from reaching the highlands and for the next two centuries Ethiopia was again virtually cut off from Christian Europe.

After a century of partial consolidation, reunification and 'glorious isolation' under relatively gifted emperors, Ethiopia again entered a period of anarchy in the second quarter of the eighteenth century. Fortunately for Christian Ethiopia, this coincided with a further disintegration of government, law and order along the Muslim coast which was probably accelerated by the general economic and political stagnation of the countries of the Red Sea basin.

As the Galla who invaded Ethiopia in the sixteenth century were deeply disunited, had no 'ideology' and were only seeking a better land to settle in, the Ethiopian rulers considered the Galla invasion far less serious than the Muslim threat. However, the fact was that the Galla migration had far-reaching consequences for the future of Ethiopia. From the sixteenth century until the nineteenth the Galla advancing from the south along the Rift Valley lakes occupied part of the Harar plateau, subjugated most of Showa, advanced as far as Lasta and penetrated the Sidama countries. They methodically displaced or absorbed the Amhara Sidama and Agaw peoples in the provinces they conquered and by the second half of the eighteenth century they had begun to invade the heart of the Christian Amhara-Tigrean provinces in the north. While this was happening the Solomonic dynasty had deprived itself of some of its most important assets. Since the beginning of the seventeenth century it had completely given up its mobility and settled for the comforts of a court life in Gondar, and after the expulsion of the Portugese, it had cut itself off from the material resources of the Christian world. In the eighteenth century the emperors began to rely more and more upon Galla troops and had slowly allowed the Galla chiefs to replace the Tigrean and Amhara nobility in their courts. Once the court of the Solomonic rulers in Gondar became dominated by Galla elements whose daughters the emperors married, it no longer represented the Christian Semitized Ethiopia and was no longer able to provide the link which held the country together. Thus, since about the middle of the eighteenth century the disuniting factors in the country completely triumphed, and had it not been for the fact that the Galla themselves lacked a unifying 'ideology', the country would have passed altogether into the hands of the Galla immigrants.[1]

The term *Zamana Masafint* means literally the era of the princes. However, in Ethiopian history the period called *Zamana Masafint* is understood by many to be the era of the judges, in the Biblical sense. This term usually pertains to the period from 1769 to 1855 when the regional rulers held the real power in the country and the King of Kings in Gondar became but a puppet in the hands of his regents, who, from the last decades of the eighteenth century, were of Galla origin.

During the *Zamana Masafint* the deeply divided Christian Amhara-Tigrean Ethiopia faced the threat of submersion and Islamization as a result of a growing fusion of Galla and Muslim interests in the highlands.

The Zagwe Agaw dynasty, which ruled Ethiopia in the twelfth and thirteenth centuries, tried to adapt itself to the Christian Semitic heritage of Axum, but was nevertheless not completely accepted by the Semitized Christian population. The Galla rulers in northern Ethiopia, although some superficially adopted Christianity, never genuinely accepted the heritage of Axum and were always considered intruders by the Semitized population. The Galla masses, in most cases, were not attracted by the Ethiopian church in its debased state in the *Zamana Masafint*, especially as it represented part of the culture of their enemies. On the other hand, the defusion of Islam in Ethiopia, which had been revived from the beginning of the nineteenth century, was very successful with the Galla, because, among other reasons, Muslim society was a society of equals, irrespective of culture and origin. Moreover, Muslim elements, indigenous and foreign, monopolized the economy of the country and made their trading caravans the vehicle by which the principles

[1] For further reading on this period, see: Chihab ed-Din Ahmed Ben Abd el-Qader (Arab Faqih): Futuh al-Habasha—*Histoire de la conquête de l'Abyssinie*, translated and edited by René Basset, Paris, 1897 (Vol. I, Arabic text); Cerulli, E.: *Documenti arabi per la storia dell'Ethiopia*, Rome, 1931; Huntingford, G. W. B.: *The Glorious Victories of Amda Seyon*, Oxford, 1965; Basset, R.: 'Études sur l'histoire d'Ethiopie', *Journal Asiatique*, Paris, 1882; Kammerer, A.: *La Mer Rouge, l'Abyssinie et l'Arabie depuis l'antiquité*, Cairo, 1929–52; Budge, Sir E. A. Wallis: *A History of Ethiopia, Nubia and Abyssinia*, London, 1928; Trimingham, J. S.: *Islam in Ethiopia*, London, 1965; Beckingham, C. F., and Huntingford, G. W. B.: *Some Records of Ethiopia 1593–1646*, London, 1954; Ullendorff, E.: *The Ethiopians*, London, 1965.

of Islam were brought to the remotest parts of the highlands. This coincided with the great changes in Galla society, which necessitated the adoption of a unifying 'ideology' which Galla lacked in the past.

The threat to traditional Ethiopia became even more ominous with the conquest of the Sudan and most of the Red Sea littoral by Muhammad Ali. Although the Egyptian ruler was not driven by religious zeal, the fact that Ethiopia was surrounded by an aggressive Muslim power indirectly furthered the spread of Islam and brought nearer the fusion of Galla and Muslim interests. The Egyptians, who had an exaggerated idea of the economic potentialities of Ethiopia because of the character of the trade of this country, might have wanted to conquer Ethiopia; but faced with the opposition of the strong European powers, they were content to control the outlets of Ethiopia's trade and meddle with its politics through contacts with the leadership of the Muslim population and some of the Galla rulers.

The failure of the Galla to establish their hegemony in Ethiopia in the nineteenth century was due, aside from the traditional Galla disunity, mainly to three factors.

While the Galla still abhorred the use of firearms even in the nineteenth century, the Tigreans and the Amhara adopted this revolutionary instrument of war at an early stage. Moreover, following Bonaparte's invasion of Egypt, European powers made their appearance in the Red Sea and gradually changed the whole political balance in the area. In truth, although the Europeans might have had a sentimental attitude towards Christian Ethiopia engulfed by the Muslim sea, their policy concerning Ethiopia was mainly motivated by power politics and, to a lesser extent, by the possibility of developing profitable trade relations with the highlands. Still, the European interests restrained and confined the Muslim power around Ethiopia and enabled the Tigrean and Amharan nobles to acquire large quantities of firearms. The final, but most important factor to influence developments in northern Ethiopia, was the reaction of the Amhara Tigrean nobility, population and clergy to the growth of Galla power and to the Islamic tendencies of the Galla rulers. It was especially the continuous territorial expansion of the Galla tribes at the expense of the Amhara and the Tigreans which convinced the latter of the need to revive the Christian kingdom.

The Christian church, which might have provided the core around which such a movement could have united, was occupied with ecclesiastic controversies and rather added to the confusion and disunity of the Christian masses. The nobility of Tigre was first to try to achieve unification, but was far too divided within its ranks and was above all unable to build a common front with the Amhara. The Amhara lords and people, who were at first slower to react to the Galla pressure, finally took the initiative after the death of Seb'agadis in 1831, a course which led to the emergence of King of Kings, Teodros.

Today, more than ever, Teodros is considered among the Ethiopian intelligentsia as the father of modern Ethiopia, the unselfish revolutionary idealist and great reformer. In fact, however, by the time of his death in 1868 Teodros was completely rejected by his own people, and Ethiopia was then at least as disunited and as torn by internal wars as it had been in the past. The battle of Maqdala, which brought an end to the reign of Teodros, was but the final death blow to a kingdom which was dying anyway. In an effort to reunify Christian semitized Ethiopia and adapt it to the nineteenth century, Teodros challenged Islam and the Galla and tried to reform overnight institutions and traditions which had existed practically unchanged for hundreds of years. Thus from the beginning of his reign, without even consolidating his hold over the territories he had conquered, he involved himself in a struggle with the most powerful elements in Ethiopia: the church, the nobility, Islam and the Galla, all at one time. Finally, through his impatience and harshness he lost even the support of the simple people whose imagination he had fired in his rise to power.

The Showan dynasty which rules Ethiopia today is also in many ways a product of the *Zamana Masafint*, but its methods and approach were evolutionary and more traditional. The rulers of this dynasty had methodically built up a territorial base with a highly centralized administration from which they could launch further expansion. Much as they wanted to rid themselves of the traditional nobility, they were realistic and bided their time, only slowly limiting the authority of the regional rulers. They pampered the church but at the same time tried to control it and use its power for their own ends. They also wished to modernize their country but they comprehended that this could not be done overnight. Finally and most importantly, they realized that the Muslims and the great masses of Galla who outnumbered the Christian Amhara and Tigreans put together were in Ethiopia to stay and could be neither annihilated nor ignored. They therefore formulated a policy of complete religious tolerance alongside an effort to Amharize and Christianize the Galla. This policy, which still guides the Ethiopian authorities today, was aimed at bringing some cohesion to the deeply divided country while still preserving Amhara Christian predominancy.

Teodros and the house of Showa represent the age-old conflict between the revolutionary approach and the evolutionary approach. Which is preferable and which is the more suited to the complex situation of Ethiopia is still an open question.

The decline of the Muslim coast
of Ethiopia

Even after the Portuguese became the virtual masters of the
Indian Ocean in the sixteenth century some of the trade with
India and the Far East continued to reach the Red Sea. The port
of Jedda and to a lesser degree the port of Mokha were the
centres of this trade, which was to a large extent transit trade.
From Jedda large quantities of Indian products as well as
Mokha coffee were reshipped to Egypt, to the Near East, and
even to Europe. Still, a sizeable part of the products of the Far
East were destined for the inhabitants of Arabia and for the
pilgrims who came to the Hijaz from all corners of the Muslim
world.

The Ethiopian foreign trade was, during the same period, only
a minor branch of the Red Sea trade. Boats from Mokha and
Jedda supplied Ethiopia through its different ports with small
quantities of Indian and European products, mainly cloth, beads,
metals and metal products and a small number of matchlocks.
The same boats carried away the limited but lucrative produce
of Ethiopia, gold, ivory, musk, skins, some agricultural products
and slaves.[1] 'Abyssinian slaves' were in great demand in the
Muslim world. The males were esteemed for their courage, hon-
esty and loyalty. However, the demand was above all for young
Ethiopian females who became concubines and wives of their
owners. Many were bought by pilgrims returning from Mecca
to their own countries. Others were acquired by the local popu-

---

[1] Bruce, J.: *Travels to Discover the Sources of the Nile in the Years 1768,
1769, 1770, 1771, 1772 and 1773*, Edinburgh, MDCCXC, Vol. III, p. 54;
Valentia, V. G.: *Voyages and Travels in India, Ceylon, the Red Sea, Abyssinia
and Egypt in the Years 1802, 1803, 1804, 1805 and 1806*, London, 1809,
Vol. II, pp. 55–6, 362–3; India Office: Home Miscellaneous, 436, p. 76,
Taylor, 30.9.1791; India Office: Factory Records, Egypt and Red Sea, Vol.
VI, No. 393, 'A sketch, etc.'; Ibid., p. 301, Sir Home Popham, 26.7.1802;
India Office: Marine Miscellaneous, Vol. 891, report from 15.7.1790, p. 117;
Ibid., pp. 281–6, Lt. Maxfield, 22.7.1805; Public Record Office: Foreign
Office, Abyssinia, 1/1, pp. 4–9, Valentia, 13.9.1808.

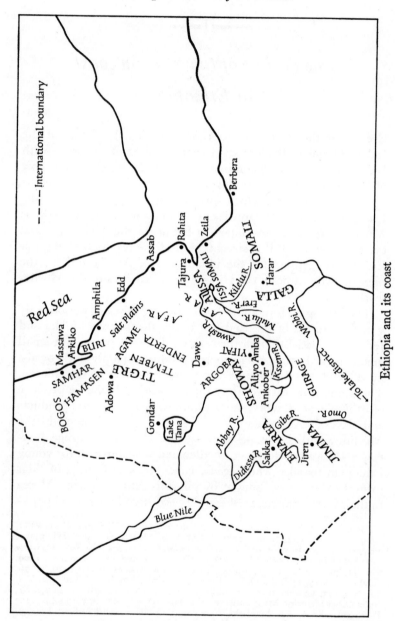

Ethiopia and its coast

lation in Arabia so that by the nineteenth century only few Arabs in the towns of the Hijaz did not have some Ethiopian blood in their veins.[1]

Although the limited quantities of Ethiopian gold and ivory and much of the coffee produced in the Yemen were taken by the Indian merchants in exchange for the produce of the Far East, Arabia had a very unfavourable balance of trade with India. In consequence large quantities of specie were carried away each year by the 'India fleet' returning from the Red Sea to Bombay, Surat, Calcutta, Mangalore and the Far East.[2] However, as a consequence of the political and economic decline of the Ottoman Empire since the seventeenth century, the constant monetary drain on the Empire could not continue for ever. Moreover, the gradual failure of law and order in many parts of the Empire and especially in Arabia affected the *Haj*, since potential pilgrims and merchants were reluctant to risk their life and property in the dangerous trip to the Hijaz. Therefore this important source of revenue to the Red Sea countries was gradually shrinking. Furthermore, the unstable political situation in Egypt and the growing rapacity of the Mameluks brought ruin upon this once rich country. In the eighteenth century the Mameluk *Beys* endeavoured to supplement their dwindling income by imposing heavier taxes on trade, and by exacting from the foreign merchants loans which they never intended to repay. The natural outcome of this situation was that most of the foreign merchants left Egypt, and the trade in this country came nearly to a standstill.

By the last quarter of the eighteenth century it was quite evident that the economy of the Red Sea basin was stagnating, and bewildered Indian merchants were looking for reasons for the great decline in the volume of their trade with this area.[3]

[1] Burckhardt, J. L.: *Travels in Arabia*, London, 1829, pp. 120, 186–8; Sulivan, G. L.: *Dhow Chasing in Zanzibar Waters and on the Eastern Coast of Arabia*, London, 1873, pp. 399–400, 410; Wellsted, J. R.: *Travels in Arabia*, London, 1838, Vol. I, p. 389; India Office: Bombay Secret Proceedings, Range Series, 385, Vol. 49, p. 3339, Finlay, 1823.

[2] Marine Misc., Vol. 891, p. 182, report from 15.8.1790; P.R.O.: Foreign Office, Abyssinia, 1/1, p. 5, Valentia, 1808; Factory Records, Egypt and Red Sea, Vol. VI, Fisher's papers, No. 234, pp. 45–60, July, 1801.

[3] Factory Records, Egypt and Red Sea, Vol. VI, Fisher's papers, No. 234, pp. 45–60, July, 1801; Marine Misc., Vol. 891, p. 183, report from 15.8.1790; Valentia, Vol. III, pp. 271–2.

In 1811 Muhammad Ali, the Pasha of Egypt, embarked upon the reconquest of the Hijaz from the Wahabis in the name of his master, the Ottoman Sultan. Within a few decades Muhammad Ali succeeded in uniting most of the coast of the Red Sea under his rule. For the first time in centuries the area enjoyed relative security and was open to direct European trade through Egypt. The expenditure of the Egyptian government by far surpassed its revenues from taxation in the Hijaz, and the soldiers of the large Egyptian corps in Arabia spent most of their pay (when they received it) on local produce and services.[1] The coffee trade of the Yemen was revived, and large quantities of coffee were sent through Jedda to Egypt, Turkey, and Europe, while American ships arriving at Mokha took sizeable quantities of Yemeni and Harari coffee to the United States.[2]

With the establishment of a mild, unfanatical government in the holy places, the relative order and security in the areas under Muhammad Ali, and the growing safety on the sea and land routes, the *Haj* not only recovered its past dimensions but by far surpassed them. Tens of thousands of pilgrims from all over the Muslim world flocked to Mecca and Medina[3] and the fair of Jedda was renewed and was visited by many merchants from Turkey, Albania, Iraq, Persia, Egypt, the Maghreb, India, Indonesia and other places.[4] Within a decade of Muhammad Ali's invasion of Arabia the economy of most of the Red Sea basin began to revive, and by the 1830's this revival reached its peak.[5]

[1] France, Ministère des Affaires Étrangères: Correspondance Commerciale (et Consulaire), Jidda, Vol. I, Fresnel, 9.3.1840; Burckhardt, *Arabia*, pp. 50–1.

[2] Valentia, Vol. II, pp. 363, 402; Range, 383, Vol. 16, p. 1811, 29.12.1809; *Annales Maritimes*, 1er semestre, 1853, p. 243; Home Misc., 494, p. 511, William Jacob, 8.12.1807.

[3] Burckhardt, *Arabia*, pp. 187–8; Wellsted, J. R.: *Travels in Arabia*, London, 1838, Vol. II, pp. 264–5, 269–70; France, Ministère de la Marine: Dossier Lefebvre, C.C. 7, Ancienne carton, No. 1467, Instruction pour Lefebvre; France, Ministère de la France d'Outre-Mer: Océan Indien, Carton 22–117, 1846–52, memorandum from 14.1.1850; France, Ministère des Affaires Étrangères: Mémoires et Documents, Afrique, pp. 330–40, Fresnel, September, 1845.

[4] Wellsted (*Arabia*, Vol. II, pp. 265, 269) estimated the number of pilgrims in 1831 to be 120,000. See also: Burckhardt, *Arabia*, pp. 187–8; France, Ministère des Affaires Étrangères: Correspondance Commerciale, Jidda, Vol. I, Fresnel, 9.3.1840; Ministère des Affaires Étrangères: Mémoires et Documents, Afrique, Vol. 13, pp. 330–40, Fresnel, September, 1845.

[5] Wellsted, *Arabia*, Vol. II, pp. 264–5, 269–70; Low, C. R.: *History of the Indian Navy*, Vol. II, p. 30; C. & C., Jidda, Vol. I, Fresnel report, 1839–40; Correspondance Commerciale, Massouah, Vol. I, Degoutin, 2.9.1843.

MASSAWA AND ARKIKO

The plain of the Samhar, which separates the Ethiopian highlands from the sea, is only about fifty miles wide at a point opposite Massawa. It is at this point that the Ethiopian escarpments are nearest to the sea. Although the Samhar had been overrun by the Beja and other nomadic peoples since the end of the seventh century, and the port of Massawa had been in Ottoman hands since 1557, Massawa with its excellent harbour had served for many centuries as the main port of Ethiopia. The people of the highlands, coming down to the coast for trade and other purposes, always preferred to descend to the sea at this point, as they were able to make most of their journey through the familiar highlands.

During the seventeenth and eighteenth centuries, the Samhar came gradually under the Belau aristocrats who were the offspring of Belau women and the Ottoman soldiers originally brought to garrison Massawa. The chiefs of the Belaus who usually resided in the village of Arkiko were given the title of *Na'ib*[1] and were recognized by the Ottomans as the rulers of the plain of Samhar in the name of the Sultan. The Belaus preserved their military organization in the form of a militia, theoretically at the service of the Ottoman Empire, and under the command of a *Kyahia* and a *Sirdar*.[2] While the *Na'ib* was appointed by the Pasha of Jedda, the *Sirdar* and the *Kyahia* in their turn were appointed by the governor of Massawa. The power of the *Na'ib* of Arkiko steadily grew during the eighteenth century, until by the second half of the century he was considered the most powerful local ruler on the Ethiopian coast. His authority was recognized to some degree by all the nomadic tribes in the Samhar plain, and extended into the coastal belt as far as Sawakin. In fact, having accepted to some extent the overlordship of the rulers of Tigre, the authority of the *Na'ib* extended into parts of the province of Hamasen, within the Ethiopian highlands.[3]

[1] Literally, deputy.
[2] The *Sirdar* was the actual commander of the troops while the *Kyahia* was some sort of a judge of the soldiers and their families. See: Ministère des Affaires Étrangères: Correspondance Politique, Égypte, Massouah, 1840–53, Degoutin, p. 119, 15.5.1844.
[3] Lejean, G.: *Voyage en Abyssinie*, Paris, 1868, p. 56; Trimingham, J. S.: *Islam in Ethiopia*, London, 1965, p. 169; Ruppell, E.: *Reise in Abyssinien*, Frankfurt am Main, 1838, Vol. I, pp. 167–8; Combes, E., and Tamisier, M.: *Voyage en Abyssinie*, Paris, 1838, Vol. I, pp. 92–3.

The town of Massawa was built on an island separated from the mainland by a few hundred feet of water. As the island was waterless and was economically dependent on Ethiopian trade going through the Samhar, the Ottomans reached an agreement with the *Na'ib* by which the Belaus were paid the sum of 1,050 thalers per month to supply the island with water and to protect the caravans crossing the Samhar. As a result of the general decline of the trade of the Red Sea in the second half of the eighteenth century, the revenue of Massawa was so reduced that the Ottoman governor was withdrawn from the island and it was left in the hands of the *Na'ib*. When the British traveller Bruce reached Massawa in 1769, the *Na'ib* of Arkiko was the *de facto* ruler of Massawa and could be considered semi-independent.[1] This situation prevailed until the end of 1808 when *Sharif* Ghaleb of Mecca sent troops to Massawa to establish his authority.[2] After the Egyptians invaded the Hijaz in 1811 a small Wahabi fleet tried to capture Massawa, but it was repulsed by the Belaus and by the population of Massawa.[3] Massawa was occupied by the Egyptians at the end of 1813 following the appointment of Ahmad Tusun Pasha, the son of Muhammad Ali, as governor of the *Wilaya* of Jedda and *al Habasha* by a Sultanic *Firman*.[4] As Muhammad Ali could not spare more than sixty soldiers and a *Kaimakam* to garrison Massawa,[5] and as the people of Arkiko held the key to the trade of Massawa, the authority of the *Na'ib* over the Samhar was confirmed, and the monthly payment to the people of Arkiko was continued. The tiny Egyptian garrison in Massawa hardly affected the situation in the area. On the contrary, as a result of a quarrel between the governor of Massawa and the *Na'ib* of Arkiko in 1826 over the monthly payment to Arkiko, the Egyptian garrison was forced to withdraw from Massawa. Only some time later, after an

[1] Bruce, Vol. I, p. 275; Ibid., Vol. III, pp. 4–5; I.O., F.R., Egypt and Red Sea, Vol. VI, No. 393, 'A sketch, etc.', from the end of the eighteenth century; Valentia, Vol. II, pp. 249–50; Combes and Tamisier, Vol. I, p. 92.
[2] F.O., Abyssinia, 1/1, p. 80, Salt, 1810. Salt, H.: *A Voyage to Abyssinia, etc., in the Years 1809 and 1810*, London, 1814, p. 496; Range, 383, Vol. 32, p. 835; Combes and Tamisier, Vol. I, p. 92.
[3] Ruppell, E.: *Reise in Abyssinien*, Frankfurt am Main, 1838, Vol. I, p. 188.
[4] Amin Sami: *Taqwim al-Nil*, Cairo, 1927, Vol. II, p. 252, on the fifth of Shawal, 1230 A.H. (1813); A.E., C. & C., Mokha, Vol. 1710–1829, p. 44.
[5] See: Ruppell, Vol. I, p. 188.

6

appeal by the population to the governor of the Hijaz, was an Egyptian detachment sent again to garrison the island.[1]

The significance of Massawa was its being the most important outlet for Ethiopia's exportable produce. The island of Massawa, its markets and shops served as a meeting-place between the merchants of Ethiopia and merchants from India and Arabia. Massawa's mercantile community was made up of a handful of Banyan merchants, a number of Arabs from the Yemen and Jedda, and a few hundred local Muslims. Most of the local merchants, the so-called *Jabartis* (Ethiopian Muslims), were small-scale retail merchants. But some took a very active part in the caravan trade with Adowa, Gondar, Gojjam and south-western Ethiopia. Others owned a number of boats which traded with Arabia, and went as far east as the Persian Gulf and India.[2]

Three factors greatly influenced the trade of Massawa. The first was the rainy season in the interior between June and October, which brought all caravan trade in Ethiopia to a halt. The second was the season of the *Haj* in the Hijaz, which brought a large number of pilgrims to Massawa on their way to or from the Hijaz. The presence of the pilgrims in Massawa greatly increased commercial activities, and provided for more frequent communication with the opposite Arab coast. The final factor was the departure of the Indian merchants from Massawa towards the end of August, before the Monsoon changed its course in the Indian Ocean and made it impossible to reach India within the same year. Besides those constant factors governing the trade of Massawa, the economy of the island was greatly influenced by the political situation in northern Ethiopia. Wars in the interior usually caused a reduction of trade in Massawa, whereas in years of peace the trade of Massawa increased.

In the second part of the eighteenth century and the first

---

[1] Ruppell, Vol. I, p. 189. For a few months in 1832/3 the island was in the hands of the rebel Turkchi Bilmas. Combes and Tamisier, Vol. I, pp. 93–4.
[2] Ministère des Affaires Étrangères: Correspondance Commerciale (et Consulaire), Massawa, Vol. I, Degoutin, 20.4.1841; Bibliothèque Nationale, Paris: d'Abbadie Papers, Catalogue France, Nouvelle Acquisition No. 21301, p. 68, para. 201, p. 28, para. 69; Ibid., p. 145; F.N.A. 21300, pp. 1, 236–238, 295, 335; *Athenaeum*. London Literary and Critical Journal, No. 1105, from 1848; Range, 388, Vol. 61, No. 2709, Nott, 1838; Rochet d'Héricourt, M. & D., Vol. 63, p. 250.

7

decades of the nineteenth, the trade of Massawa declined and became of little importance, although Massawa was still the main commercial outlet of Ethiopia.[1] Massawa, like the other trading centres of the Red Sea, suffered from the general stagnation of the trade of the region. In addition Massawa was affected by the absence of a strong authority in the area, by the growing greed of the *Na'ib* and by the continuous civil wars in northern Ethiopia. Not until the conquest of the Hijaz and the Sudan by Muhammad Ali and the renewal of the *Haj*, and its unprecedented growth after the second decade of the nineteenth century, did trade revive in the Red Sea.[2] By the 1840's the town, which at the beginning of the century had a population of about 2,000, had nearly 5,000 inhabitants. The island of Massawa became too small for such a population and for the many caravan merchants visiting the coast. Many of the inhabitants, especially the rich merchants, moved to the mainland where they built their permanent homes. Larger quantities of gold, musk, ivory, and agricultural products were brought to the island; however, the most noticeable development was in the slave trade there, probably as a result of the growing demand for Ethiopian slaves in the Hijaz and in other markets of the Muslim world. Nevertheless, according to the customs returns of Massawa, the trade of the island did not amount to even half a million thalers per year.[3]

An observer could not but be impressed by the quantities of gold, musk and ivory, and the number of slaves passing through Massawa. To anyone who did not know the potentialities of the Ethiopian highlands it would have appeared that much more could be gained from the Ethiopian trade if a stronger government could be established along the main caravan routes, and if a curb could be put on the wholesale smuggling which went on through Massawa itself and through the many little harbours along the coast.

[1] India Office: Home Misc., 436, p. 76, Taylor, 30.7.1791; I.O.F.R., Egypt and Red Sea, Vol. VI, pp. 301–2, Home Popham, 20. 7. 1802; F.O., Abyssinia, 1/1, p. 9, Valentia, 13.9.1808. 'Massawa is at present the only port through which any article can be conveyed to Abyssinia, and there are no Banyans or other merchants in the place who could purchase the cargo of a ship and make immediate payment.'
[2] F.O., Abyssinia, 1/2, Mount Norris, 19.3.1831, pp. 80–2.
[3] Ruppell, Vol. I, p. 191.

HARAR

After the disintegration of the great Harar kingdom in the second half of the sixteenth century, and until the second half of the nineteenth century, the town of Harar was the seat of an Amirate which, although small in size, was noted as a centre of trade and Islamic learning on the Horn of Africa. However, even after Galla pressure and internal wars caused the centre of the old Harar empire to be moved to Aussa in the Afar country, the rivalry within the local ruling house of Harar continued; and this, combined with other political, military and economic factors, caused the Amirate to decline steadily during the seventeenth, eighteenth and nineteenth centuries until its conquest by the Egyptians in 1875.[1]

The original population of Harar was of Hamitic stock called Adere. Although it was supplemented throughout the eighteenth and nineteenth centuries by Somali, Galla and Afar settlers, the number of inhabitants in the town slowly diminished. By the second quarter of the nineteenth century the town, which could hold 40,000 to 50,000 people, had only about 12,000 to 14,000 inhabitants.[2]

Harar was surrounded by a constantly irrigated belt of gardens and orchards, many kinds of fruits and vegetables, coffee, saffron and *qat*[3] were grown. Beyond the circle of the town gardens the Hararis had cultivated a belt of cereals. Beyond this, as far as the borders of Showa on the one side, and to the limits of the Harar plateau in the direction of the sea on the other, the land belonged nominally to the Amir but was in fact in the hands of Galla and Somali tribes.

Although it employed a smaller proportion of the population of Harar, trade was as important to the town's economy as was

[1] Cerulli, E.: 'Gli Emiri di Harar dal secolo XIII alla conquista egiziana', *Rassegna di Studi Ethiopici*, Anno 2 (1942), Rome, pp. 3–20. See: 'Deterioration of Quality of Coins in Harar', *University College of Addis Ababa Ethnological Society, Bulletin No. 10*, July–December, 1960; Yusuf Ahmed: *An Enquiring Into Some Aspects of the Economy of Harar (1825–75)*, p. 35, footnote.

[2] Rochet d'Héricourt: *Voyage sur la côte orientale de la Mer Rouge, dans le pays d'Adel et le royaume de Choa*, Paris, 1841, p. 332; Kielmaier, *The Friend of Africa*, published by the Society for the Extinction of the Slave Trade, Vol. I, p. 90, November, 1840.

[3] A plant of low narcotic content whose leaves are chewed by the people of southern Arabia and the Horn of Africa as a stimulant.

agriculture. Harari caravans traded with the rich provinces of southern Ethiopia, with Showa, and with the Ogaden. From Harar, caravans went to Zeila and to the fair of Berbera, driving hundreds of slaves and carrying products of the Ethiopian plateau as well as sizeable quantities of coffee, saffron, *qat* and cereals produced in the vicinity of Harar.

Towards the end of the eighteenth century, the Galla tribes in the region of Harar were still slowly expanding their territories at the expense of their neighbours. They squeezed the Afar out of the last fertile areas which they possessed on the edges of the Harar plateau. They completely overran the region between Harar and Showa, which was considered the property of the *Amir*. They fought the Somalis to the south and to the west of the town, and they slowly penetrated even the lands held by Hararis a short distance from the town.[1]

Many Galla tribes in the Harar district adopted Islam at an early period and settled down on land which they conquered or received from the Amir. The growing sedentary element among them was called *Qottu*, while those remaining nomadic cattle-breeders were called *Prontuma*. The *Qottu* Galla, who lacked central authority and who were an easier prey for the Amir's army, tended to recognize the authority of the Amir, as did some of the more sedentary Somali tribes in the vicinity of Harar. They paid some tribute and from time to time gave the Amir presents for recognizing their rights to the land, and for the investiture of their chiefs. The *Prontuma*, on their part, continued to be completely independent and did not recognize any authority but that of their elected office-holders.[2] Probably in order to pacify the Galla and strengthen their authority, the Amirs married into neighbouring Galla and Somali tribes. Thus the influence of the surrounding tribes on the affairs of Harar was slowly growing.[3]

[1] Abbadie, F.N.A. 21302, p. 346; Ibid., 21303, p. 186, letter from Taurin Cahagne, 2.8.1881; Cruttenden, C. J.: *Memoir of the Western Edour Tribes*, Bombay, 1848, p. 181; Barker, W.: *Journal of the Royal Geographical Society*, Vol. 12, pp. 238, 240; M. & D., Vol. 13, pp. 192, 230–2, Combes, 20.4.1840, 1.7.1840.
[2] *Bulletin de la Société Khédiviale de Géographie du Caire*, 1876; Moktar, M.: *Notes sur le Pays de Harar*, p. 381; *University College of Addis Ababa Ethnological Society, Bulletin No. 10*, July–December, 1960; Yusuf Ahmed: *An Enquiring Into Some Aspects of the Economy of Harar (1825–75)*, p. 21.
[3] For many years the Amirs of Harar intermarried with the Bartiri tribe.

At the end of the eighteenth century and the beginning of the nineteenth, during the reign of the strong Amir, Ahmad Muhammad, the Galla were kept at bay and the caravan routes into the interior were opened to trade and travellers.[1] However, after the death of Ahmad Muhammad, the authority of the Amirs was badly shaken as a result of internal strife within the ruling family, a problem which had affected the stability of Harar since the death of Nur Ibn Mujahid. As the succession to the Amirate could be either primogeniture or through the eldest member of the family, the authority of each Amir was challenged by many claimants to the throne. According to the practice in Ethiopia, the Amirs imprisoned all their male relatives in order to ensure the succession to their sons.[2] Nevertheless, as some claimants to the throne had the support of their mothers' tribes, many wars of succession broke out.[3] The Galla and Somali tribes took advantage of the confused situation and invaded the area adjacent to the town. The small standing army of the Amir was helpless in the face of the many incursions of the tribes, and the Amir was forced to carry out constant raids against his neighbours in order to preserve the little authority that he still had, and to keep the fields around the town safe and the caravan routes open. However, even the harshest measures did not succeed in containing the Galla. By the second quarter of the nineteenth century the people of Harar were not even safe in their own fields and orchards within sight of the town's walls. Herds were driven away in broad daylight while grazing near the walls and military escorts had to be provided for those working in the fields.[4] If

---

Cruttenden, C. J.: *Memoir of the Western Edour Tribes*, Bombay, 1848, p. 198. The grandfather of Amir Abu Baker (1834–52) was from the Alla Galla. Abbadie, F.N.A. 21302, p. 25.

[1] Salt, H.: *A Voyage to Abyssinia, etc., in the Years 1809 and 1810*, London, 1814, Appendix V.

[2] Cruttenden, *Edour*, p. 181; Abbadie, F.N.A. 21302, p. 15, para. 21, 23.11.1840; Paulitschke, P.: *Harar*, Leipzig, 1888, p. 205. See similarity in the dynasty of Showa, p. 165 below.

[3] Harris, W. C.: *The Highlands of Aethiopia*, London, 1844, Vol. I, pp. 381–2; India Office: Bombay Proceedings, Lantern Gallery 166, No. 2482, para. 17, Harris, 1841; Paulitschke, P.: *Harar*, Leipzig, 1888, p. 227; Burton, R. F.: *First Footsteps in East Africa*, London, 1894, Vol. II, p. 18, footnote 2; L.G., 301, No. 482, para. 5, Playfair, 7.4.1856; *Bulletin de la Société Khédiviale de Géographie du Caire*, 1876; Moktar, M.: *Notes sur le pays de Harar*, pp. 385–6.

[4] Abbadie, F.N.A. 21302, p. 346; Cruttenden, *Edour*, p. 181; Barker,

orchards and fields were not destroyed and if the trade routes were kept open at all, it was due to the payment of many 'presents' to the neighbouring Galla chiefs.[1] Even in Harar itself the Amir did not feel completely secure. Fortunately Harar was the only town in the region surrounded by a wall[2] and having a few pieces of artillery. Thus the marauding tribes were kept from penetrating the town itself. Still, Harar needed the trade of the Galla and the Somali. Small caravans of Galla and Somali were allowed to enter the town, but they had to leave their arms at the gate and the number of foreigners allowed in at one time was always controlled. At sunset all visitors had to leave, and on rare occasions when foreigners were permitted to stay overnight they were lodged in special houses as 'guests' of the Amir.[3]

In spite of the growing power of the Galla, the Amirs of Harar maintained some authority over them, since the absence of a central authority of their own, and their having lived within the Amir's authoritative realm for a few centuries led the Galla to accept him as a part of their own social structure. Therefore, their chiefs, like some of the nearby Somali tribes, sought investiture and title to their land from him.[4] Harar was also necessary to the Galla economy since by the nineteenth century Galla agriculturalists and pasturalists had surpluses of coffee, saffron, hides and cattle as well as some ivory and occasionally slaves. As they could not travel through the lands of their enemies, the Somalis or the Afar, to Zeila, Berbera or Aussa, and the commercial centres of Showa were too far away, Harar was the natural market for their surpluses and the source of supply for those foreign

---

Journal of the Royal Geographical Society, Vol. 12, pp. 238, 240; M. & D., Vol. 13, pp. 192, 230-2, Combes, 20.4.1840, 1.7.1840.

[1] Yusuf Ahmed MS., pp. 48, 53. Lists of payments under title: '*Ma'arafat al-Ababin Haq al-Safar.*'

[2] If one ignores the low, crumbling mud wall of Zeila.

[3] Cruttenden, *Edour*, p. 181; Barker, J.R.G.S., Vol. 12, p. 240; L.G., 209, No. 2336, Christopher, 8.5.1843, last pages of dispatch; Burton, L.G., 294, No. 158, 22.2.1855; Harris, W. C.: *The Highlands of Aethiopia*, Vol. I, pp. 38, 381-3. According to oral evidence, if the price of bread went up in Harar as a result of abnormal demand the authorities immediately investigated whether Somali or Galla stayed in town.

[4] Harris, Vol. I, p. 153; Cruttenden, *Edour*, p. 179. See also tribute from Galla chiefs receiving 'head dresses' (investiture) and land: Yusuf Ahmed MS., p. 53. Tribute received in the time of Amir Abdul Karim and Amir Abu Baker from Galla: Yusuf Ahmed MS., pp. 45, 49.

products that they needed. Thus it was in the interest of the Galla to preserve Harar. Nevertheless, the Galla still wanted more land, a larger share in the town's income and more prestige and influence in the court of the Amir, so they continued to put pressure on the town.[1]

By the nineteenth century relations between Harar and Showa were on the whole quite friendly. Until the first decades of the nineteenth century Showa was largely dependent on Harar for its foreign trade and for its communications with the coast.[2] However, because of deterioration of security resulting from Galla and Afar raids along the route between Showa and Harar, this route was much less in use than in earlier times.[3] Furthermore, a new trade route opened by the southern Afar from Tajura to Showa greatly contributed to the decline in importance of the Harari route. Finally, the rich markets in the Soddo area and northern Gurage, exceedingly important for the Harar trade, came under the sway of Showa in the 1830's as a result of Showa's expansion southwards. Although the direct route from Harar to Gurage was left untouched by the Showans, the instability created by the frequent raids in the area made conditions very difficult for Harari merchants. As a result, many Harari merchants preferred to trade with the rich markets of the south through Showa, and thus a large Harari community was to be found in the town of Aliyu Amba, the central market of Showa. The rulers of Harar and of Showa co-operated in endeavouring to keep the route between Showa and Harar open. Frequent messages were exchanged, and the head of the Harari community in Aliyu Amba was appointed by the Amir of Harar and

[1] L.G., 209, No. 2336, Christopher, 8.5.1843, last pages of dispatch; Paulitschke, p. 228; Moktar, pp. 376–7; Burton, R. F.: *First Footsteps in East Africa*, London, 1894, Vol. I, p. 205. It seems that since the death of Amir Abu Baker in 1852, the Amirs were completely in the power of the Galla chiefs (Moktar, pp. 386, 390). Rivalry and payments of Galla chiefs to sit near the Amir (Moktar, pp. 376–7).

[2] Abbadie, F.N.A. 21302, p. 346; F.O., Abyssinia, 1/1, pp. 206–7, Salt, 22.8.1811; Combes and Tamisier, Vol. II, p. 351; *Church Missionary Records*, publication of Church Missionary Society of England, Vol. 1839, Krapf, 28.5.1837.

[3] This is true especially after Amir Abu Baker came to power in 1834. J.R.G.S., Vol. 12, p. 242; Harris, Vol. I, p. 379; L.G., 225, No. 5, Cruttenden, 24.11.1847; Compare Abbadie, F.N.A. 21302, p. 346; Barker, J.R.G.S., Vol. 12, pp. 238, 242; Rochet d'Héricourt: *Voyage sur la côte orientale de la Mer Rouge dans le pays d'Adel et le royaume de Choa*, Paris, 1841, pp. 330–1; Barker, L.G., 189, No. 2037.

recognized by the ruler of Showa as a 'consul' representing his master and having jurisdiction over Harari subjects in Showa.[1]

Although decaying, depopulated, and impoverished, Harar was still at the beginning of the nineteenth century the most important Islamic centre in the area. The town boasted many mosques and a great number of shrines of venerated saints (*Awliya*) who were supposedly the protectors of the town and its people. The town attracted many learned sheikhs from Arabia and most of the male population of the town visited the holy places of Islam and had a right to the title *Haj*.[2] While European Christians were barred from reaching the highlands through Harar, the town served as an avenue, and its trading caravans as a vehicle, by which Islamic teaching reached the furthest corners of southern and south-western Ethiopia.[3] In fact merchants and *Fuqaha* coming from Harar, or through Harar, were partially responsible for the peaceful Islamization of the Galla in southern and south-western Ethiopia, after the beginning of the nineteenth century.[4]

THE NORTHERN SOMALI COAST

In the first half of the nineteenth century Zeila was just a shadow of its past glory when it had been the seat of a great Muslim kingdom. It was a large village surrounded by a low mud wall, with a population that varied according to season from 1,000 to 3,000 people.[5] Since 1630, Zeila had been a dependency of the town of Mokha[6] and was farmed out for a small sum to one

[1] Harris, Vol. I, pp. 379, 383; Johnston, C.: *Travels in Southern Abyssinia*, London, 1844, Vol. II, p. 247; L.G., 185, No. 1440, para. 15, Barker, 7.1.1842. Chief of Hararis told Barker that with a letter from Sahle Selassie he would be safe in Harar.
[2] Barker, J.R.G.S., Vol. 12, pp. 238, 240, 243; M. & D., Vol. 63, pp. 18–19; *Bulletin de la Société Khédiviale de Géographie du Caire*, Série II, p. 463; Harris, Vol. I, pp. 379, 381; Abbadie, F.N.A. 21302, p. 15.
[3] In 1840 the Amir announced that he would execute anyone who brought a European to his country. M. & D., Vol. 13, p. 192; Ibid., Vol. 63, pp. 18–19; See also Rochet d'Héricourt: *Second Voyage*, Paris, 1846, p. 263; Cruttenden, *Edour*, p. 181; Abbadie, F.N.A. 21303, p. 393, para. 217; Ibid., 21303, p. 365, para. 184; Trimingham, pp. 239–40.
[4] See below, pp. 76–7.
[5] Isenberg, C. W., and Krapf, L.: *Journals of the Rev. Messrs. Isenberg and Krapf, 1839–42*, London, MDCCXLIII, p. 3; Cruttenden, *Edour*, p. 182; M. & D., Vol. 63, p. 10, Linant, 10.8.1839; Abbadie, F.N.A. 21301, p. 161, para. 533.
[6] Trimingham, p. 97.

of the more important office-holders in Mokha. It was governed by an Amir who had some vague claim to authority over all the *Sahil*,[1] but whose real authority did not extend very much beyond the walls of the town. With the help of a small troop of mercenary matchlockmen and a number of cannon, the governor defended the town against the disunited Somali nomads who roamed in the area, and against pirates who operated in the Gulf of Aden. Although his army was quite small, he was a power to be reckoned with in the area because he represented the Yemeni government, and because of the firearms his soldiers possessed.

Zeila was essentially a merchant colony with a mixed Arab, Somali and Afar merchant population, some of whom were quite important and owned boats which traded with Jedda, the Persian Gulf and even with India.[2] Because Zeila was unrivalled along the Somali and Afar coast, as the only town with permanent trading facilities and government, its shallow harbour was frequently visited by Arab, Afar and Banyan ships. In fact, until the second quarter of the nineteenth century the Banyans used Zeila as their trading headquarters for the whole area.[3] The Issa Somali and other nomads who roamed in the neighbourhood of Zeila continually visited the town in order to sell their surpluses and make purchases. Other nomads came to Zeila during the period of the *Haj* 'to perform their pilgrimage there, which among them was considered quite as efficacious as a pilgrimage to Mecca'.[4] But most important was the large number of trading caravans that came to the town from the interior during the period of the local fair during October and November. However, with the opening of the Berbera fair in November, the nomads left Zeila, and

[1] Literally, coast, but in this area it meant the northern Somali coast from the Bay of Tajura to Cape Guardafui. Abbadie, F.N.A. 21302, p. 346; Ibid., 21303, p. 186; M. & D., Vol. 63, pp. 10–11. Linant, 10.8.1839; L.G., 251, No. 537, para. 25, Cruttenden, April, 1847.

[2] Ali Shermerki, who was exporting coffee to India and slaves to the Persian Gulf belonged to this class. L.G., 145, No. 4618, Moresby to Haines, 24.8.1840; L.G., 255, No. 5, para. 10, Cruttenden, 24.11.1847; Rochet d'Héricourt: *Second voyage*, Paris, 1846, p. 288; L.G., 153, No. 412, Barker, 8.12.1840, enclosed in Haines dispatch from 1.1.1841; Range, 388, Vol. 40, No. 2726, 7.4.1837.

[3] M. & D., Vol. 13, pp. 229–30, Combes, 1.9.1841.

[4] L.G., 167, No. 2710, Cruttenden and Barker, 26.4.1841.

nearly half of the permanent population of the town moved to Berbera.[1]

Zeila's relative importance on the *Sahil* was derived mainly from the fact that it served as the port of Harar and because until the first quarter of the nineteenth century the old-established route from Zeila through Harar to the highlands was the only one used extensively between southern Ethiopia, Showa and the coast. In 1808 the traveller, Henry Salt, wrote the following:

Zeila is a port under the Imaum of Sana or the dola of Mocha. This is of some consequence as being the only point of communication with the Mohammedan kingdom of Hurrur and through that to the kingdom of Shoa and Efat.[2]

No doubt, the decline of the trade in the Red Sea area had a very serious effect on Zeila, especially because of the decline of Harar and the opening of a direct route from Tajura to Showa.[3] By the second quarter of the nineteenth century, as a result of the constant decrease in revenue, the government of Zeila as well as the merchant community of the town tried to supplement their dwindling incomes by exactions and rapacity. The natural outcome of such practices was that wherever possible the nomads and the long-range caravans preferred to trade with Berbera and other ports, and the Banyans turned their backs on Zeila and traded directly with the Somali coast from their centres in Mokha and Aden.

The fair of Berbera, which took place between the months of October and April, was among the most important commercial events of the east coast of Africa. Berbera had no permanent population; during the season of the fair the sub-tribes of the Haber Awal, who claimed ownership of Berbera, gathered on the coast as early as September and provided the nucleus for the temporary town which sprang up overnight on the empty shores. From October to April many caravans of Somali tribes and others from Harar, the Ogaden and from other places on the Ethiopian

---

[1] L.G., 153, No. 412, Barker, 8.12.1840, enclosure in Haines dispatch from 1.1.1841; Johnston, C.: *Travels in Southern Abyssinia*, London, 1844, Vol. I, p. 33.

[2] See also: F.O., Abyssinia, 1/1, pp. 206–7, Salt, 22.8.1811. Salt, Appendix V; Range, 383, Vol. 52, pp. 2912–14, Pearce, 15.2.1814; Abbadie, F.N.A. 21302, p. 346.

[3] See below, pp. 24–5.

plateau arrived and departed. Contrary winds did not allow shipping to enter the harbour of Berbera before the second part of October. Some Zeilan merchants, who wanted to be the first to meet the caravans, went to Berbera by land.[1] However, most Zeilan merchants, and merchants coming from the Gulf of Aden, came only at the end of October, while the larger boats from the Red Sea and from the Persian Gulf reached Berbera only in December, when the most important caravans started to arrive from the interior. Last to arrive were the Indian merchants from Porbunder, Mangalore and Bombay.[2]

It is not known when the fair of Berbera was established. In fact very little was known by Europeans about Berbera until the first decades of the nineteenth century. Banyan and Arab merchants who were concerned with the trade of this fair closely guarded all information which might have helped new competitors; and actually through the machinations of such merchants Europeans were not allowed to take part in the fair at all.[3] It seems, however, that the trade of Berbera received new impetus at the end of the eighteenth century, when it began to attract many more Indian merchants who were disappointed in the decreasing Red Sea trade, and who may have also been attracted because no customs duties were levied at Berbera. The arrival of American merchants at Mokha from the beginning of the nineteenth century and the revival of trade in the Red Sea area and the Ethiopian highlands further stimulated the growth of the fair.

The importance of the northern Somali coast drew the attention of Muhammad Ali, ruler of Egypt, as early as 1821. However, a landing party dispatched by Muhammad Ali to Berbera was forced to abandon the place in the face of local opposition.[4] Muhammad Ali continued to keep an eye on Berbera throughout the 1820's while its importance grew steadily, but his preoccupation with the Morea diverted his attention from this remote though important place. When the Egyptians conquered

---

[1] Speke, *Blackwood's Magazine*, 1860, Vol. 87. See also: L.G., 209, No. 2336, 8.5.1843.
[2] Cruttenden, *Edour*, p. 186.
[3] F.O., Abyssinia, 1/1, p. 6, Valentia, 1808; Range, 385, Vol. 61, Nos. 20–2, from 25.4.1825, registered 6.7.1825; Ibid., Vol. 60, No. 66, registered 15.6.1825.
[4] Range, 385, Vol. 20, p. 1901, para. 7, 2.1.1822; Ibid., p. 4098, 27.6.1823.

the Yemeni coast in the 1830's, they also took over the government of Zeila. But, because of their preoccupation with Syria and their continuous troubles in the Yemen, they continued the practice of farming out Zeila to Al Bar family, which for some time held the governorship of the town,[1] and did not interfere with Berbera.

After the withdrawal of the Egyptians from the Yemeni coast in 1841, the rights to the farming of Zeila were bought by an important Somali merchant, *Haj* Ali Shermerki.[2] The change in the governorship of Zeila had an immediate effect on the whole *Sahil*. For the first time in many decades the executive power in Zeila rested in the hands of a successful and ambitious merchant, who immediately tried to divert as much of the coastal trade as possible to his own town. Being a slave merchant, he jealously observed the successful slave trade of the Tajurans, and incited the Issa Somali to attack their caravans on the Tajura route.[3] Moreover, he contrived to monopolize the trade of Harar and the Ogaden by using the shadowy authority which the governor of Zeila supposedly had over the *Sahil*. In 1845, taking advantage of the constant wars between the branches of the Haber Awal, who were the protectors[4] of the Berbera fair, Ali Shermerki joined forces with one of the sub-tribes, and garrisoned Berbera with a few score of matchlockmen. The Amir of Harar, who had already quarrelled with Shermerki over financial matters, was greatly disturbed by the possible consequences of Shermerki's activities on the trade of Harar. He therefore encouraged the Haber Awal to make up their differences and thereby prevent Shermerki from taking over Berbera altogether.[5] While the Amir was mobilizing the resistance to Shermerki's ambitions, the latter plotted with Somali tribes inimical to

[1] Cruttenden, *Edour*, p. 183; Rochet, *Voyage*, pp. 339–40; Abbadie, F.N.A. 21301, p. 161, para. 533; Burton, Vol. I, p. 24.

[2] L.G., 210, No. 2740, para. 14, Christopher, 9.7.1843; Rochet, *Second Voyage*, p. 284.

[3] On the Tajura route, see below, pp. 24–6; Burton, Vol. I, p. 10, footnote 2; Ibid., p. 208, footnote 1; Shermerki's letters: L.G., 301, enclosure in 482, 28.11.1855.

[4] *Abbans*. See my article, 'Brokers and Brokerage in Ethiopia in the First Half of the Nineteenth Century', *Journal of Ethiopian Studies*, Vol. III, No. 1, 1965, p. 3.

[5] Burton, Vol. I, p. 208, footnote; L.G., 256, No. 389, Cruttenden, 4.4.1848; M. & D., Vol. 63, pp. 10–11, Linant, 1839, probably from 1848. The Somali tribesmen had no firearms (Wellsted, *Arabia*, p. 362).

Harar to block the Harar route to Berbera and to unseat the Amir.[1]

Meanwhile, the Egyptians made plans to occupy the whole Afar and Somali coast as far as Cape Guardafui, after reoccupying Massawa and Sawakin at the end of 1846. Messengers were sent to the local dignitaries to inform them of the Egyptian intentions, but the sharp British reaction resulting from Shermerki's protest, and the death of Muhammad Ali's gifted son, Ibrahim Pasha, who was the Regent of Egypt, prevented the Egyptians from putting their plans into action.

The Haber Awal finally succeeded in driving Shermerki's soldiers out of Berbera in 1852, and in 1854 Shermerki himself was banned from attending the fair. When Shermerki retaliated by blockading Berbera, he was strongly reprimanded by the authorities of Aden.[2] The British interest in Berbera had been growing since the conquest of Aden at the end of 1838. Berbera was an important source of income to the Indian and other merchants under British protection. The Somali coast on the whole had some strategic importance once Aden was occupied by the British, and it was also the main source of food supplies for the Aden garrison. This interest finally led to the conquest of Berbera by the British in the 1880's and to the founding of the British colony in Somaliland.

In 1855, as a result of complaints by the merchants of Tajura, who also insinuated that he was a British agent, Shermerki was arrested by the Ottoman authorities in Mokha and the governorship of Zeila was given to the Afar slave merchant, Abu Baker, from the village of Ambabo near Tajura. Abu Baker became the Pasha of Zeila under the Egyptians after the conquest of the northern Somali coast and Harar by the army of Khediv Ismail, and his family took a very active part in the history of the region in the second half of the nineteenth century.[3]

THE SOUTHERN AFAR COAST

Of the handful of Europeans who succeeded in reaching Showa

---

[1] L.G., 294, No. 158, para. 9, Burton, 2.2.1855.
[2] L.G., 277, No. 1, 6.12.1851; L.G., 278, No. 445, Cruttenden, 7.4.1852; L.G., 289, No. 161, 26.1.1854.
[3] L.G., 301, enclosure in 482, 28.11.1855; L.G., 297, No. 697, 14.10.1855; L.G., 294, 158, Burton, 2.2.1855.

during the second quarter of the nineteenth century, nearly all went by way of the Sultanate of Tajura. Although some tried to reach the highlands through Zeila, Berbera and other Afar villages, they found soon enough that the only point on the coast, besides Massawa, having direct and constant communications with the highlands was Tajura.[1] Studying all the materials left by those travellers, one tends to receive an exaggerated impression of the importance of Tajura.

Although Tajura was the seat of the Ad-Ali Abli Sultanate it was no more than a medium-sized village consisting of about 200 or 300 huts with a population which might have numbered 2,000 during the Tajura fair, but which usually did not consist of more than a few hundred people.[2] The Sultan of Tajura, whose title was *Dardar*, claimed authority over all the northern Adoimara Afar to the borders of Showa. However, although it was true that some sub-clans of the Ad-Ali and Abli Adoimara roamed as far as the borders of Yifat,[3] even the staunchest supporters of the Sultan agreed that his actual authority did not stretch beyond Lake Assal, a short distance from Tajura.[4] In fact, it is doubtful whether the *Sultan* had any authority beyond the limits of Tajura itself, and even in Tajura his authority was nominal. The real authority among the southern Adoimara rested in the hands of the clans' chiefs (*ukal*s), some of whom gathered from time to time in Tajura to discuss affairs concerning their clans.[5] Moreover, although claiming complete independence, the Sultanate of Tajura seems to have been a dependency of Zeila. The Sultan received a small annual stipend from the governor of Zeila, and the merchants of Tajura had to pay a tax on all imports and exports, particularly on slaves, to the governor.[6] Nevertheless, while all the other so-called Afar

[1] For example Krapf, Isenberg, Rochet d'Héricourt, d'Abbadie, Dr Beke, Johnston and others. See also: L.G., 146, dispatch No. 4858, 1840.
[2] L.G., 146, No. 4858, 1840; L.G., 145, No. 4618, Haines, 28.8.1840, report by Moresly (probably Moresby) from 24.8.1840.
[3] J.R.G.S., Vol. 10, p. 462.
[4] Harris, Vol. I, p. 173.
[5] Johnston, Vol. I, pp. 10, 45, 48; Harris, Vol. I, pp. 48, 65; L.G., 165, No. 2276, Young, 8.6.1841.
[6] Isenberg, C. W., and Krapf, L.: *Journals of the Rev. Messrs. Isenberg and Krapf, 1839–42*, London, MDCCXLIII, p. 13; L.G., 145, No. 4618, Haines, 28.8.1840; Lt. Barker report; Ibid., Moresby report, 28.8.1840; L.G., 165, No. 2316, Haines, 5.7.1841; M. & D., Vol. 13, p. 191, Combes,

sultanates along the coast were described in the nineteenth century as small decaying villages of no political or commercial importance, and Zeila was continuing to decline, Tajura retained relatively steady connections with Showa.[1] In addition to other lucrative goods arriving from the highlands, Tajura exported between 1,500 and 3,000 slaves annually,[2] a number which equalled, if not surpassed, the number of slaves exported through Massawa.[3] Tajura merchants owned a number of sea-going boats, and many of them were to be found in the ports of the Red Sea, in Zeila, Berbera, and even in the Persian Gulf.

Tajura is not even mentioned in all the material discussing the Red Sea in the late eighteenth and early nineteenth centuries. In the beginning of the nineteenth century the customary line of communication with Showa was through Zeila and Harar.[4] The question therefore arises as to what happened within a few decades to turn Tajura into a centre of communication and trade with the highlands, while its neighbours remained the same dilapidated villages, and while Zeila's importance was decreasing from day to day.

The Afar, who are called Danakils or Ada'il by the Ethiopians and the Arabs, are Hamitic people of the same branch as the Somali. They are nomadic herdsmen, whose stock consists chiefly of goats, sheep and some camels. They occupy the coastal plains of Ethiopia from the Buri Peninsula in the north to the Gulf of Tajura and the slopes of the Harar plateau in the south. The Afar are divided into two main groupings, Asaimara (the red house) and Adoimara (the white house). These again are subdivided into a large number of tribes and kinship groups. Their political system, probably resulting from the physical nature of their country, is based on the kinship group rather than on the tribe;

20.4.1840; Ibid., p. 230, 20.4.1840; Ibid., p. 225, Combes, 26.4.1841; M. & D., Vol. 63, pp. 10–11, Linant, 10.8.1839 (probably from 1848); Abbadie, F.N.A. 21300, p. 488, 1841; L.G., 301, appendix to No. 482, Shermerki, 28.11.1855; Ibid., No. 396 of 1855. See also: L.G., 297, No. 787, paragraphs 79–87, Coglan, 8.11.1855.
[1] Rochet, *Voyage*, p. 35; M. & D., Vol. 63, pp. 10–11, Linant, 10.8.1839; Ibid., p. 33, Combes, 26.4.1841; L.G., 146, No. 4858, 1840; M. & D., Vol. 13, pp. 184, 225, Combes, 1.3.1840.
[2] See below, p. 65.
[3] L.G., 165, No. 2316, 5.7.1841.
[4] Range, 383, Vol. 52, pp. 2912–14, Pearce, 15.2.1814; Abbadie, F.N.A. 21302, p. 346; F.O., Abyssinia, 1/1, pp. 206–7, Salt, 22.8.1811.

therefore the heads of the kinship groups have the only real authority among the Afar, and the loose tribal organization exists mainly for the purpose of war.[1]

The new developments in the Red Sea basin in the first half of the nineteenth century had of course an impact on the Afar coast. New blood was infused into the veins of the old trade routes to the interior, and coastal settlements that had direct connections with the highlands grew in importance.

Not less important for the Afar coast was the rapid expansion of the kingdom of Showa from the middle of the eighteenth century onwards, when the borders of the kingdom were extended to the verge of the Afar desert. By the second quarter of the nineteenth century the expansion of Showa southwards and westwards brought within its realm some important trade routes leading to the rich south, and diverted to Showa part of the lucrative trade of south-western Ethiopia. In Showa salt, beads, copper, cloth and other foreign products were greatly in demand for local consumption and for the transit trade of the country. The growing court of the Showan king, and the households of the provincial governors, created additional demands for foreign merchandise while the constant wars with the fierce Galla enhanced the importance of firearms which, from about the middle of the eighteenth century, became a decisive factor in the struggle to reconquer the Showan provinces lost to the Galla.

Nature has not favoured the country of the Afar. It is an arid, sterile, broken and volcanic country. It is as forbidding as a desert can be; most of it is not even fit for grazing, and the little rain that falls evaporates because of the scorching heat. It can support only a limited number of nomads and their herds, and consequently the battle for survival is far fiercer here than in other places on the Horn of Africa. However, the country of the southern Afar possessed two assets: its geographical position between the plateau and the sea, and a number of salt deposits, the most important of which is Lake Assal,[2] which from time immemorial provided the southern Afar with the salt which they

---

[1] Trimingham, pp. 171–5; Lewis, I. M.: *Peoples of the Horn of Africa*, London, 1955, p. 160.
[2] A short distance from Tajura.

exchanged in the Ethiopian highlands for foodstuffs, local products, and slaves. No wonder that in a country so poor the possession of Lake Assal and the mastery over the routes to the
highlands was a matter of life and death and gave cause for
never-ending wars.

Some time in the beginning of the eighteenth century, the
Mudaito tribe of the Asaimara group overran the fertile valley
of Aussa in the heart of the Afar country, and drove out the
dynasty of Harari Imams which had come to the area in 1577.[1]
The chief of the Mudaito, Kedafu, became the first Sultan of the
Afar dynasty of Aussa, probably after first establishing some
unity between the Mudaito and the Aussan peasantry.[2] Throughout most of the eighteenth century, the Sultanate of Aussa,
under its Mudaito Sultan, was the strongest and most important
Afar political unit. The valley of Aussa was the only fertile and
cultivated area in the country of the Afar, and it produced crops
which supplied the needs of the inhabitants as well as those of
the visiting caravans and the nomads of the neighbouring area.
The relative peace and stability afforded by the strong Sultans,
the abundance of food and water, and Aussa's geographical position in relation to the highlands attracted many merchants who
traded with the highlands, some of whom settled in Aussa. However, towards the end of the eighteenth century it seems that the
Mudaito sultanate of Aussa was past its peak. In its heyday it
was to a certain extent a commercial sultanate, and afterwards it
was affected by the general economic stagnation in the area. The
powerful Sultan Ijdahis, who ruled Aussa in the last decades of
the eighteenth century, kept the Adoimara Afar, always jealous
of the relative prosperity of their enemies, the Mudaito, at bay.
When the Debene–Wema, the strongest tribes among the southern Adoimaras, reinforced by a few hundred Yemeni matchlockmen obtained from Zeila, attacked Aussa, Ijdahis still
managed to wipe out the Yemeni force and to drive away the

---

[1] Trimingham, p. 97; *Fitaurari* Yayo, who is today the highest ranking
Afar next to the Sultan of Aussa and other Afar elders, told me that the last
Imam was Imam Salman; before him ruled Imam Ali, and before him Imam
Omar, the family of which came from Arabia (?).

[2] Kedafu, according to Yayo (see above), ruled fifteen years. His son,
Kedafu Muhammad, ruled about thirty years, his grandson, Ijdahis, about
twenty-two years, his great-grandson, Ijdahis Muhammad, one year, and his
second great-grandson Anfari, who died in 1862, ruled about sixty years.

Adoimara, even though Aussa was taken by surprise.[1] Nevertheless, the decline of Aussa could not be stopped. After the death of
Ijdahis, followed shortly by the death of his son, Ijdahis Muhammad, the very young Anfari came to power at the beginning
of the nineteenth century and Aussa was plunged into a period
of anarchy and instability. Lacking the strong hand of Ijdahis,
the union of the Mudaito tribes and the settled peasantry broke
up and Sultan Anfari could therefore only claim the obedience
of the people of the valley of Aussa.[2] The Wema were quick to
take advantage of the situation and probably around 1810 they
sacked Aussa and forced the Mudaito Sultan to share his authority with an Adoimara chief.[3]

The Wema victory enforced the claims of the Adoimara to a
share in the salt of Lake Assal. Combined with the opportune
decline of Mudaito power and the rise of the kingdom of Showa,[4]
it also provided for the opening of a new and more direct trade
route from Tajura to Yifat in Showa in addition to the traditional
route through Aussa to Dawe in Wollo-Galla country. The new
route, completely by-passing Aussa, caused the Mudaito tribes
to lose much of the income which they had derived in the past
from the caravans trading with the highlands. On the other hand,
Tajura, the seat of the decaying Adoimara sultanate, grew in

---

[1] Krapf, F.O., Abyssinia, 1/3, pp. 83–4, 1840. In his letter Krapf writes
that this happened sixty years ago, i.e., 1780–90; also Isenberg, p. 24; Harris,
Vol. I, pp. 175–81, 187; Johnston, Vol. I, p. 240.

[2] According to Krapf and Harris (ibid.) both of them writing in the 1840's,
the Sultan of Aussa in the last decades of the eighteenth century was Yusuf
Ali bin Ijdahis. While Harris claimed that the Yemeni force was wiped out
by Yusuf Ali but that *later* Aussa was sacked by the Wema, Krapf and Isenberg claim that the Yemenis were victorious, but after maltreating the wives
of their allies were sent away. Yayo and the Afar elders, on the other hand,
completely disclaim the existence of Yusuf Ali bin Ijdahis. They knew about
the Yemeni force which was sent against Aussa in the time of Ijdahis and they
claim (as did Harris) that this force was wiped out. Harris's version probably
telescoped the defeat of the Yemeni force with the weakening and sacking of
Aussa. The sacking of Aussa might have occurred at the beginning of the
nineteenth century, when Anfari, who must then have been a young child,
came to power. Yayo and the other Afar elders claim that after the death
of Ijdahis at the end of the eighteenth century, or the beginning of the nineteenth, his son, Ijdahis Muhammad, ruled for one year and then Anfari came
to power and ruled for sixty years (died 1862). The beginning of the nineteenth century was probably a difficult time for the sultanate of Aussa. The
unruly Mudaito took advantage of the unstable situation and of the rule of a
child-sultan, to renew their independence.

[3] Harris, Vol. I, p. 175.

[4] See below, Chapter VIII.

importance and became a centre of trade and communications with the Ethiopian highlands, and especially with the kingdom of Showa.

The sacking of Aussa and the opening of the new trade route only intensified the bitter and constant wars between the Mudaito and southern Adoimara. Above all the Galela Mudaito, who seem to have lost most from the opening of the new trade route with Showa, constantly harassed the Adoimara tribes and attacked their caravans in order to re-establish their former domination of the area.

From the third decade of the nineteenth century, it appears that the sedentary Aussans and the southern Adoimara grew nearer to each other, mainly for economic reasons. The Aussan merchants and farmers suffered just as much as the Adoimara from the attacks of the Galela Mudaito.[1] The Aussans needed large quantities of salt for their trade with the highlands and for their own use, and the salt found near Aussa, being impure, was not liked in Ethiopia. Better-grade salt was regularly brought to Aussa by Adoimara caravans from Lake Assal. These same caravans took back to Tajura the agricultural surpluses of Aussa and merchandise acquired by Aussan caravans in the highlands. The Aussans preferred Tajura and its smaller sister village Rahita to the Mudaito coast between Edd and Rahita,[2] and Aussan merchants joined Adoimara caravans on the route to Yifat. The Tajurans themselves depended to a large extent on Aussa for foodstuffs, and Adoimara merchants were constantly using the trade routes from Aussa to Argobba, Wollo and Massawa.[3]

Throughout the second quarter of the nineteenth century, the Galela Mudaito, the Issa Somali, the Itu and other Galla tribes

[1] *Fitaurari* Yayo and other Aussan elders agreed that Aussans were not originally Mudaito but immigrants from many places including Harar and Arabia. They kept their identity by settling in separate parts of the valley. Thus there were many 'communities' in Aussa like Sharifa, Kabirto, Saido, Harara, etc., each having a sheikh of its own. Abbadie, F.N.A. 21302, p. 27; Johnston, Vol. I, p. 382.

[2] Krapf, F.O., Abyssinia, 1/3, pp. 83–4, October, 1840; Harris, Vol. I, p. 139; Johnston, Vol. I, pp. 382, 441; L.G., 166, No. 2482, 25.6.1841; Isenberg, C.M.R., Vol. 1841, p. 4; Licata, G. B.: *Assab e i Danachili*, Milan, 1885, p. 239.

[3] Abbadie, F.N.A. 21300, pp. 477–9, 1841; Abbadie, F.N.A. 21302, p. 27, para. 41; L.G., 193, No. 2918A, para. 8, Harris, 8.5.1842; M. & D., Vol. 13, p. 230, Combes, 1840; Beke, Dr C. T.: *Letters on the Commerce and Politics of Abyssinia, etc.*, London, 1852, p. 8.

constantly harassed caravans along the Tajura trade route to Showa. In some cases they succeeded in blocking the route for months, and even for a number of years. But the Adoimara, uniting under one chief, always managed ultimately to reopen the route to Showa which was so important for their livelihood.[1]

CONCLUSION

From the time of Grañ and the conquest of Massawa by the Ottomans until the first decades of the nineteenth century, it seems that Christian Ethiopia had no interest in the coast, or at least made no effort to regain a foothold there. The barren, hot and unhealthy coastal plains were left unchallenged in the hands of nomadic tribes and a number of inconsequential Muslim principalities whose existence depended to a large extent on the trade of Ethiopia. The zeal of the *Jihad* among the coastal Muslims was long forgotten, and because of mutual interest and interdependence, relations between Christian Ethiopia and the Muslim coastal population were on the whole relatively good. As a result of the economic decline in the whole region in the eighteenth century, even the lucrative trade of Ethiopia decreased. Thus, although Christian Ethiopia itself was torn by internal strife and church controversies[2] and was constantly under pressure of the expanding Galla tribes, the degenerate Muslim coastal principalities and the failing power of the Ottomans in the Red Sea area could no longer constitute a threat to the Christian highlands.

[1] Johnston, Vol. I, pp. 380–3, 432–3; J.R.G.S., Vol. 10, Diary, p. 459; F.O., Abyssinia, 1/3, pp. 83–4, Krapf; Isenberg, pp. 44–5, 49; Harris, Vol. I, pp. 130–1, 246; L.G., 153, No. 412, Barker, 1.1.1841; L.G., 145, No. 4618, Haines, 28.8.1840, Barker and Cruttenden report; L.G., 166, No. 2842, Harris, 25.6.1841; Rochet, *Voyage*, p. 99.
[2] See below, pp. 38–40.

II

The growth of Galla power in northern Ethiopia

Although the Muslim threat to Christian Ethiopia subsided during the seventeenth and eighteenth centuries, the emperors of Ethiopia were still faced with the continuous Galla expansion in various parts of the highlands. While the Sidama highlands were penetrated by the Mecha and other Galla tribes, the Yejju and Wollo Galla—some of whom accepted Islam after invading central Ethiopia—continued their slow penetration of the Amhara provinces in the north. From the eighteenth century on, they became enmeshed in the already intricate political web of the country. The Gondarine rulers came more and more to depend upon their Galla troops, and the Galla nobility was an accepted feature in the Gondar courts.

In the past, the King of Kings conferred upon army commanders, office-holders and court favourites fiefs and governorships which in most cases were not hereditary. The more important governorships came with the title of *Dejazmatch*[1] and their importance was signified by the number of *Negarit*s that the governor was allowed to display.[2] Each *Negarit* represented the authority of the governor over one district. Proclamations by the governor were made in market-places to the sound of his *Negarit*s. When the governor wanted to collect an army, his *Negarit*s were beaten in all the important villages and whenever the governor travelled or marched to battle his *Negarit*s, attached in pairs to mules, were sounded continuously before him.[3]

[1] Literally, warrior of the door, next to *Ras* in the Ethiopian hierarchy of nobility, headed by the *neguse negest* (king of kings).

[2] The *Negarit*s were kettledrums. Notice similarity to the number of horsetails of the Pashas of the Ottoman Empire.

[3] Mondon Vidailhet: *Chronique de Theodros II, roi des rois d'Éthiopie*, Paris (no date), p. 86, footnote 14; Lefebvre, C. T.: *Voyage en Abyssinie executé pendant les Années 1839, 1840, 1841, 1842, 1843, 1845–51*. Vol. I, p. xliv; Plowden, W. C.: *Travels in Abyssinia and the Galla Country*, London, 1868, pp. 41, 47; Harris, Vol. III, p. 291; Ferret and Galinier, Vol. I, p. 340.

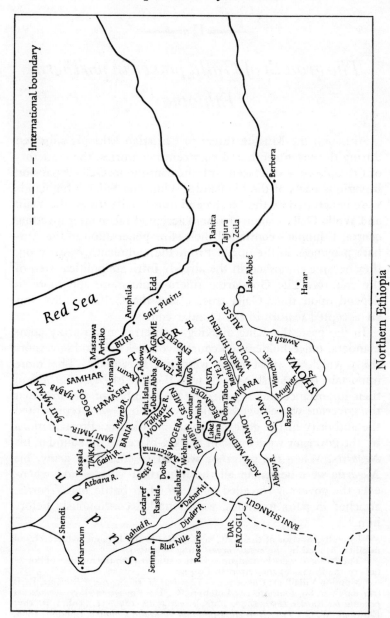

Northern Ethiopia

Each governor was responsible for the preservation of law and order within his territories. He had the power of life and death over the population as he was the highest judicial and executive authority in the area. In theory, the people were protected to some extent by the Church and could, if they had the means of reaching Gondar, appeal even to the Emperor. The governor was also responsible for the collection of taxes in his provinces for the imperial treasury, but in lieu of tribute each governor was required to bring his army to fight for the Emperor whenever called to do so. Each district (*Negarit*) was in its turn divided into a number of parishes, each under a *Chiqa Shum*, usually an ex-soldier and old retainer of the *Dejazmatch* who owed allegiance only to him.[1]

The army of each lord was made up of units of infantry and cavalry. The soldiers provided their own armament and horses, but the select troops of matchlockmen, who were the pride of each governor, were not only provided with arms by their master but also received comparatively generous pay.[2] As there was never a shortage of recruits, the size of the army of each governor depended on his financial means; but as each unit was quartered with a parish which was responsible for supplying it with provisions, the size of the army of each noble also depended on the extent of his territory.

With the decline of imperial authority, the regional governors, although officially still owing allegiance to the King of Kings and through him to his guardian, strengthened their position within their own provinces to the point where they could be considered semi-independent, and the governorship of each province became hereditary. While the most powerful regional lords were warring among themselves, especially for the position of the guardian of the Emperor, the provincial governors would transfer their allegiance from one important leader to another, according to circumstances. However,

---

[1] Parkyns, M.: *Life in Abyssinia*, London, 1853, Vol. II, p. 229; Ferret and Galinier, Vol. II, p. 332.
[2] The matchlockmen were usually Tigreans and the best came from the Agame district. Lefebvre, Vol. I, pp. xlviij, xxx, xxxiij; Plowden, *Travels*, pp. 41, 47, 65–6; Hotten, J. C.: *Abyssinia and its People*, London, 1868, p. 182; Harris, Vol. III, p. 291; Ferret, P. V. A., and Galinier, J. G.: *Voyage en Abyssinie*, Paris, 1847, Vol. II, pp. 227, 332; Abbadie, F.N.A. 21303, pp. 436–7; Parkyns, M.: *Life in Abyssinia*, London, 1853, Vol. II, p. 113.

even the authority of the different provincial rulers was not secure. District governors tried to establish their own little empires; and the many claimants to power in each region expedited the process of fragmentation and disintegration of the empire.

In a situation of continuous war, when districts and provinces often passed from one hand to another, law and order were nonexistent. The armies of many nobles, who in most cases had to live off the land, ravaged not only the domains of their master's enemies, but the country which belonged to him as well. Desperate farmers, seeing their crops burnt or taken away from them time and again, often became soldiers or highwaymen preying upon the caravans and ravaging the land of their neighbours. Thus the economy of the country continually declined, and the population decreased.[1]

When the British traveller Bruce visited Ethiopia between 1769 and 1772, the real power in Gondar lay in the hands of *Ras*[2] Michael Suhul, governor of Tigre, and not in the hands of the King of Kings. Earlier, *Ras* Michael was called upon to save his master from Galla domination. But instead, he assassinated one emperor and replaced another in succession, thus initiating the *Zamana Masafint*. Shortly after the departure of Bruce, Michael Suhul was defeated by a Galla Amhara coalition, but was allowed to return to his province of Tigre. In the coming decades the guardianship of the King of Kings passed into the hands of a Yejju Galla family, who, though in most cases superficially Christians, still derived most of their power from their Muslim and pagan Galla kinsmen in Begamder, Amhara, Wollo, and Yejju. The founder of this new dynasty of Galla regents was *Ras* Ali I, who ruled the province of Begamder and Amhara from his centre in Debra Tabor. However, as long as *Ras* Michael was alive he was a power to be reckoned with, and the regency was

[1] Isenberg, p. 487; Gobat, S.: *Journal of a Three Year's Residence in Abyssinia*, London, 1834, p. 312; Abbadie, F.N.A. 21303, pp. 493–6, immigration of farmers of Lasta to Dembya. Also: Combes and Tamisier, Vol. II, pp. 153–4; Ibid., Vol. III, p. 161; Isenberg, p. 458; Plowden, *Travels*, p. 130; Parkyns, Vol. I, pp. 219, 223, 248; Ferret and Galinier, Vol. II, pp. 293–4, 332; M. & D., Vol. 61, p. 182, report of Bardel; Ministère des Affaires Étrangères (Bruxelles), Archives, Dos. 2024, Annexe 40, Blondeel, 24.9.1841; Lefebvre, Vol. I, pp. xxx–xxxij.
[2] Literally—head, the highest position in the heirarchy of Ethiopian nobility.

not secure in the hands of the Galla nobles. *Ras* Michael died in
1779–1780. His son Wolde Gabriel took up the battle against
Galla authority in Gondar, but fell in the battlefield in 1788
fighting *Ras* Aligaz, who had succeeded his brother *Ras* Ali I on
the latter's death. With the death of Wolde Gabriel and following a period of struggle for power among the Tigrean nobility,
the governorship of Tigre passed into the hands of *Ras* Wolde
Selassie of Enderta. Though Wolde Selassie had cooperated
with Aligaz in his early days,[1] he became now a serious challenger
to the guardianship of the King of Kings. Especially after the
death of Aligaz in 1803, when Aligaz's nephew Gugsa rose to
power, *Ras* Wolde Selassie at the head of the Christian nobility
of Tigre and supported to some extent by the rulers of Showa,
Lasta and Wag, led the struggle against the Galla and their
Amhara supporters.[2]

The journey of the British traveller Bruce to Ethiopia in the
eighteenth century was an isolated incident. Only since the
beginning of the nineteenth century, as a result of the growing
interest of Britain in the Red Sea littoral, have Europeans
seriously tried to breach the walls of isolation around Ethiopia.
The first to be affected by this turn of events was *Ras* Wolde
Selassie of Tigre, who was visited twice by Henry Salt. The
British traveller[3] brought him modern firearms and tried to
impress upon him the necessity of opening an avenue to the
coast in order to facilitate commercial and political relations with
Christian Europe. However, *Ras* Wolde Selassie showed no
enthusiasm for conquering the coast and was happy to leave the
situation as it was, unless the British were willing to take Massawa themselves. Wolde Selassie nevertheless applied to King
George III for firearms and for help in getting an *Abuna*[4] whose
support he wanted to recruit against the Yejju Galla nobles and

[1] Parkyns, Vol II, p. 108; Halls J. J.: *The Life and Correspondence of
Henry Salt*, London 1834, Vol. I, p. 105; *The Royal Chronicles of Abyssinia*,
editor: H. Weld Blondell, Cambridge 1922, pp. 424–425; Ruppell, Vol. I. pp.
272–273; Combes et Tamisier, Vol. II, p. 138.
[2] Pearce, Vol. I, pp. 72–73, 105–106, 108; Range 384, Vol. 52, pp. 2912–
2914, Pearce, Adowa, 15.2.1814; Arnauld d'Abbadie: *Douze Ans dans la
Haute Ethiopie*, Paris 1868, p. 403; Combes et Tamisier, Vol. III. pp. 146–
147, 150; F.O. Abyssinia 1/1, pp. 155, 188, Salt, 2.4.1810, 24.4.1811.
[3] Later British Consul-General in Egypt 1816–27.
[4] The head of the Ethiopian Church was always obtained from the Coptic
Church of Egypt (until 1949) against certain payments.

their Christian and Muslim allies.[1] Ethiopia had been left without an *Abuna* from the death of *Abuna* Joseph III in 1803 until the arrival of *Abuna* Kerilos in 1816.[2] Shortly after *Abuna* Kerilos finally arrived, the old *Ras* became sick and died, after which Tigre fell into complete chaos. The descendants and followers of Wolde Selassie fought the descendants and followers of *Ras* Michael Suhul and both parties fought many new claimants to power in the different provinces.[3]

Beyond the Takkaze, the provinces of Semien and Wolkait were governed by *Dejazmatch* Haile Mariam. After succeeding his father, *Dejazmatch* Gebru, in 1815, Haile Mariam tried to consolidate his father's possessions in the face of continuous pressure from *Dejazmatch* Maru of the house of Fenja. From the beginning of the nineteenth century Maru managed to carve himself a little empire to the north and north-west of Lake Tana. He also expanded his territories to include Wogera and Belassa,[4] and before the invasion of the Sudan by Muhammad Ali he received tribute from Metemma and fought the Sultanate of Sennar. Both Maru and Haile Mariam as well as most of the Christian nobility of Begamder and Amhara co-operated with *Ras* Gugsa and recognized his overlordship. In order to cement his relationships with the most potent Christian rulers on the western side of the Takkaze, Gugsa gave his daughters in marriage to *Dejazmatch* Maru and *Dejazmatch* Haile Mariam.[5]

While the internal wars sapped the energy of Tigre, and while the Amhara lords fought each other and vied for the favour of Gugsa, the Wollo, Yejju, and Raya Galla, with the acquiescence of the Galla Regent, continued their slow expansion into Amhara, Lasta and, to a lesser degree, Tigre. When *Dejazmatch*

---

[1] F.O., Abyssinia, 1/1, pp. 155, 181, 201, 202, 204, Salt, Antalo, 1810; Halls, J. J.: *The Life and Correspondence of Henry Salt*, London, 1834, Vol. I, pp. 148–9.

[2] See below, pp. 41–2.

[3] Ruppell, Vol. I, p. 273; *The Royal Chronicles of Abyssinia*, ed. H. Weld Blondell, Cambridge, 1922, p. 527.

[4] Conti Rossini Carlo: *Nuovi documenti per la storia d'Abissinia nel secole XIX*, Rendiconti dell'Accademia Nazionale dei Lincei, 1947, Ser. VIII, Vol. II, p. 372; Plowden, *Travels*, p. 82.

[5] Conti Rossini Carlo: *Nuovi documenti per la storia d'Abissinia nel secolo XIX*, Rendiconti dell'Accademia Nazionale dei Lincei, 1947, Ser. VIII, Vol. II, p. 376; Parkyns, Vol. I, p. 184. There is also a story that Haile Mariam was given a daughter of Aligaz, Hirut, whose brothers Faris Aligaz and Birru Aligaz ruled the Yejju of Lasta (Ferret and Galinier, Vol. I, p. 424).

Zawde of Gojjam and Damot tried to oppose the Galla ascendancy and the Galla spread into eastern Gojjam, he was defeated by *Ras* Gugsa and his territories were given to Gugsa's son, Alula. Thus, at least for a time, even this important Amhara and Agaw region came under direct Galla rule.[1]

The descendants of Aligaz, who lost the leadership of the northern Galla to Gugsa, governed most of Yejju and the southern parts of Lasta. Whereas many of the Yejju chiefs, like their kinsmen of Begamder and Amhara, were superficially converted to Christianity,[2] the Wollo Galla rulers with few exceptions were staunch Muslims and openly anti-Christian. In fact, the chief of the Wollo of Warra Himenu, *Dejazmatch* Ahmade, who succeeded his father, *Imam* Liban, on his death in 1815, was such a zealous Muslim and so anti-Christian that he was considered by many the most important Muslim ruler, if not the leader, of all the Muslims of Ethiopia.[3]

Until the death of *Ras* Gugsa in 1825, northern Ethiopia was relatively quiet. The death of Gugsa was, however, the signal for a renewed struggle for power among all the important lords of the country. *Dejazmatch* Maru allied himself at first with *Dejazmatch* Haile Mariam, the governor of Semien and Wolkait, in order to overcome the Galla nobility of Begamder and Amhara. However, as was usual in those days, Maru soon changed sides, and joined *Ras* Yimam, Gugsa's son and heir, although he was openly sympathetic to Islam. Haile Mariam was defeated at the beginning of 1826 and soon after died in his mountain stronghold of Semien.[4] The designated heir of Haile Mariam was his third son from his Yejju Galla wife, Merso, but in the struggle which ensued among the heirs, the second son, Wube, governor of Wolkait, defeated his brother's supporters and was recognized as ruler of Semien. While the struggle for succession was going on in Semien, *Dejazmatch* Maru tried to take advantage of

[1] M. & D., Vol. 61, p. 87, Gilbert, 28.8.1861.
[2] One of their chiefs changed his religion four times in the second decade of the nineteenth century (Pearce, N.: *Life and Adventures of Nathaniel Pearce*, London, 1831, ed. J. J. Halls, Vol. II, pp. 46–7.
[3] *Royal Chronicles*, p. 488; Isenberg, p. 437; Abbadie, F.N.A. 21300, pp. 346, 796; Combes and Tamisier, Vol. II, pp. 168, 300–1; L.G., 159, February, 1841, Krapf; *Nuovi documenti*, pp. 378–9.
[4] Plowden, *Travels*, p. 82; Parkyns, Vol. I, pp. 163–5; *Royal Chronicles*, p. 485; *Nuovi documenti*, pp. 370–3.

the situation and expand his authority beyond Wogera into Wolkait and Semien. At first the young Wube tried to fight off both Maru and Yimam, but his desperate situation finally brought him to seek an alliance with *Ras* Yimam. The latter was ready to help Wube because he feared the ambitions of Maru, who allied himself with *Dejazmatch* Goshu, who had in the meantime become the ruler of Gojjam and Damot.[1] In October 1827, the combined armies of Wube and Yimam met the combined armies of Goshu and Maru at Kosso Ber in Gojjam and defeated them. Goshu escaped to his mountain fortress but Maru was killed and his territories were given to Yimam's brother, *Dejazmatch* Marye. Soon after (1828) Yimam died and Marye became the guardian of the Emperor and the ruler of Begamder and Amhara.

The internal war in Tigre terminated only at the end of 1822 with *Dejazmatch* Seb'agadis from the house of Agame emerging triumphant. Seb'agadis had already gained some notoriety in the first decade of the century when he rebelled a number of times against the authority of *Ras* Wolde Selassie. But just before the death of Wolde Selassie it seems that he made it up with his master and became one of his loyal lieutenants.[2] It was already becoming evident while he was trying to overcome his many competitors in Tigre that Seb'agadis intended to form a Christian Tigrean–Amhara coalition to oppose the Galla expansion and fight the Galla rulers of Begamder and Amhara, whom he accused of being Muslims.[3] However, as long as Gugsa was alive and the coalition between the Galla and Amhara rulers of the provinces beyond the Takkaze was solid, he bided his time.

Seb'agadis was convinced that only firearms could tip the scales against the fierce Galla cavalry, and following the example of *Ras* Wolde Selassie, he continuously accumulated firearms. For this he very much needed European support. Therefore, in 1827 he dispatched Salt's servant Coffin, who had remained in Ethiopia, with a letter to King George IV in which he requested

[1] His father, *Dejazmatch* Zawde, was imprisoned by Gugsa and died in prison. See: *Royal Chronicles*, p. 486; *Nuovi documenti*, p. 371; Ferret and Galinier, Vol. I, p. 524.

[2] Halls, *Salt*, Vol. I, pp. 109, 478; Pearce, N.: *Life and Adventures of Nathaniel Pearce*, London, 1831, ed. J. J. Halls, Vol. I, p. 103.

[3] *Royal Chronicles*, Appendix H; Ruppell, Vol. I, p. 273; Combes and Tamisier, Vol. III, pp. 152–3.

military and technical aid. Having had stronger relations with the Muslim coastal population, and having extended his authority into the Taltal and Saho country, he was more aware of the possibilities and importance of opening an avenue to the coast than was *Ras* Wolde Selassie.[1]

The evacuation of the Egyptian garrison from Massawa in 1826[2] presented Seb'agadis with a godsent opportunity to gain a foothold on the coast. Seb'agadis therefore concluded his letter to the British monarch by writing: 'I hope you will take the port of Mussowa, and give it to us or keep it.'[3] Thus for the first time in the modern era an Ethiopian ruler seriously attempted to breach the wall of isolation around Ethiopia and create a bridge to Christian Europe.

By the end of the 1830's Seb'agadis was considered the champion of Christianity in northern Ethiopia.[4] Following again the policy of his predecessor in Tigre he tried a number of times to obtain a new *Abuna* from Egypt, but as *Abuna* Kerilos, with whom he had quarrelled, was still alive he was unsuccessful. Meanwhile he kept up continuous communications with the most important Christian lords of Ethiopia,[5] until in 1830 he succeeded in forming a loose coalition with the Christian rulers of Gojjam, Lasta, and Semien against *Ras* Marye. However, Marye, who was forewarned of the plot, dealt with his opponents singly. After defeating *Dejazmatch* Goshu in Gojjam, he marched with the bulk of his army to Lasta, and then quickly turned to Semien and attacked Wube. Seb'agadis, who was watching his border with Lasta,[6] did not come to the aid of his ally and Wube preferred to submit to the *Ras* rather than face him alone. After his success in isolating Seb'agadis,

---

[1] Plowden, *Travels*, p. 26; Combes and Tamisier, Vol. III, p. 152; Ruppell, Vol. I, p. 273; F.O., Abyssinia, 1/1, p. 204, Salt, 22.8.1811; *Nuovi documenti*, p. 376.

[2] See above, p. 6.

[3] F.O., Abyssinia, 1/2, Adowa, 24.4.1827.

[4] Gobat, S.: *Journal of a Three Year's Residence in Abyssinia*, London, 1834, pp. 303–4; *Nuovi documenti*, p. 376; Abba Tekla Haimanot: *Abouna Yacob*, Paris, 1914, p. 91.

[5] See below. See also: Tagher, J.: *Cahiers d'histoire égyptienne*, Vol. I–II, 1948–9. Mohamad Ali et Les Anglais, pp. 472–4; Cadalvene and Breuvery: *L'Égypte et la Turquie 1829–1836*, Paris, 1836, Vol. II, pp. 446–7; F.O., 78/511, para. 7, Harris, 28.2.1842; *Nuovi documenti*, p. 575.

[6] Ruppell, Vol. I, p. 213; Combes and Tamisier, Vol. III, p. 153; *Nuovi documenti*, p. 375; Parkyns, Vol. II, pp. 114–5.

Marye decided to put an end to the Tigrean threat. At the head of Galla contingents from Wollo, Yejju, Begamder and Amhara, and supported by the armies of Wube and Goshu, he advanced beyond the Takkaze into Tigre. Seb'agadis had meanwhile mobilized his forces and in the beginning of 1831 the two armies met at Mai Islami near Debra Abbai. Although the Tigreans had by far the greater number of firearms, the matchlockmen were poorly employed and the Galla cavalry won the field after a most bloody fight in which Marye was killed. Seb'agadis, who surrendered to Wube, was handed over to the Galla and was executed in retaliation for the death of Marye.[1]

Nearly a year after his death, although he was a Tigrean, people all over the Amhara countries were still lamenting Seb'agadis:

> Alas! Sabagadis, the friend of all,
> Has fallen at Daga Shaha, by the hand of Aubeshat!
> Alas! Sabagadis, the pillar of the poor,
> Has fallen at Daga Shaha, weltering in his blood!
> The people of this country, will they find it a good thing
> To eat ears of corn which have grown in the blood?
> Who will remember (St) Michael of November (to give alms)?
> Mariam, with five thousand Gallas, had killed him
> (him, i.e., who remembered to give alms)
> For the half of a loaf, for a cup of wine,
> The friend of the Christians has fallen at Daga Shaha.[2]

The Galla contingents under the command of Dori, Marye's brother, ravaged Tigre, but because of Dori's serious illness they finally withdrew and left Tigre to Wube. Seb'agadis's many enemies and rivals now turned against his offspring. Moreover, even Seb'agadis's own sons and supporters fought each other for ascendancy, and in the chaos which ensued Tigre became an easy prey for the ambitious Wube. Between 1831 and 1835 Wube succeeded in establishing his rule in this most important region, making use of the traditional aristocracy, including Seb'agadis's sons, as tributary provincial governors. Actually, Wube's authority in Tigre was continuously challenged thereafter by the descendants of the previous dynasties, but Tigre's aristocracy was

[1] Plowden, *Travels*, p. 65; Gobat, p. 289; Ruppell, Vol. I, p. 274.
[2] Gobat, p. 304.

so deeply divided that Wube managed to preserve his hold over the entire region for the following two decades.[1] But although Tigre lost its leadership in the struggle against the Galla predominancy, the final outcome of the death of Seb'agadis was that for the first time all of northern Ethiopia from Tigre to Wogera was united under one ruler and presented a far more formidable opposition to the Galla nobility than it had in the past.

Throughout the 1830's and until the last years of the 1840's the three most important rulers of Ethiopia were *Dejazmatch* Wube of Tigre, Semien, Wolkait, and Wogera, *Negus* Sahle Selassie of Showa,[2] and *Ras* Ali II, Gugsa's grandson by his son Alula, who came to power in 1831 upon the deaths of his uncles Marye and Dori. Lesser rulers like *Dejazmatch* Goshu of Gojjam and Damot, *Dejazmatch* Ahmade of Warra Himenu, Faris Aligaz, the ruler of the Yejju of Lasta, and *Dejazmatch* Kinfu, who received his great-uncle Maru's territories from *Ras* Ali in 1831, played a secondary role in the development of events. Goshu was quite successful in fighting the Mecha Galla beyond the Abbay nearly as far as the borders of Enarea.[3] He tried from time to time, especially when pressured by his ambitious son, Birru Goshu, to assert his independence and replace *Ras* Ali. However, his talents and the size of his army did not match his ambitions. Most of the time Faris Aligaz was in open revolt against his kinsman, Ali, who (he thought) had cheated him of his rightful inheritance. Although he joined a number of coalitions directed against Ali, most of the time he was kept on the run by the *Ras* or by his two Muslim uncles, Beshir and Ahmade.[4] *Dejazmatch* Ahmade, of the Wollo of Warra Himenu, had at first immense powers as regent to *Ras* Ali, and leader of the Muslim party, but he lost much of his influence when *Ras* Ali took over the reins of the government, and he died at the beginning of 1839. As for *Dejazmatch* Kinfu, he was far too occupied with his

---

[1] Ruppell, Vol. I, p. 274; Combes and Tamisier, Vol. III, pp. 158–60; Ibid., Vol. IV, p. 132; Ferret and Galinier, Vol. I, p. 430; Parkyns, Vol. II, pp. 119–23; L.G., 189, No. 2031, Harris, 10.11.1841; *Nuovi documenti*, p. 376.

[2] See below, Chapter VIII.

[3] L.G., 189, No. 2031, para. 23, Harris, 10.11.1841; L.G., 159, No. 1518B, Krapf, 22.2.1840; A.E.B., Dos. 2024, Annexe 39, 41, Blondeel.

[4] Ruppell, Vol. II, p. 229; Gobat, p. 305; Combes and Tamisier, Vol. III, pp. 158, 160; A.E.B., Dos. 2024, Annexe 38, p. 8, Dembya, 6.8.1841; *Nuovi documenti*, pp. 378–9, 381.

'Arab', Tekruri and Egyptian neighbours, and just when he achieved some prominence after defeating an Egyptian army in 1837, he became sick, and he too died at the beginning of 1839.

Ras Ali II was still a minor when he became the ruler of Begamder and Amhara and the guardian of the King of Kings.[1] In fact, at first he himself was put under the guardianship of a council of the most powerful Wollo and Yejju Galla lords, who had elected him. Nevertheless, with the help of his mother, Mennen, Ali was soon able to shake off the control of the regents, and his authority was recognized to some extent by most of the rulers of northern Ethiopia. As only Begamder and Amhara were under his direct control, however, Ali had to walk the tightrope between the Amhara Christian nobility of those provinces and the Muslim and newly converted Christian-Galla nobility, without whose support he could not keep his predominant position in Ethiopia. This delicate balance was preserved mostly through the machinations of Mennen, who was born a Muslim but was converted to Christianity and in fact ruled Ethiopia through her irresponsible young son.[2] The *Ras* himself did not take his position seriously and practised a system of *laissez faire*. As he surrounded himself with his mother's Muslim kinsmen, and showed the same indifference to his religion as to state affairs, it is not surprising that it was continuously rumoured that he had reverted to Islam and was about to surrender the whole country to the Muslims. However, as long as he did not openly declare for Islam, the leadership of the Ethiopian clergy in Gondar, appointed by the *Ras* at will and needing his support in its theological controversies, was ready to co-operate with Mennen.[3] Christian Ethiopia was thus left in the hands of an infantile and

[1] Twelve years old, according to Ruppell, Vol. II, p. 59.
[2] *Douze ans*, pp. 402–3; F.O., 78/343, p. 279, Isenberg; M. & D., Vol. 61, p. 182, Bardel report; C.M.R., Vol. 1833, p. 8, Gobat; Combes and Tamisier, Vol. I, pp. 88–9; Ibid., Vol. II, pp. 56, 93–4; M. & D., Vol. 61, p. 286, Rochet d'Héricourt; Ferret and Galinier, Vol. II, p. 243; Blanc, H.: *A Narrative of Captivity in Abyssinia*, London, 1868, p. 28; Tubiana, J.: Deux fragments du tome second de 'Douze ans dans la Haute-Éthiopie' d'Arnauld d'Abbadie, p. 44. *Rocznik Orientalistycny*, Tom XXV, Zesztt 2.
[3] Plowden, *Travels*, p. 88; *Nuovi documenti*, p. 375; *Royal Chronicles*, pp. 451, 490–1; Gobat, p. 260; Combes and Tamisier, Vol. II, p. 92; Ferret and Galinier, Vol. II, pp. 228–9; Tubiana, J.: Deux fragments du tome second de 'Douze ans dans la Haute-Éthiopie' d'Arnauld d'Abbadie, p. 37. *Rocznik Orientalistycny*, Tom XXV, Zesztt 2; Lefebvre, Vol. I, p. xxij; Harris, Vol. III, p. 141; Rochet, *Voyage*, p. 148; Rochet, *Second voyage*, p. 222.

above: Danakil girls tending camels at Batie market, Wollo

below: A market scene in Gurage

A monk-hermit in Showa

lethargic ruler and a church which was too busy with its own petty quarrels to provide the much-needed leadership and inspiration for its people.

The Ethiopian Church, which was a branch of the Coptic monophysite church of Egypt, was plagued throughout its history by theological controversies. Most of those controversies revolved around the dogma of Christ's having only one nature, and probably stemmed from the need to reconcile pure monophysitism with the Catholic dogma of the two natures of Christ supported by what seems to be evidence in the New Testament regarding the human nature of Christ.

In the eighteenth and nineteenth centuries the Ethiopian theologians became deeply divided over the question of the number of births of Christ, a problem which had its roots in the previous controversies. Some theologians developed a theory that Christ was first born in eternity as a divine being (the eternal birth), was born again in the womb of Mary and anointed by the Holy Ghost, and nine months later was born by Mary into the world as a perfect man and a perfect divinity united in one nature.

The followers of the theory of the three births (*Tsega Lij* or *Sost Lidet*)[1] were connected with the monastery of Debra Libanos in Showa, whence came their leader, the *Ichege*, who was the head of all the monks in Ethiopia. The *Ichege*, who since the seventeenth century lived in Gondar, was second only to the *Abuna* in the Church hierarchy, and was in fact more powerful because while the *Abuna* was an Egyptian Copt, he was an Ethiopian.

To the followers of the pure monophysitism the theory of the three births of Christ was unacceptable as it could be interpreted that Christ was not inherently perfectly divine, and that at one time he had had two natures, divine and human. They claimed that being divine, Christ anointed himself and was born by Mary through his own divine wish. Moreover, being divine he had no need to receive the Holy Ghost at his incarnation in the womb of Mary and therefore the second and the third births were in fact one. The followers of this theory were called *Wold*

---

[1] *Tsega Lij* literally means the son of grace. *Sost Lidet* literally means the three births.

Qib or *Karra Haymanot*,[1] and their stronghold was the province of Tigre. There was still another theory widespread in the province of Gojjam, which claimed that Christ had only two births (*Hulet Lidet*). It also accepted the eternal birth as the first birth of Christ, but claimed that at the moment of his incarnation, when he was born into the world, he was anointed by the Holy Ghost (*Qibat*); thereafter he was a perfect man and a perfect god united in one inseparable nature.[2]

As very often happens, this ecclesiastical controversy soon took on a political character. During the regency of *Ras* Michael Suhul of Tigre, who was a follower of the *Karra Haymanot*, this theory triumphed in Gondar because of the predominant position of *Ras* Michael. Thus the *Karra Haymanot* became synonymous with Tigrean rule and was rejected by all those nobles who strongly opposed the power of Tigre, particularly the Amhara and the converted Galla lords. Immediately after the defeat of *Ras* Michael Suhul and after the death of *Abuna* Yusuf (Yosab) in 1803, who was a supporter of the *Karra Haymanot* because of its stricter monophysitism, the school of the three births led by *Ichege* Wolde Yonas again became predominant in the capital of the empire. The *Ichege* excommunicated the followers of the two births theory and banished them from the capital with the help of the Galla rulers of Begamder and Amhara.[3] Moreover, Asfa Wossen, the ruler of Showa (died 1807), was promised through his father confessor, who was a Gondarine monk, that the Church would support his efforts to annex the principality of Marra Biete if he would accept the theory of the three births.[4] Asfa Wossen accepted the offer, and a lot of blood was shed in

[1] *Wold Qib* means the son anointing, while *Karra Haymanot* literally means the belief of the knife as they have cut off the third birth. The geographical division between *Tsega Lij* and *Wold Qib* reflected, in a way, the division between the two monastical orders of the Ethiopian church: the followers of the teachings of Tekla Haymanot and of Ewostatewos.

[2] Dimotheos, R. P.: *Deux ans de séjour en Abyssinie*, Jerusalem, 1871, part II, pp. 64–8; Harris, Vol. III, p. 190; *Royal Chronicles*, Appendix H; Combes and Tamisier, Vol. III, p. 175; A.E.B., Dos. 2024, rapport de Blondeel, Annex No. 40, p. 3, 24.9.1841; *Bulletin Académie des Sciences Coloniales*, Bruxelles, p. 1150, Blondeel, 20.6.1843. *Qibat* means anointed.

[3] *Royal Chronicles*, pp. 474–5, 484; the *Abuna* and previous *Ichege* were, it seems, at the head of an anti-Galla movement in the 1790's. *Royal Chronicles*, p. 421.

[4] See below, p. 148. See also: Harris, Vol. III, p. 190; Rochet, *Second voyage*, p. 226.

Showa as a result, but the following of the *Sost Lidet* remained exclusively within the court circles in Showa and in the monastery of Debra Libanos.[1]

In the beginning of the nineteenth century a strange alliance emerged in Gondar, drawing together the followers of the *Ichege*, the Christian Galla nobles, and the Muslim lords of Begamder and Amhara, who, each for his own reason, wanted to prevent the 'importation' of a new *Abuna*. Thus after the death of *Abuna* Yusuf, Ethiopia was left without an *Abuna* until 1816, when the new *Abuna* arrived mainly as the result of the initiative of *Ras* Wolde Selassie of Tigre, who wanted his support in his struggle against the Galla guardian of the Emperor.[2] In the meantime a new theory related to the *Sost Lidet* was developed by a Gondarine monk. According to this theory, the human soul possesses knowledge, fasts, and worships already in the womb and immediately after its separation from the body it renders account on high.[3] This theory was adopted by the *Ichege* and his followers in Gondar but was not accepted by many of the supporters of the *Sost Lidet*, particularly in Showa.[4] Consequently a new controversy broke out in the 1830's which threatened the existence of Showa. Subsequently, it is claimed, because he feared an attack by *Ras* Ali, the king of Showa decided to apply to the European Powers for military aid and particularly for firearms.[5]

When *Abuna* Kerilos (Cyril) reached Tigre from Egypt in 1816, he openly supported the Tigrean ecclesiastics against their Gondarine rivals. Although the death of *Ras* Wolde Selassie soon after meant the loss of important political support, the *Abuna* and the Tigrean ecclesiastics found a new champion in *Dejazmatch* Seb'agadis, who was emerging as the most serious contestant for power in Tigre. In 1819 the *Abuna* went to Gondar and tried to bring unity to the Church by forbidding the continuation of all discussions regarding the number of births of Christ. But the Gondarines challenged his decision as they con-

[1] F.O., 78/468, Krapf, 20.4.1811.
[2] F.O., Abyssinia, 1/1, Wolde Selassie to King George III, p. 202; Halls, *Salt*, Vol. I, p. 249.
[3] *Royal Chronicles*, Appendix H; Harris, Vol. III, p. 190.
[4] L.G., 190, No. 2060F, Harris, 31.12.1841; Harris, Vol. III, pp. 190–1; Isenberg, p. 413.
[5] See below, pp. 158–9. See also: L.G., 159, No. 1486B, Krapf, 15.12.1840 17.12.1840; F.O., 78/468, Krapf, 20. 4.1841.

sidered it favourable to the *Wold Qib* (*Karra Haymanot*), and with the help of *Ras* Gugsa, the *Ichege* and the Gondarine clergy finally forced the *Abuna* to return to Tigre.[1]

Ichege Wolde Yonas, who was the main opponent of the *Abuna* and who co-operated with *Ras* Gugsa, died in 1821. *Ichege* Yohannes, who was appointed to succeed him, resigned in 1823. The next *Ichege*, Phillipos, was considered more liberal and open-minded and was finally forced to abdicate in 1830 by *Ras* Marye. Meanwhile, the *Abuna*, who meddled with the politics of the country and quarrelled with Seb'agadis, again came to Gondar. There, the actions and behaviour of Kerilos so enraged the clergy and the population that *Ras* Yimam, who succeeded his father Gugsa in 1825 and who was openly sympathetic to Islam, had no qualms about banishing him to a monastery on Lake Tana. There Kerilos remained until his death about 1829.[2]

By the end of 1822 *Dejazmatch* Seb'agadis established himself as the unquestioned ruler of Tigre. Having parted ways with Kerilos, he tried to get a new *Abuna* from Egypt. But the Coptic Patriarch in Alexandria was not willing to send one as long as Kerilos was alive.[3] Soon after the death of Kerilos, Seb'agadis hurriedly despatched an embassy to Egypt to get an *Abuna*,[4] but before achieving any success, Seb'agadis died in 1831. The Galla lords of Begamder and Amhara, again with the full co-operation of the *Ichege*, did their best to prevent the coming of a new *Abuna*, and Christian Ethiopia was left without the guidance of an *Abuna* until the end of 1841.[5]

[1] *Royal Chronicles*, Appendix H; Rochet, *Second voyage*, p. 226.

[2] *Nuovi documenti*, pp. 372–3; *Royal Chronicles*, Appendix H; Lefebvre, Vol. I, p. xxij; Rochet, *Second voyage*, p. 223; Gobat, p. 261; Combes and Tamisier, Vol. III, p. 190; Pearce, Vol. II, pp. 67, 150. Massaia (*I miei*, Vol. I, p. 51) wrongly claims that Kerilos died in 1834. Another version (Guidi, I.: La Chiesa Abissinia, *Oriento Moderno*, Rome, 1922, p. 16) claims that Kerilos was banished to Tigre where after meddling with politics he was killed by Seb'agadis in 1824, or was murdered as a result of a quarrel over some property with one of Seb'agadis's governors—Coulbeaux, J. B.: *Histoire politique et religeuse d'Abyssinie*, Paris, 1829, Vol. II, p. 383.

[3] Tagher, J.: Mohammad Ali et les Anglais. *Cahiers d'histoire égyptienne*, Vol. I–II, 1948–9, p. 473.

[4] Cadalvene and Breuvey: *L'Égypte et la Turquie 1829–1836*, Paris, 1836, Vol. II, p. 446.

[5] Besides obvious political and religious reasons for the objection to 'importing' an *Abuna*, several rulers had taken over the estates of the *Abuna* and stood to lose financially if a new one came. Rochet, *Second voyage*, p. 224; *Royal Chronicles*, Appendix H, p. 474; Ruppell, Vol. II, p. 96; *Douze ans*, p. 403; Plowden, *Travels*, p. 87.

CONCLUSION

Until the 1830's the Galla elements in northern Ethiopia slowly
continued their advance into the Christian Amhara and Tigrean
provinces. This infiltration was faciliated to a certain extent by
the Yejju Galla lords, who consolidated their hold over Begamder
and Amhara and their position as guardians of the King of Kings.
The only serious opposition to the growth of Galla power, which
was also accompanied by the spread of Islam, came from Tigre.
However, the hopes of Christian Amhara and Tigrean Ethiopia
were smashed at Mai Islami with the death of Seb'agadis, and
Islam continued to spread in the country with the active support
of many Galla rulers who, though superficially Christians, were
secretly, and in some cases even openly, opposed to Christianity,
which was part of the heritage of their enemies.[1] Moreover,
while Islam was being spread all over the highlands, the Ethiopian Church, in the past a source of inspiration around which the
Christian population rallied in times of crisis, was now incap-
able of putting up any serious opposition. It was deeply torn
by theological controversies in which both the rulers and the
population were involved. Its clergy was uninspiring, to some
degree illiterate, and in some cases even immoral, and monas-
ticism became the refuge of many who did not seek spiritual
fulfilment but preferred the idle life of poor but respected para-
sites to fruitful and honest labour.[2] While Islam was being
spread all over the highlands by merchants and sheikhs who
carried with them the newly revived spirit of Islam in its
different *Sufi* interpretations, the Christian population and the
great masses of pagan Galla were offered by the Ethiopian
Church only dead formalism.[3]

[1] Gobat, p. 360; Pearce, Vol. II, p. 150; Arnold, T. W.: *The Preaching of
Islam*, London, 1913, pp. 117–19; *Bayana al-Habasha*, p. 201.
[2] *Bulletin Académie des Sciences Coloniales*, Bruxelles, pp. 114–18, Blondeel
quoting *Dejazmatch* Goshu, 20.6.1843: 'Il m'a dit lui-même que ses prêtres
sont des imbéciles et des lâches qui ne feraient rien ni pour dieu ni pour leur
prochain'. See also: Pearce, Vol. II, p. 155; Harris, Vol. III, pp. 134, 141–2,
266; Combes and Tamisier, Vol. III, p. 201; Demotheos, R. P.: *Deux ans
de séjour en Abyssinie*, Jerusalem, 1871, part II, pp. 63, 65, 80–1.
[3] Cederquist: Islam and Christianity, *Moslem World*, Vol. II, London,
1912, p. 154.

III

The revival of the highland trade

The development in the Red Sea basin since the first decade of the nineteenth century had an immediate impact upon Ethiopia. The continuous demand for the limited quantities of Ethiopian luxury products which reached the coast grew quickly. Moreover, while the increased number of pilgrims to Mecca enhanced the demand for slaves in the markets of Arabia, the conquest of the Caucasus by the Russians closed this important source of supply of concubines for the harems of the Ottoman Empire. Consequently the demand for the highly esteemed Ethiopian slaves became insatiable[1] and the foreign trade of the highlands received a new impetus. The merchant communities in the north flourished to some extent and a number of rulers increased their revenue from passing caravans. But as most of the exportable products of Ethiopia came from the Galla and Sidama areas of the south-west and south, the mass of the Ethiopian people were hardly touched by the new prosperity and remained just as poor as they had been in the past.

SALT MONEY

During the *Zamana Masafint*, as in the past, much of the trade in Ethiopia's markets was carried on by barter.[2] However, in the more important trading centres, especially in northern Ethiopia and Showa, the Maria Theresa thaler was accepted by merchants. For smaller change people used pieces of cloth, black pepper, beads and, above all, salt money, called *amoleh*. Salt, having been essential to Ethiopia's economy since the Axumite period and probably before it,[3] retained its importance in the eighteenth and nineteenth centuries. The *amoleh* could be considered to

---

[1] Madden, R. R.: *Travels in Turkey, Egypt, etc., in 1824–1827*, London, 1829, Vol. I, p. 6; Burckhardt, *Arabia*, p. 120; Ferret, P. V. A., and Galinier, J. G.: *Voyage en Abyssinie*, Paris, 1847, Vol. II, p. 371.

[2] The absence of coined money was a feature of the Ethiopian economy since the decline of the Axumite Empire. See: Pankhurst, R.: *An Introduction to the Economic History of Ethiopia*, London, 1961, p. 260.

[3] Ibid.

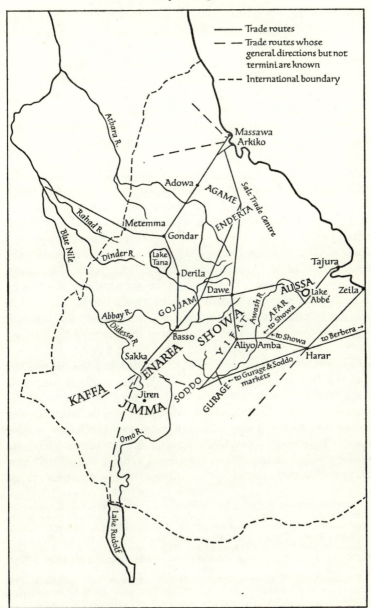

Main trade routes of Ethiopia in the nineteenth century

have been the official currency all over the highlands from Tigre to Kaffa and from Wollaga to Argoba. In many cases taxes and tribute were paid in *amoleh*. For certain articles only *amoleh* were accepted[1] and even when barter was practised it served in many instances as a medium of exchange. It was indispensable to the long-range caravan trade, because the further the merchants penetrated into the interior the less ready were people to accept thalers, while the *amoleh* was always welcomed. Thus *amoleh* merchants were to be found even in the remotest markets of the Ethiopian plateau.[2]

The *amoleh* during the *Zamana Masafint* had the shape of a prism, about twenty centimetres long and two-and-a-half thick. In the centre it was about five centimetres wide, but only two-and-a-half at the ends. The accepted weight of the *amoleh* was about half a kilo and it was usually protected from damage by a strip of leather bound across it.[3] During the rainy season the *amoleh* tended to become moist and fall to pieces. Moreover, with continuous use it decreased in weight until it would not be accepted any more at its full value or would not be accepted at all. The difference in value between the *amoleh* and raw salt was such that people tried to preserve their *amoleh* by burying them in ashes or by suspending them above a fire.

The source of all the *amoleh* in circulation in Ethiopia was the Taltal salt plains, nearly one hundred miles south of Massawa. An ancient agreement existed between the Taltal and the Tigreans by which the latter, for a small payment, had been allowed to descend to the Taltal plains to extract as much salt as they could. Thus each year large caravans left Agame and Enderta under the protection of an important official whose title was *Balgada*.[4] Because of weather conditions the Tigreans only stayed

[1] Rochet, *Second voyage*, p. 261; Harris, Vol. II, p. 170. On the salt currency used during the Portuguese period in Ethiopia, see: Pankhurst, *An Introduction*, pp. 261–2; Pankhurst, R.: Primitive Money in Ethiopia. *Journal de la Société des Africanistes*, 1963, pp. 214–15.

[2] Abbadie, F.N.A. 21303, pp. 260–2, para. 106; Ferret and Galinier, Vol. II, p. 414; Cecchi, E.: *Da Zeila alla frontiere del Caffa*, Rome, 1886–7, Vol. II, p. 298.

[3] Ruppell, Vol. I, p. 302; Abbadie, F.N.A. 21301, p. 118, para. 346. The size, shape and protective cover of the *amoleh* were different in different periods.

[4] F.O., Abyssinia, 1/4, pp. 124–6, Plowden, 17.11.1847; Salt, p. 325; Ferret and Galinier, Vol. II, p. 58.

a few weeks in the Taltal area and then returned to the highlands with many thousands of salt blocks which they shaped into the accepted form. The Taltal themselves brought to Agame great quantities of rock salt which they sold to the local population, who later formed them into the desired *amoleh*. The quantity of *amoleh* introduced each year into Ethiopia depended to a large extent on the political, climatic and economic conditions in the area. Because of the instability in Ethiopia during the *Zamana Masafint*, it is only to be expected that the supply of *amoleh* greatly varied from year to year, but estimates of the amount range from three-quarters of a million to thirty million.[1] However, as the salt plains were flooded during the rainy season in Ethiopia and were unbearably hot during the hot months of the year, the salt mines were actually exploited less than three months of the year and one could safely assume that the average number of *amoleh* introduced annually into the highlands probably did not exceed a few million.[2] Being very fragile and easily corroded, a great number of *amoleh* went constantly out of circulation and the number of available *amoleh* probably did not increase very much from year to year. Thus, especially in the light of the slow expansion of trade in Ethiopia in the nineteenth century, the danger of inflation was avoided.

The most important centres of the *amoleh* trade were the villages of Ficho and Atsbi on the border between Agame and Enderta, overlooking the Taltal plains. Here, *amoleh* were exchanged at the rate of eighty to 100 per thaler, depending on the season.[3] From this area the *amoleh* were carried by donkeys,

---

[1] According to Munzinger and Arakel Bey, thirty million. See: Douin, G.: *Histoire du règne du Khédiv Ismail*, Cairo, 1936, Tome 3, p. 709. According to Antoine d'Abbadie, who travelled extensively in Ethiopia in the second quarter of the nineteenth century, three-quarters of a million. Abbadie, F.N.A. 21300, p. 385. See also: Pankhurst, R.: Primitive Money in Ethiopia, *Journal de la Société des Africanistes*, 1963, pp. 218–22.

[2] The annual revenue of *Dejazmatch* Kassai, ruler of Agame (overlooking the salt plains) in the late 1830's, from all sources, was about 10,000 thalers. The customs duty levied by Kassai on *amoleh* was 20 per cent (Abbadie, F.N.A. 21302, p. 28, para. 69). The market of Aliyo Amba, the most important in Showa, which was also the centre of *amoleh* trade in that country and where 10 per cent tax was paid on all sales, is said to have yielded to the government of Showa 3,000 thalers in cash and about 2,000 in kind annually (L.G., 185, No. 1140, para. 18, Barker, 7.1.1842). See also: Pankhurst, *Primitive Money*, pp. 219–20.

[3] Ferret and Galinier, Vol. II, pp. 58–9; Abbadie, F.N.A. 21300, p. 385; Lefebvre, Vol. II, pp. 25–6.

mules and porters to Antalo, Lasta, the Yejju and the Wollo areas. On the borders of Wollo the salt merchants of the north were met by caravans coming from Showa. These caravans took the *amoleh* into Showa and beyond it to southern Ethiopia, the Sidama areas and even to Kaffa.[1] Another route led from Atsbi to Ifag in Begamder and from there to Gondar. No less important was the route of distribution from Begamder to the market of Basso in Gojjam and thence to all the provinces of south-western Ethiopia. The limits of *amoleh* diffusion in southern and south-western Ethiopia were probably the limits of the penetration of caravan merchants from the north, that is, the Sidama lake area on one hand, and Kaffa on the other.[2]

The rate of exchange of *amoleh* for the thaler, at any trading or administrative centre, differed according to its distance from Agame and Enderta. This resulted mainly from the cost of transportation and the unavoidable damage to the fragile *amoleh* on the road; but also from the heavy taxes laid upon the *amoleh* merchants by governors and by customs authorities all along the caravan routes. Therefore, while at Ficho up to 120 *amoleh* were received per thaler, at Sokota in Lasta or Adowa in Tigre, fifty to seventy were given per thaler, in Begamder thirty to forty, in Gojjam and Showa about twenty and in Enarea ten to twelve.[3] Because of their increased value, the *amoleh* reaching south-western Ethiopia were broken into four and sometimes even into six smaller units.[4]

The revenue from the *amoleh* trade was of great importance to the governors of Tigre and especially to the rulers of the provinces of Agame and Enderta overlooking the salt plains. Income from the salt trade enabled them to defray part of the cost of keeping a sizeable army[5] and to pay for the large stock of fire-

[1] L.G., 189, No. 2034, 12.12.1841; Combes and Tamisier, Vol. IV, p. 125; Abbadie, F.N.A. 21303, pp. 260–1, para. 106.

[2] According to d'Abbadie (F.N.A. 21303, p. 421, para. 277) *amoleh* were rare in Kambat. The population of Kulo, south of Kaffa, we are told, had no use for *amoleh* and there is no evidence of any trade in *amoleh* with the negroid areas to the south and west of the Ethiopian plateau. See: Abbadie, F.N.A. 21303, pp. 277, 357, paras. 118, 178, respectively.

[3] Ferret and Galinier, Vol. I, p. 453; Ibid., Vol. II, p. 59; L.G., 185, No. 1440, Barker, 7.1.1842; Harris, Vol. I, pp. 376–7, 379; Johnston, Vol. II, p. 248; Lefebvre, Vol. II, Appendix Mer Rouge, p. 82.

[4] Abbadie, F.N.A. 21303, pp. 260–1, para. 106.

[5] Pearce, N.: *Life and Adventures of Nathaniel Pearce*, London, 1831, ed.

arms which they managed to acquire in the nineteenth century. In fact the rulers of Tigre, taking advantage of their position in the highlands and making use of the income of the salt trade, had a larger number of firearms than the ruler of any other province in Ethiopia.[1] No doubt the bitter and continuous struggle for power among the descendants of *Dejazmatch* Seb'agadis of Agame, *Ras* Wolde Selassie of Enderta and *Dejazmatch* Wube of Semien was enhanced by European intrigues around the road from Edd and Amphila on the coast to Agame on the plateau;[2] but it received great impetus from the fact that this was also a struggle for the all-important revenue from the salt plains.

It is quite evident that the regular and continuous supply of *amoleh* was vital to Ethiopia's economy and to the efficient administration and governing of the different provinces. The quantity of thalers imported into Ethiopia was relatively small,[3] while Ethiopian exports barely covered its imports and a certain quantity of thalers was continuously taken out of circulation by the silversmiths of Ethiopia. Moreover, a number of rulers tended to hoard thalers, while others used all the thalers they could get for the purchase of firearms.[4] The salt *amoleh*, being produced in Ethiopia, did not present the same problem as the silver, all of which had to be imported.

The fact that the sources of *amoleh* lay beyond the limits of the recognized or effective authority of Ethiopian rulers might have served as an invaluable weapon in the hands of the enemies of Ethiopia. However, as long as the salt was in the hands of the weak and divided Afar, some sort of a balance existed. The Afar needed Ethiopian products just as much as the Ethiopians needed their salt. Even more important, the Afar were far too weak to threaten Ethiopia, whereas the Ethiopians in their turn abhorred

---

J. J. Halls, Vol. II, p. 14. See also above, p. 47, footnote 2, for the income of *Dejazmatch* Kassai from the salt trade.

[1] Plowden, W. C.: *Travels in Abyssinia and the Galla Country*, London, 1868, pp. 65, 75–7; Abbadie, Arnauld: *Douze ans dans la Haute Éthiopie*, Paris, 1868, p. 300; Pearce, N.: *Life and Adventures of Nathaniel Pearce*, London, 1831, ed. J. J. Halls, Vol. I, pp. 87, 113.

[2] See chapters II, V, VI. See also: India Office: Political and Secret Records, *Letters from Aden*, Vol. 28, Christopher, 15.12.1834.

[3] Valentia, Vol. III, p. 268; Pankhurst, R.: 'The Maria Theresa Thaler in Pre-War Ethiopia,' *Journal of Ethiopian Studies*, Vol. I, No. I.

[4] Ibid., Rochet, *Voyage*, p. 287; M. & D., Vol. 8, p. 286.

the climate of the coastal plains, and having great respect for the ferocity of the Afar, preferred to remain on their plateau.

CARAVAN TRADE

As in other parts of Africa, especially in some regions of the Savanna, internal trade in Ethiopia was carried on at weekly markets which took place near every important village and town. The markets of Ethiopia were an institution which fulfilled important economic, political and social functions. The rural population attended the markets not only to sell their surpluses and satisfy their limited needs, but also to meet their neighbours, inspect their produce and livestock, and hear the latest news and announcements made by the governor. To the governors the markets were an important source of income, as taxes were levied on all produce displayed in the market for sale.

In every district the markets were usually held on different days of the week, so that the inhabitants could attend any market within a reasonable distance from their village on any given day. Most markets were visited by merchants who travelled in caravans. Some caravans would cover several important markets within a province. Others would visit markets within a number of neighbouring provinces. A few caravans, organized by the most daring entrepreneurs, would push to the limits of the trading routes, striving to reach the sources of the most lucrative items produced in Ethiopia.

During the rainy season, between June and October, trade in Ethiopia came almost to a standstill. Some exchange of commodities would still take place between neighbouring villages and towns, but caravans would not risk the deep mud and the treacherous rivers swelled by the continuous rains. However, at the end of each rainy season caravans would again be organized in all the commercial centres. Usually a merchant of some importance, known for his experience, wisdom, and bravery, would announce his intention of organizing a caravan, publicizing the place of assembly and the date of departure. Smaller merchants and travellers of various sorts would then take advantage of this opportunity and would gather before the day of departure at the appointed place. The initiator of the caravan would usually be elected as the *Negad Ras*, the merchants' chief, and would be responsible for the organization of the caravan, for its protection, and for relations with the different rulers and chiefs along the road.

While northern and central Ethiopia produced hardly any exportable commodities, southern and south-western Ethiopia were the source of musk, ivory, gold, and the slaves for which Ethiopia was famous throughout history. The most important caravan route besides the traditional but degenerating one from southern Ethiopia to Harar, Zeila and Berbera was the one starting from the Gibe area. Here many trade routes from the south and west converged and from here the route led to Basso in Gojjam and northward across Gojjam to a number of commercial centres in the provinces of Begamder and Amhara with a branch going to the town of Dawe in Wollo, and from there to Aussa and the Afar coast. From Begamder and Amhara the trade routes either led to the Sudan through Metemma or through Tigre to Massawa.[1] Gondar, Derita and Adowa were considered important centres of the caravan trade in northern Ethiopia but Gondar surpassed them all and was the most important commercial centre in the whole of the Ethiopian highlands. Sudanese itinerant merchants (*Jalaba*) frequented the town but were not allowed to proceed beyond Gondar.[2] Their caravans together with those organized by Ethiopian merchants (*Jabartis*) brought into Ethiopia gold in rings, called *Sennari* and considered the purest (for re-exportation), ivory, silk, Maria Theresa thalers, and an assortment of products from Europe and Egypt similar to that which reached Ethiopia by way of Massawa. In Gondar they bought coffee, wax, musk, and above all, female slaves for the harems of Egypt and the Ottoman Empire.

After the rainy season, in the month of November, when the houses of the merchants in northern Ethiopia were bulging with produce from the interior and their stock of foreign goods was nearly exhausted, caravans were organized to go to Massawa. These caravans varied greatly in size, and carried with them gold from Sennar, Fazogli, and Wollaga, ivory and musk from

[1] Of the route from Showa to Tajura, see below: Slave Trade, pp. 62–4.
[2] Katte, A. Von: *Reise in Abyssinien im Jahre 1836*, Stuttgart, 1838, pp. 130–1; M. & D., Vol. 61, p. 404, Lejean, 15.5.1863; Matteucci, P.: *In Abissinia viaggio di . . .*, Milan, 1880, p. 270; Combes and Tamisier, Vol. I, pp. 110–11.

southern and south-western Ethiopia, coffee from south-western and western Ethiopia, tanned skins, wax and about 1,000 to 2,000 slaves, mainly of Galla and Sidama origin.[1] On their return journey the caravans would take into the interior copper, brass, knives, swords, other metal products, spices, beads of diverse sizes and colours, bottles, shawls, silk and, above all, cotton cloths of different shades and qualities. The Turkish and later the Egyptian government of Massawa forbade, or at least tried to control, the exportation of firearms to Ethiopia; nevertheless, because of the great demand among the lords of northern Ethiopia many caravans carried powder and matchlocks hidden among their merchandise.

In most of the Galla areas in southern and western Ethiopia, where a centralized system of government was not known or was just emerging, merchant caravans could not travel without a patron (*Gofta* or *Mogasa*), and many weeks were expended arguing with individuals regarding the presents to be given to families and tribes through whose area the caravan intended to pass. In the north the development of caravan trade was greatly hindered by the continuous wars and by the archaic system of customs. Before the disintegration of the imperial power in the eighteenth century, a number of customs houses were farmed out by the Emperor to the highest bidder. However, after the second half of the eighteenth century, the income of each province, including that coming from the customs houses, went to the provincial rulers. In addition, a great number of toll houses or customs barriers, called *Ber* (pass, gate), were established at suitable narrow passes or commanding positions.[2] Besides the customs houses and the toll barriers, there were still other places where local chiefs had a traditional right to exact what they could from the passing caravans.

The customs rates, even at the official customs houses, were never fixed. Merchandise was not inspected and the *Negad Ras*[3] or his representatives arbitrarily estimated the tax on each caravan. Naturally, the amount due was always a cause for unceasing

---

[1] See below, pp. 58, 66–7.
[2] Public Records Office: Foreign Office, 401.1, Confidential Print, 'Abyssinian Correspondence 1846–1868', enclosure in No. 256, Plowden, 20.6.1852.
[3] Literally, the merchants' head. In this context the farmer of the customs, not to be confused with the chief of a caravan who had the same title.

haggling between the officials and the head of the caravan. And while this was going on the merchants were forced to camp at the spot for many days. The merchants had the right to appeal to the local governor, but such a procedure usually took weeks, and in most cases the governor sided with his *Negad Ras*, who not only paid heavily for his position but could always prove that the merchants were engaged in the smuggling of gold, musk and other articles of great value. As the merchants never agreed to pay what the *Negad Ras* demanded there were always arguments and quarrels at each customs barrier. In order to enforce his demands, the *Negad Ras* therefore employed a few score armed retainers. However, when the caravan was large and well armed, the merchants could still force their way through the customs barriers, and more consideration was given to large caravans. For this reason as well as for reasons of convenience and security, merchants travelling long distances preferred to organize themselves into large and well-armed caravans, which in many cases resembled small armies.

There is little doubt that Ethiopia's caravan trade and exports grew noticeably in the first half of the nineteenth century. This is easily proved by the hoards of thalers in the treasuries of some of the rulers on the plateau.[1] And although the quantities of gold, ivory and musk which could be produced in Ethiopia were limited, the number of slaves could always be supplemented to meet the demand of the market. It seems therefore that the growth in Ethiopian foreign trade was mainly the result of the growing number of slaves exported from the country.

SLAVE TRADE

Ethiopia has always been known for its slaves, who were much sought after in the Muslim world. In fact, the most important item in the Ethiopian foreign trade was probably the exportation of slaves, the annual number of which depended on political conditions in the highlands and the demand in the slave markets. The *Habasha* slaves, as Ethiopian slaves were called, were not actually Ethiopian in the strict meaning of Amhara and Tigrean, as they came mainly from the Galla and Sidama areas in sou-

[1] Pankhurst, R.: The Maria Theresa Thaler in Pre-War Ethiopia, *Journal of Ethiopian Studies*, Vol. I, No. I, p. 10.

thern and western Ethiopia, and to a lesser extent from the negroid areas surrounding Ethiopia proper. The slave trade was forbidden to the Christian population of Ethiopia by ecclesiastical and civil law and in some cases even involved the death penalty, but the buying and keeping of slaves, however, were not forbidden to Christians. The Muslims of Ethiopia had no qualms about trading in slaves, and although Islam forbade the enslavement of Muslims, and, theoretically, Christian Amharas and Tigreans were protected by the civil law of Ethiopia,[1] they could still enslave the pagan Galla and Sidama.

The Galla and the Sidama were of a far lighter colour than the negroid *Shanqalla* and their temperament was considered by the Arab slave-dealers far more suitable to the demands of the slave markets than that of the Amhara, who were believed to be quarrelsome and haughty. They were acquired especially to be trained as personal servants, doormen, bodyguards and soldiers. Even more sought after were the Galla and Sidama girls, for whom the demand in the slave markets was second only to the demand for white slave girls from the Caucasus. And after the conquest of the Caucasus by the Russians, Ethiopian slave girls took first place in the slave markets of the Muslim world.

Warfare could be considered the most important factor influencing the source of supply for the slave trade. The continuous wars which took place in the areas of the fragmented Galla and Sidama societies always produced a great number of captives who were inevitably enslaved. The growing number of slave-merchants from the north and from the coast who, from the beginning of the nineteenth century, penetrated deeper and deeper into the interior enhanced the demand for slaves, and when the normal supply could not match the demand, the acquisition of slaves through warfare was further encouraged. In some cases it was the institutions of the Galla and Sidama principalities themselves which were an incentive to the slave trade. The economy of many of these principalities depended on the supply of slave labour for agriculture, and the profits from the sale of

---

[1] Hundreds of Christians were nevertheless either kidnapped by passing caravans or sold in secrecy by Christian Ethiopians. Northern and central Ethiopia were continuously engrossed in civil wars but the local rulers still afforded some protection to their subjects against the avidity of the slave-merchants who were to be found in every important commercial centre.

Priests singing during Epiphany celebrations

One of the many Gondar castles built during
the seventeenth and eighteenth centuries

slaves to foreign merchants covered, to some extent, the cost of imported goods consumed by the ruling classes. According to the laws of the Galla and Sidama kingdoms, the population could be sold into slavery as punishment for minor offences and for non-payment of taxes. Furthermore, in contrast to the Amhara kingdom of Showa, the rulers of the Galla and Sidama kingdoms in the nineteenth century did not have the paternal sense of responsibility for their subjects.[1] In years of famine, which occurred from time to time, it was not unusual for poor Galla and Sidama subjects to sell their own children into slavery when they were not able to feed them. Occasionally, children were taken from their parents by the government in lieu of unpaid taxes.[2]

Once the cash value of human bodies was realized, it was not long before bands of marauders specialized in kidnapping young people from the fields, and in some areas people used trickery to sell even their own kin and neighbours into slavery. 'Many on their way from one village to another are stolen and sold by their own relations and houses are frequently set on fire at night and the inmates, in endeavouring to escape, are seized and sold.'[3]

Although most of the slaves coming from south-western Ethiopia were called 'Enarea slaves', it is quite clear that they originated in the many Galla and Sidama principalities and tribes of south-western Ethiopia and above all in the kingdom of Kaffa.[4] Enarea, and to a lesser degree the other Galla kingdoms of the Gibe, served as centres of the slave trade and the merchant villages (*Mander*), which sprang up near the more important markets and political centres of the Gibe area, were always crowded with slaves brought by the many caravans from all over south-western Ethiopia.

In southern Ethiopia, Gurage was probably the most important target of slavers because of the great demand for 'Gurage

[1] See below, p. 160.
[2] Abbadie, F.N.A. 21300, pp. 235, 710; Ibid., 21301, p. 24; Combes and Tamisier, Vol. IV, p. 98; India Office: Bombay Secret Proceedings, Lantern Gallery, Vol. 196, No. 3491, Harris Slave Report, 20.7.1842, para. 7; M. & D., Vol. 61, p. 404, Lejean, 15.5.1863; Beke, Dr C. T.: *Letters on the Commerce and Politics of Abyssinia, etc.*, London, 1852, p. 23.
[3] Krapf, L.: *Travels and Missionary Labour in East Africa*, London, 1860, p. 46; Isenberg, p. 180.
[4] Cecchi, E.: *Da Zeila alla frontiere del Caffa*, Rome, 1886–7, Vol. II, pp. 517–18.

6

slaves'.[1] One tends, however, to suspect that, as in the case of the 'Enarean slaves', the slaves passing through the Gurage and the markets of southern Showa acquired the name Gurage irrespective of their Sidama or Galla origins:

Guráguê, whence are obtained the 'red Ethiopians' so much prized in Arabia. Kidnapping has consequently been there carried to an extent so frightful as to impart the name of the unhappy province as a designation for slaves generally.[2]

Another source of supply to slave-merchants who could not afford, or did not want to pay for slaves, or who found out that the supply could not meet the demand, were the negroid areas surrounding Ethiopia. Slave-raiding expeditions into these areas were organized by merchants coming from Kaffa and from the Galla principalities. These expeditions marched southwards and south-westwards into the so-called Doqo countries,[3] where they rounded up hundreds of unsuspecting and defenceless people and without opposition drove them northwards.[4] These negroid slaves were intended mainly for 'local consumption', especially for field work. Similarly, the slaves captured by the Amhara rulers of Gojjam and northern Ethiopia, who from time to time raided the adjacent *Shanqalla* area of Barea, Kunama and the peripheral areas of Damot and Dembya, were intended for the same purpose.

Small numbers of eunuchs were also acquired by the Muslim slave-merchants in southern Ethiopia. These unfortunates were mostly young children, who fetched the highest prices in the Muslim world markets. Some became eunuchs as a result of the barbaric practices of war in the area, but most of them came from the principality of Badi Folla in the Jimma area south-east of Enarea. Even the despotic rulers of the Galla kingdoms were disgusted by the terrible practice of deformation and drove out of their country those who engaged in it. Nevertheless, the

---

[1] Abbadie, *Bulletin de la Société de Géographie, Paris*, Vol. 17, 1859, p. 174.
[2] Harris, Vol. I, p. 228.
[3] 'Doqqo c'est le nom de plusieurs peuplades qui vivent au sud du Kullo, dont ils sont séparés par la rivière Uma.' Abbadie, *Bulletin de la Société de Géographie, Paris*, 1859, Vol. 17, p. 172.
[4] L.G., 184, No. 1098, Harris, 1.1.1842; India Office: Bombay Secret Proceedings, Lantern Gallery, Vol. 196, No. 3491, Harris Slave Report, 20.7.1842, para. 21; Krapf, L.: *Travels and Missionary Labour in East Africa*, London, 1860, p. 51; Johnston, Vol. II, p. 383.

ardent slave-merchants, although they claimed that in principle they opposed the deformation of children, did not refrain from buying the poor youngsters, who brought an enormous price on the coast.[1]

The markets of the Gibe area of Showa and of Basso in Gojjam were the meeting points of the many small Galla caravans coming from all over southern Ethiopia and the larger caravans of the Muslim merchants of northern Ethiopia, Harar and the coast. Here slaves were sold either privately in the huts of the merchants and brokers of the merchant villages (*Mander*), or in the open market to the highest bidder.[2] The slave-merchants had a very elaborate terminology and classification for slaves according to their age, origin, sex and qualities. There was a clear distinction between 'red' and 'black' slaves, Hamitic and negroid respectively; the *Shanqalla* (negroids) were far cheaper as they were destined mostly for hard work around the house and in the field, while the Sidama and Galla slaves were far more costly and were carefully sorted. Very young children up to the age of ten were called *Mamul*. Their price was slightly lower than that of young boys between the ages of ten and sixteen, who were called *Gurbe*, and were marked for training as personal servants. Young men in their twenties were called *Kadama* and although they still fetched a handsome price they were not as prized as the *Gurbe* because potential slave-buyers considered them beyond the age of training. The older the man the lower the price he fetched. As for females, the most esteemed and most in demand were girls in their teens, who were called *Wosif*, and if comely enough, were destined to become concubines and wives. Older women were judged according to their strength and ability to perform household duties.[3]

Payment for slaves in the southern Ethiopian markets was rarely made in cash. The accepted forms of payment were in a

[1] Abbadie, F.N.A. 21300, pp. 219–20, 236, 797; d'Abbadie, Antoine: *Géographie de l'Éthiopie*, Paris, 1890, pp. 79–80; C. & C., Massawa, Vol. I, Degoutin, 10.9.1844.
[2] Krapf, p. 51; Harris Slave Report, para. 21; Cecchi, Vol. II, p. 194.
[3] Katte, pp. 130–2; C. & C., Massawa, Vol. I, Degoutin, 10.9.1844; Abbadie, F.N.A. 21300, pp. 219, 236; Cecchi, Vol. II, p. 195; Beke, *Commerce*, p. 22; Beke, F.O.T.A., published by the Society for the Extinction of the Slave Trade, Vol. I, 1843, p. 135. Compare to prices in 1870's: Cecchi, Vol. I, p. 490; Ibid., Vol. II, p. 60.

cloth called *hindi*, or in *amoleh*, copper or beads.[1] The slave-merchants were always very careful to inquire about the origins of their 'merchandise', so as not to have in their caravans any slave belonging to the people whose country they intended to cross. In fact one of the most important principles of the slave trade was to remove the slave as far and as soon as possible from his home area in order to lessen the possibility of escape or attack by any of his kinsmen.[2]

Most of the slave caravans going northwards from the Galla areas carried quantities of the products of the south, gold, ivory, musk, skins and coffee. As for the slaves they led, the proportion of females to males was usually about two to one, the demand for female slaves in the markets of Arabia and the Sudan being nearly insatiable.[3] Young men, moreover, were harder to come by, since many were killed in battle, while women and children were spared. Those males who survived and were taken prisoner were either needed as field labourers in the Galla areas, or were adopted into families in order to strengthen the power and prestige of the family or the tribe.[4]

Before starting on the long march northwards, the slaves were sorted according to age and size. They walked in a double file, but only the older and the stronger slaves were tied in pairs by their hands to a forked stick.[5] The young slaves were unbound, gaily walking along the road, carrying in some cases small loads of food and merchandise. At the end of the day the caravan would camp in a great circle. The outer perimeter was guarded by the servants and followers of the merchants. Within the perimeter, the slaves were grouped, each having some water gourds, wooden plates and materials for building rough shelters for the night and for rainy days. All the transport animals were kept

[1] Abbadie, F.N.A. 21300, pp. 387–8; Ibid., 21302, pp. 330, 333; Beke, F.O.T.A., published by the Society for the Extinction of the Slave Trade, Vol. I, p. 135; Beke, *Commerce*, p. 26; Bianchi, G.: *Alla terra dei Galla (1879–1880)*, Milan, 1886; Cecchi, Vol. I, p. 491.

[2] Abbadie, F.N.A. 21300, pp. 222–3, 230; Ibid., 21303, p. 384, para. 268; Cecchi, Vol. II, p. 372.

[3] M. & D., Vol. 61, p. 404, Lejean, 15.5.1863; Krapf, p. 74.

[4] C. & C., Massawa, Vol. I, Degoutin, 10.9.1844; Abbadie, F.N.A. 21300, pp. 219, 236; Ibid., 21302, pp. 330–3; Cecchi, Vol. II, p. 289; Massaia, G.: *I miei trentacinque anni di missione nell'alta Ethiopia*, Rome, 1925, Vol. II, p. 155.

[5] Matteucci, P.: *In Abyssinia viaggio di . . .*, Milan, 1880, pp. 273–4; Harris Slave Report, para. 21.

within the inner circle, and were tended by a number of slaves. The food and merchandise were kept covered by skins around the tents of the slave-dealers in the centre of the camp.[1] During the night the older slaves would have their hands and feet bound, but the younger ones were left free. On the whole, the slaves were not badly treated on the road and were given sufficient food. The girls were usually given preferred treatment and only light tasks to perform so that they should not lose their looks and lessen their value. On the other hand, many served as concubines for the merchants and their servants, whereby they automatically depreciated in value, having lost their virginity.[2]

Slaves in caravans which reached one of the market villages on the borders of the Amhara areas were usually taken to the huts of the local brokers. The merchant village of Yejube, near the important market of Basso in Gojjam, which could be considered typical, had seventeen recognized brokers, and it was claimed that 5,000 to 10,000 slaves passed through the hands of these brokers annually. In nearby Basso the slaves were exposed to the inspection of potential customers who examined the teeth of the slaves, felt their bosoms and touched the palms of their hands while the slaves stood completely passive. Then they were returned to the huts of the brokers, where the actual bargaining took place.[3]

The principals or their brokers seated on the ground take each other's hands, the hands being covered with their cloths . . . by grasping or pressing the fingers they make known the price which they are respectively willing to give or to accept. . . . Having first settled between themselves whether the price in question is to be in gold (ounces), silver (dollars) or in salt (*amolehs*) . . . for 50 grasp the whole 5 fingers, for 40 only four. For 60 they first grasp the whole five and say 'this' and then after a momentary pause add 'and this' accompanying the latter words with pressure of one finger only . . . subdivisions of the wokiet are made known by pressing the nail of the forefinger on the forefinger of the other party, the end joint being $\frac{1}{4}$, the second joint or middle of the finger $\frac{1}{2}$ and the middle of the first

[1] Cecchi, Vol. II, pp. 539–40; Harris Slave Report, para. 24.
[2] Virgin slave girls were called '*Bakr*' and non-virgins '*Karag*'. The *Bakr* were worth about one-sixth more than the *Karag*. Abbadie, F.N.A. 21300, p. 220. On the practices of slave-dealers in Enarea, see: Abbadie, F.N.A. 21300, p. 236; Cecchi, Vol. II, p. 194.
[3] Beke, *Commerce*, pp. 21, 23; Beke, F.O.T.A., Vol I, p. 135.

phalanx $\frac{3}{4}$. As it mostly happens that several persons are interested or if not so, at all events take part in the transactions as friends or advisors, its progress is communicated to them by the principals through the other hands which are in like manner hidden under their clothes. . . . When any of these think the amount offered sufficient, they cry out 'sell', 'sell' and if the conclusion of the bargain be long delayed, this cry is repeated.'[1]

While in the houses of the brokers, the slaves were on the whole well treated. In order that they should fetch a better price, they were washed, fed and given a scanty dress. The girls were even adorned with all kinds of gaudy jewellery which would be taken from them when sold. They were taken each day to a meadow near a river and left there to play under the watchful eyes of their masters. The slaves, frightened out of their wits by the new environment and by tales of the fierceness and cruelty of the population, clung to their masters, and never dreamed of escaping.[2]

From the borders of the Amhara provinces the slaves reached northern Ethiopia with the caravans plying the main routes of the country. Most of the slaves brought to the markets south of Showa would be taken across the country to a number of villages in Argoba, clustered around Showa's main market of foreign trade, Aliyo Amba, and especially to the great slave market of Abdul Rasul, only a few kilometres from Aliyo Amba. Others were taken through Debra Libanos to the markets of Wollo, where caravans coming from northern Ethiopia, Aussa and Tajura were awaiting the arrival of the inland caravans. The caravans from the south and south-west were the source of the thousands of slaves sold in Showa annually, not the military expeditions undertaken by the Showan rulers as mistakenly claimed by some authors. The slave trade was strictly forbidden to Christians, and it was not likely that Sahle Selassie would condone the sale of the captives by his soldiers. Sahle Selassie himself with his strong attachment to the Church would not

[1] Beke, *Commerce*, p. 19. Compare to similar practice in Mecca: Burckhardt, *Arabia*, p. 191. See also my article: 'Brokerage and Brokers in Ethiopia in the First Half of the Nineteenth Century', *Journal of Ethiopian Studies*, Vol. III, No. I, pp. 4–5.

[2] Beke, *Commerce*, p. 22; Beke, F.O.T.A., Vol. II, p. 8. A very different picture of the conditions of slaves in the late 1870's is presented by Matteucci, p. 274.

have dared to sell his captives. On the contrary, the captives from each raided tribe would be released once their tribe came to terms with Sahle Selassie. Those who were kept as slaves by the king were emancipated according to customary law after seven years, and were never sold.[1]

It was estimated that between 3,000 and 4,000 slaves were sold annually at the market of Abdul Rasul, which was attended by Muslim merchants from Harar, Tajura, Aussa, Rahita, Wollo and northern Ethiopia.[2] For some reason the slave-merchants preferred to cloak their trade in mystery although it was completely legal (to Muslims) and was even encouraged by the government.[3] As in other merchant villages the sale of slaves took place in the huts of the brokers and prices varied according to age, sex and qualities.

. . . Examined like cattle by their purchaser, the sullen Shankela fetches a price proportioned to the muscular appearance of his giant frame; and the child of tender years is valued according to the promise of future development. Even the shame-faced and the slenderly-clad maiden is subjected to every indignity, whilst the price of her charms is estimated according to the regularity of her features, the symmetry of her budding form, and the luxuriance of her braided locks. . . .[4]

The Galla slave-merchants from the south would not accept the thalers of the coastal merchants. The latter usually invested their thalers in salt *amoleh*, beads, copper and certain types of cloth which were in demand in the Galla areas.

The growing demand for Abyssinian slaves, especially concubines, in the Arabian markets was probably the main cause of Tajura's economic development after the second quarter of the nineteenth century. Fortunately for the Tajurans this growing demand coincided with the expansion of the kingdom of

[1] Beke, F.O.A., published by the Society for the Extinction of the Slave Trade, Vol. I, pp. 168–9. Harris Slave Report, paras. 15, 17, 20. In para. 15 of his Slave Report Harris claims that moral standards in Showa had deteriorated and the slaves who did not accept Christianity were sold.
[2] L.G., 185, No. 1440, Barker, 7.1.1842; Rochet, *Voyage*, p. 300; Johnston, Vol. II, p. 129; L.G., 189, No. 2060G. Report on trade, paras. 16–17, Harris, 5.1.1842; Bernatz, J. M.: *Scenes in Ethiopia*, Munich-London, 1852, Vol. II, Plate 24.
[3] Rochet, *Voyage*, p. 300; Cecchi, Vol. I, p. 303.
[4] Harris, Vol. I, pp. 377–8.

Showa, which opened new routes to trade in the interior and created a demand in Showa for foreign products and firearms.[1] Although the Tajurans going to Showa took with them many loads of salt from Lake Assal, it seems that the salt supply of the highlands was mainly in the hands of the nomad Adoimara. As one camel-load of foreign products and metals could buy the same number of slaves as a whole caravan loaded with salt, many Tajuran merchants brought to the highlands with them blue and white cotton cloth, copper, beads, metals and other foreign-made products available at Mokha and Berbera, or preferably thalers.

Unlike the *Jabartis* and Arab merchants coming from Massawa, the Tajurans were prevented from reaching the sources of supply by the rulers of the kingdom of Showa and the principality of Wollo Argoba. Consequently Tajuran merchants often used the services of local agents, who acquired the slaves for them in the markets to the south of the Amhara regions. In some cases the Tajurans bought their slaves directly from Galla and *Jabarti* merchants, whose caravans came to the markets of Abdul Rasul, Dawe and Ein Amba in northern Argoba.[2]

In Showa the Tajurans were not allowed to penetrate beyond the villages on the eastern border of Yifat. Peace and security may have been an important reason for this,[3] but the king was probably motivated to a large extent by his wish to turn Showa into an emporium of trade where merchants from different parts of Ethiopia would meet and trade and consequently enrich the Showan treasury. Thus the village of Chanoo was allotted to the Tajurans and the village of Aliyo Amba to the Hararis, while Tigreans and northern merchants had to live in Ankober.

The slaves acquired by the Tajurans in Showa were mostly highly valued 'Guragens', the red Ethiopians 'so much prized' in Arabia, and to a lesser degree Galla and Sidama from southwestern Ethiopia. Nearly all of them were under twenty and the majority were between the ages of seven and fourteen. The proportion of females to males in the Tajuran caravans was even

[1] See below, pp. 172–3.
[2] Abbadie, F.N.A. 21300, pp. 224–5; Beke, *Commerce*, p. 8; Beke, F.O.A., Vol. I, p. 168. Abbadie, F.N.A. 21303, p. 349, para. 171, 21.10.1843.
[3] Harris, Vol. I, p. 324; Johnston, Vol. II, pp. 89–90.

higher than in the ones going to Massawa.[1] Until their departure for the coast, the slaves were housed in the huts of Chanoo and on occasions when the roads to the coast were blocked, there would be over a thousand slaves awaiting transportation in the village.[2]

Some of the more prominent Tajuran merchants, who served as a nucleus for each caravan, led to the coast a few score of slaves. However, most Tajurans could not afford to buy more than five or six slaves, which in Showa represented an invest-ment of about one hundred thalers. The average Tajuran slave caravan to the coast was made up of thirty to fifty Afar merchants and their attendants leading on the average about 200 slaves.[3] Such a caravan was far too small to travel alone through the dangerous area beyond the Awash, and the Tajurans would usually join forces with smaller Harari caravans and with the much larger nomadic Adoimara caravans returning to their home areas with foodstuffs and livestock exchanged for salt.

Although usually very young, and having already covered a few hundred miles before reaching Abdul Rasul, the newly acquired slaves had to traverse on foot the very difficult, hot and waterless route to Tajura. Each slave carried a water gourd, some food and a head rest, while the camels of the merchants carried extra provisions, water and merchandise including ivory, hides, some musk and, on rare occasions, a little gold.[4]

En route, the Tajurans took the front, rear and the flanks of the caravan to prevent sudden attacks and escapes while the slaves of each merchant walked in the centre in small groups, under the supervision of the oldest and the strongest. When camping, the males were given charge of the camels, of prepar-ing the camp, of fuel gathering and other easy tasks. The females

[1] Harris, Vol. I, p. 228; Abbadie, F.N.A. 21300, p. 487; Beke, F.O.A., Vol. I, pp. 89, 106; Isenberg, C.M.R., Vol. 1841, p. 4; Johnston, Vol. I, pp. 220, 227; L.G., 204, No. 1146, Haines, 6.4.1843; Bernatz, J. M.: *Scenes in Ethiopia*, Munich-London, 1852, Vol. I, Plate 9; L.G., 165, No. 2316, Haines, 5.7.1841; *Transactions of the Bombay Geographical Society*, Vol. 4, Kirk, R.: Journey from Tajoora to Ankobar 1841, pp. 322, 337.
[2] L.G., 204, No. 1146, Haines, 6.4.1843.
[3] *Transactions of the Bombay Geographical Society*, Vol. 4, Kirk, R.: Journey from Tajoora to Ankobar 1841, p. 337; Abbadie, F.N.A. 21300, pp. 477, 486, 497; L.G., 185, No. 1440, Barker, 7.1.1842, para. 21; Rochet, *Voyage*, pp. 322, 331; Beke, F.O.A., Vol. I, p. 106; Johnston, Vol. I, p. 219.
[4] Isenberg, C.M.R., Vol. 1841, p. 4. Abbadie, F.N.A. 21300, pp. 477, 479, 486, 497; Johnston, Vol. I, p. 220; Beke, F.O.A., Vol. I, p. 106.

served their masters, the more beautiful becoming their concubines.[1] Although some authors give a very grim description of
the Tajuran slave caravans,[2] the more accepted version is of gay
groups of children walking unconfined along the road and usually
well treated.[3] One must admit that the Afar were not as gentle
with their slaves as were the north Ethiopian slave-merchants
and that the climate, lack of water and the dangers of the Afar
road could not be compared to the conditions in the highlands.
However, considering the very special nature of their 'merchandise' and the fact that the slaves represented most of their limited
capital,[4] it stands to reason that the Afar merchants gave them
the best care possible under the circumstances.

Upon reaching Debene-Wema territory beyond Muloo, after
crossing the most dangerous part of the route, the large caravans
would begin to break up into their original units. The nomad
Adoimara returned to their tribe and the Hararis went home by
way of Metta. However, the Tajuran slave caravans still had a
special problem providing the water necessary for the hundreds
of young children they were driving along. Just after the rainy
season caravans were certain not to lack water all along the road,
but they also stood a chance of encountering small bands of Issa
Somali and Mudaito Asaimara. If the caravan travelled in the
latter part of the dry season, it always stood in danger of finding
the most important water-holes dry, and many of the slaves
would die of thirst.[5]

Once the caravans reached the *Bahr* Assal area most of the
dangers were over. The Afar caravans began to break up into
smaller units comprising the slaves, the camels and escorts of
one or two merchants.[6] The Tajurans would enter their village
only after dark in order to preserve their property from the 'evil
eye'. On entering Tajura each merchant took his little herd of
human merchandise to his own enclosure and the ordeal of the
slaves was over.

[1] Beke, F.O.A., Vol. I, p. 169; Harris, Vol. I, pp. 218–19, 227; Kirk, p.
322.
[2] Bernatz, Vol. I, Plate 8. He accompanied the Harris Mission to Showa.
See also: C.M.R., Vol. 1841, Isenberg description, p. 4.
[3] Johnston, Vol. I, pp. 219, 227; Beke, F.O.A., Vol. I, pp. 106, 169.
[4] Beke, F.O.A., Vol. I, p. 119, December, 1843.
[5] Abbadie, F.N.A. 21300, p. 497
[6] Kirk, p. 322.

In Tajura the slaves were always kept in the merchant's house for a short while until they recuperated from the fatigue of the road and until transportation was available. Most of the Tajuran slaves were sent to Jedda, Hudieda and Mokha. However, with the decline of the Yemeni coast many more of the Tajuran slaves were taken to the fair of Berbera, where they were sold to Persian Gulf merchants. After 1840, owing to British intervention in the Persian Gulf slave trade, the number of slaves shipped from Tajura to Arabia, and from there by land to the Persian Gulf and Iraq, was on the increase.[1]

In the second quarter of the nineteenth century Tajura exported between 1,500 and 3,000 slaves annually.[2] A young male slave who was bought for about fifteen thalers in Showa fetched about forty to fifty thalers in Berbera or in Arabia. A young female bought in Showa for about twenty thalers would fetch at least forty thalers and for an exceptionally good-looking female even a hundred thalers could be got in the foreign markets.[3] One may assume that the gross profit of the slave-merchants of Tajura was about 100 per cent in Tajura and even 200 per cent in Berbera or Arabia. However, the slave-merchant spent on the average about six months in the process of buying his slaves, waiting for the caravan, travelling to the coast and waiting for the slaves to regain their strength before sending them on to Berbera or Arabia. If one considers all the risks taken by the slave-merchant, the expenses on the road and the fact that the average Tajuran could not afford to buy more than a few slaves on each trip, the profits of most Tajuran merchants were small. At the most they might have been sufficient to cover the expenses of his large family. In fact, accumulation of capital in Tajura was very slow and most of the Tajurans remained poor.

---

[1] Abbadie, F.N.A. 21300, pp. 477, 486. L.G., 301, No. 371, 20.5.1856; L.G., 256, No. 389, May, 1848, paras. 37–8, Lt. Cruttenden.
[2] Harris, Vol. I, pp. 63, 336; Beke, F.O.A., Vol. I, p. 169; Isenberg, C.M.R., Vol. 1841, p. 4; Bernatz, Vol. I, Plate 3; Rochet, *Voyage*, p. 300; L.G., 145, No. 4618, Haines, 28.8.1840, report of Captain Moresly (probably Moresby) from 24.8.1840; M. & D., Vol. 13, p. 230, Combes, 20.4.1840; Ministère de la France d'Outre-Mer: Côte Française des Somalis, Carton 129/3, commander of Génie, 16.4.1858.
[3] J.R.G.S., Vol. 10, p. 457; Beke, F.O.A., Vol. I, pp. 89, 169; Barker Report, L.G., 145, No. 4618, Haines, 28.8.1840; Abbadie, F.N.A. 21300, pp. 32, 424, 486; Krapf, p. 74; Bernatz, Vol. II, Plate 24; Isenberg, C.M.R., Vol. 1841, p. 4.

Little is known of the slave trade of Harar, probably because Europeans were not allowed into the town until after its conquest by the Egyptians.[1] Burton, who was the first European to visit the town in modern times (1855), claims that Harar was 'still of old the great half-way house' for 'slaves from Zangaro, Gurague and the Galla tribes'.[2] Nevertheless it is quite clear that the number of slaves that reached Harar in the nineteenth century was limited because of circumstances already mentioned above.[3] Slaves, especially girls, were considered a very good investment in Harar and the houses of the merchants of the town were always full of slaves. The townspeople who did not care to join the caravans going into the interior would usually entrust money to a *Wakil* (representative) of an important merchant, or to a lesser merchant who joined the caravan, to be invested in slaves.[4] The Amir of Harar himself took an active part in the slave trade. In addition to those which he received in lieu of tribute and taxation, his agents in the interior acquired for him a number of choice slaves which they sent back with each caravan returning to the town.[5] The number exported from Harar annually is not known. In the 1850's the last Harari caravan to Berbera, the 'slave caravan', usually led about 500 slaves. It is probable that other Harari caravans brought the same number either to Zeila or Berbera. From the amount of coffee, saffron, *qat* and other merchandise exported annually by the merchants of Harar,[6] it is clear that slaves were not as decisive a factor in Harar's economy as they were in Tajura's. The slave trade was none the less popular among the Harari merchants because it brought high profits and also helped with the transportation of the merchandise.

The number of slaves sold annually at the fair of Berbera in the second quarter of the nineteenth century was between 1,000 and 2,000. A few hundred slaves were shipped to the northern

---

[1] Barker, L.G., 185, No. 1440, para. 15, 7.1.1842, paras. 26, 31–40, 15.12.1841.
[2] Burton, Vol. II, p. 25.
[3] See pages 12–13.
[4] Yusuf Ahmed MS., pp. 47, 52.
[5] Yusuf Ahmed MS., p. 49. In the time of Amir Abdul Karim taxation was paid with slaves. See also: Sale of slaves and presents of slaves by the Amir: Yusuf Ahmed MS., p. 43.
[6] See above, p. 10.

ports of the Red Sea, and about 1,000 Ethiopian slaves were exported annually to the Persian Gulf area.[1] It might be said that Berbera specialized in the supply of high-quality slaves, especially females, to southern Arabia, the Persian Gulf area, Mesopotamia and to a lesser extent Persia and India.[2] Nearly every boat leaving Berbera for the above destinations had some on board.[3] Somali girls were kidnapped each year by visiting boats, but their number was insignificant when compared to the number of Gurage, Sidama, Galla and occasional Amhara slaves brought by the caravans from the highlands. Berbera was renowned as the centre of the trade of the so-called Gurage slaves, especially concubines. It was the beauty of the Gurage girls, their light colour and above all the higher moral qualities claimed for them, which pleased the Arabian buyer.[4]

A brisk trade in slaves was carried on in all the commercial centres in northern Ethiopia throughout the year. Hundreds of slaves were sold to Sudanese *Jalaba* in Gondar and many others to merchants coming from Arkiko, Massawa and Arabia. However, the bulk of the slaves brought to northern Ethiopia by each trading caravan coming from the south, and especially from Basso in Gojjam, were driven by the *Jabarti*s (Ethiopian Muslims) themselves to Massawa or to Sennar. Little is known about the slave trade between Gondar and Sennar besides the fact that over 1,000 slaves were exported by this route annually in times of peace.[5] Far more information is available about the caravans driving slaves to Massawa from the different Muslim commercial centres in the northern plateau. In fact the importance of

[1] Range, 387, Vol. 10, No. 660, para. 7, Wilson, 28.1.1831; L.G., 192, No. 2762, Edwards, July, 1842; L.G., 188, No. 1821, para. 3, Robertson, 4.3.1842; L.G., 255, No. 5, para. 10, Cruttenden, 24.11.1847.
[2] Range, 387, Vol. 10, No. 660, Wilson, 28.1.1831; L.G., 188, No. 1821, para. 3, Robertson, 4.3.1842; L.G., 192, No. 2762, Kemball and Edwards, July, 1842; L.G., 251, No. 537, Cruttenden, 1847; Abbadie, F.N.A. 21301, p. 26; Ibid., 21300, p. 477.
[3] India Office: Political and Secret Records, *Letters from Aden*, Vol. 26, p. 111, 22.2.1842; Abbadie, F.N.A. 21300, p. 487; L.G., 251, No. 537, April, 1847; L.G., 294, No. 158, para. 29, Burton, 22.2.1855.
[4] Abbadie (F.N.A. 21301, pp. 23, 26; 21300, p. 487) was told that the Gurage slave girls are the best in the Adjami (Somali) countries. It is interesting that the general name of slaves in Berbera was *Quraqa*. Abbadie, 21303, p. 23. See also: Range, 387, Vol. 10, p. 600, Wilson, 1831, paras. 26–9, of slaves from Berbera serving in armies of Persian Gulf rulers.
[5] M. & D., Vol. 61, Rochet d'Héricourt, pp. 232–3—1,200 slaves; Combes and Tamisier, Vol. IV, p. 95—over 2,000 slaves.

each caravan reaching Massawa was usually measured by the number of slaves it brought.[1] While from Hamasen, where many slave-merchants lived, the average trade caravan would bring a score or two of slaves, the great caravans coming from Gondar, Derita and Adowa usually drove over a hundred and sometimes 200 slaves at one time. Most of the slaves in these caravans were children under twenty and the ratio of the sexes was at least two females for each male.[2] The slaves in the northern caravans were mainly of Galla and Sidama origin, but a small number of *Shanqalla* were also to be found in each caravan.

On their arrival at Massawa, slaves were inspected by the customs authorities, and after payment of five thalers per slave, each merchant received an official certificate for each one.[3] A much higher tax, however, was paid for eunuchs. The average price of a Galla or Sidama *Gurbe* was between thirty-five and fifty thalers, and a *Wosif* fetched from fifty to sixty thalers, while eunuchs fetched even one hundred thalers.[4] It is difficult to estimate the number of slaves who reached Massawa and the nearby coast because many were smuggled from small harbours in the vicinity of Massawa, or were dressed as pilgrims to avoid taxation. It is noteworthy that while in the beginning of the nineteenth century about 500 to a 1,000 slaves were officially exported each year from Massawa,[5] in the 1830's and 1840's the annual number was nearly 2,000.[6]

From Massawa the slaves were usually shipped to Jedda and to Mokha. On the day of departure the hands and feet of the slaves were dipped in a solution of reddish-yellow Hina. Then they were dressed in new clothes and in the evening, probably to avoid the 'evil eye', they were put on the boats. Some Muslim merchants from the highlands preferred to travel with their slaves to Jedda, where they received a better price, and per-

---

[1] C. & C., Massawa, Vol. I, Degoutin, 10.9.1844; Katte, A. Von: *Reise in Abyssinien im Jahre 1836*, Stuttgart, 1838, p. 131; Ferret and Galinier, Vol. II, p. 427; Ruppell, Vol. I, pp. 193–4.
[2] Abbadie, F.N.A. 21300, p. 330.
[3] Ibid., pp. 330, 337, 339, 346; Ibid., 21301, p. 72, para. 227; Ibid., p. 145; L.G., 165, No. 2316, Haines, 5.7.1841.
[4] Abbadie, F.N.A. 21300, pp. 236, 337; ibid. 21301, p. 36, para. 102.
[5] Salt, p. 426; Bruce, Vol. III, p. 91; Valentia, Vol. II, p. 487.
[6] C. & C., Massawa, Vol. I, Degoutin, 10.9.1844; Ibid., Rochet d'Héricourt, 10.11.1848; Range, 388, Vol. 61, No. 2709, 20.4.1838; L.G., 186, No. 1470, Christopher, April, 1842; L.G., 301, No. 571, Coghlan, 20.5.1856.

formed the *Haj* at the same time.[1] However, this was done only rarely, as the time expended in the voyage and pilgrimage could be used for another trip into the more familiar interior. The slave trade between Massawa and the Arabian coast was thus left mainly in the hands of the *Jabarti*s of Massawa and Arab and Egyptian merchants.

As a result of the growing demand for Ethiopian slaves throughout the Muslim world it seems that about 6,000 to 7,000 slaves were exported annually in the second quarter of the nineteenth century through Metemma, Massawa, Tajura, Zeila and Berbera. Most of the so-called 'Abyssinian slaves' were actually pagans of Galla and Sidama origin. As in the past, the Ethiopian slave trade was mainly geared to supply young concubines for the harems in the Muslim countries and therefore the largest proportion of slaves exported from Ethiopia were young females. While Tajura and Berbera were the main outlets for the so-called Guragen slaves, who were exported mainly to southern Arabia and the Persian Gulf, Massawa and Metemma were the outlets for the Galla and Sidama slaves of south-western Ethiopia, who went mostly to Egypt, the Hijaz and even to Turkey.

The great development of the slave trade in Ethiopia in the second quarter of the nineteenth century was in fact the beginning of the end of this trade. The British became actively interested in its suppression in the 1830's. When Aden became a British base in 1839 the ports of the Red Sea came under closer surveillance through the frequent visits of Indian navy boats coming from this port, and one of the aims of the Harris mission to Showa (1841–3) was to study the problems of the Ethiopian slave trade. Nevertheless, fearing the reaction of the inhabitants of the Red Sea coast and not being too secure in Aden, the board of governors of the East India Company decided to act cautiously in the matter of the abolition of slavery in the area and for the time being not to press the issue.[2] British interference in the slave trade of the Red Sea became more noticeable in the late 1840's as a result of a more vigorous anti-slavery policy imposed upon the Indian government by the British government and by a new anti-slavery treaty signed with the Sultan of Muscat and

[1] Combes and Tamisier, Vol. IV, p. 93.
[2] L.G., 182, No. 837, 6.2.1842; L.G., 182, No. 836, Haines, 22.12.1841.

Zanzibar. Nevertheless, although Omani subjects were legally prohibited from taking part in the Ethiopian slave trade, there were still many other Arab merchants who could not be legally prevented from dealing in Ethiopian slaves. The final legal loophole in the battle for abolition of the slave trade in the area was closed when the Porte, under British pressure during the Crimean War, issued a *firman* in 1854/5 outlawing the slave trade all over the Ottoman Empire.[1] Just about this time Emperor Teodros of Ethiopia forbade, at least in theory, the slave trade in the Ethiopian highlands[2] and some Somali chiefs were coerced into signing an anti-slavery agreement with the British.

In reality the Ethiopian slave trade continued to exist on a very large scale even in the time of Menelik, but this was the last convulsion of a trade which had been in the past an important factor in the social and economic life of the Ethiopian highlands and of the ports of the Red Sea. If it still existed by the end of the century it was mainly because of the proximity of Ethiopia to Arabia, still the main slave market in the world.

CONCLUSION

In the Middle East the ruling Muslim society looked with contempt and scorn upon trade and traders. As a result of this attitude, trade passed to a large extent into the hands of Levantine Christians and Jews, who were excluded from the army, the administration, and other fields of government. This process was accelerated by the fact that European merchants preferred to deal with their co-religionists and employ them as their representatives and brokers. In Ethiopia, this situation was reversed. The Amhara Tigrean Christian society composed of nobles, priests, soldiers and agriculturalists had looked down for many generations on commercial activities and crafts. The Muslim authorities on the coast of the Red Sea, and Muslim traders from Arabia, Somali and Egypt on their side preferred to deal with and favoured Muslim Ethiopian merchants. And even in

---

[1] L.G., 295, No. 265, Coghlan, 13.4.1855; L.G., No. 708, Coghlan, July, 1856.
[2] Public Record Office: Foreign Office, 401.1, Confidential Print, 'Abbysinian Correspondence 1846–1868', No. 490, Plowden, 10.11.1856; Ibid., Enclosure in No. 559, Plowden, 7.11.1858. L.G., 297, No. 723, Coghlan, 8.10.1855.

The site of Jiren, the capital of Abba Jifar, King of Jimma

The rocky mountains of Tigre dotting the plateau

the highlands, the Ethiopian Christian was always at a disadvantage when competing with the Muslim.

Ethiopia's main items of export—gold, ivory and slaves—came mainly from the south-western provinces and were forwarded to the coast by means of trading caravans. The waste of time, the expense, not to speak of the dangers incurred by merchants engaged in the long-range caravan trade on this route were immense; but as the result of the unceasing wars among the different Galla tribes and the Sidama, slaves were the most available commodity in the remote markets, whereas this was not so with gold, musk and ivory. However, though slavery was always a recognized factor in Ethiopian society, the Christian was forbidden to trade in slaves while the Muslim was not.

The new political and economic developments in the Red Sea basin reawakened the interest of the surrounding Muslim world in the Ethiopian plateau with its luxurious products. Because the Ethiopian trade was to a large extent a trade in luxury items, usually carried on in secrecy, and because the sources of this trade in the first half of the nineteenth century still presented a mystery and were hardly known on the coast, the countries adjacent to Ethiopia had an exaggerated conception of its value and of the possibilities for developing the foreign trade of that country.

The revival of Islam in Arabia and elsewhere after the end of the eighteenth century, coupled with the political and economic developments in the Red Sea area, had a tremendous impact on Ethiopia. Those elements among the population of the coast who were not Muslim were thereafter quickly Islamized. But even more important, the peripheral regions of Tigre became increasingly Muslim, and Islam made deep inroads into the Amhara areas of northern Ethiopia. In truth, Muslim communities in those areas originated in some cases even before the time of Grañ, but they grew greatly in size and in importance[1] and new Muslim trading centres flourished all over the highlands. The Wollo and the Yejju Galla, who dominated large parts of central and northern Ethiopia, strengthened their ties with Islam, and many Galla rulers of the north sympathized at least with Islam,

[1] Nearly all the farmers of the customs were Muslims, and the Greek trading communities lost their importance in this period.

if they did not actually help it spread.[1] The caravans of the Muslim merchants, which penetrated deeper and deeper into the interior, served as a vehicle by which the principles of Islam, and Muslim *Ulama* from Arabia and elsewhere, reached the remotest corners of the highlands. Consequently a widespread Islamization was begun among the pagan Galla tribes of south-western and southern Ethiopia.[2]

[1] Arnold, T. W.: *The Preaching of Islam*, London, 1913, p. 117; Ruppell, Vol. I, pp. 328, 366; Ibid., Vol. II, p. 69; Beke, Dr C. T.: *Routes in Abyssinia*, London, Her Majesty's Stationery Office, 1867, pp. 51–2; Isenberg, pp. 36, 423; Abdul Majid al-Abadin: *Bayna al-Habasha wa'l-Arab*, Cairo (no date), pp. 200–1; Combes and Tamisier, Vol. II, p. 300.
[2] Abdul Majid al-Abadin: *Bayna al-Habasha wa'l-Arab*, Cairo (no date), p. 199; Cederquist: Islam and Christianity in Abyssinia, *Moslem World*, Vol. II, London, 1912, p. 153; Combes and Tamisier, Vol. II, pp. 44–7. See below, pp. 76, 79.

IV

The emergence of the Galla of the south-west[1]

Before the Galla invasion in the sixteenth century southern Ethiopia was inhabited by people of Cushitic origin called Sidama.[2] The Sidama highlands were divided into a great number of kingdoms and principalities, among which were: Hadya, Wollamo, Sidamo, Enarea and Kaffa.[3] The last two were probably the strongest and the richest, as they were situated in the area from which or through which came most of the gold, ivory, musk, incense, precious skins and slaves for which Ethiopia was famous.

By the beginning of the eighteenth century, after two centuries of constant wars, first with the Amhara and then with the Galla, Sidama resistance was broken and the Sidama plateau was overrun by Galla tribes. The Galla gradually absorbed the Sidama people left in the areas they had conquered, and in their turn largely gave up the pasturalist life and slowly adopted many Sidama customs, cultural features, and forms of social and political organization. Owing to the difficult mountainous terrain in some areas and the river valleys in others, the loosely knit Galla tribes tended to split into even smaller units lacking any cohesion. Each unit was governed by elected officers, whose authority depended completely on the good will of each individual in the tribe, a system which to the outsider seemed to border on anarchy. This political system and social organization prevailed among the Galla of south and south-western Ethiopia until the second part of the nineteenth century, and in a degenerate form

[1] This chapter is based to a large extent on my article, 'The Emergence and Consolidation of the Monarchies of Enarea and Jimma in the First Half of the Nineteenth Century', *Journal of African History*, Vol. VI, No. 2, 1965.

[2] Meaning in Galliña, foreigners, non-Galla. Trimingham, p. 179, footnote; Beckingham, C. F., and Huntingford, G. W. B.: *Some Records of Ethiopia 1593–1646*, London, 1954, p. 1. While the term Sidama describes the people of the area, the form Sidamo is the name of a single tribe.

[3] It is still debatable whether Kaffa could actually be called a Sidama kingdom.

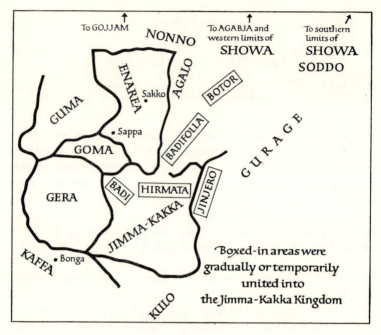

The Galla monarchies of the south-west

continued to do so, with some important exceptions, until Ethiopia was united by Menelik in the last decades of the nineteenth century. Throughout the eighteenth and most of the nineteenth centuries southern and south-western Ethiopia were in a continuous state of war. The Galla not only continued to attack Sidama areas, but even more, fought among themselves. From time to time the Mecha Galla made inroads into the Amhara provinces of Gojjam and Damot, conquered some of the peripheral areas and devastated others.

Had it not been for their political disunity, the Mecha Galla could have taken advantage of the disintegration of the Gondarine Empire and conquered Gojjam and changed the history of Ethiopia. However, the timely introduction of firearms by the weak Amhara lords of Gojjam in the middle of the eighteenth century affected the whole balance of power in that area, and the Amhara lords not only halted the Galla advance, but succeeded

74

in making deep inroads into Galla territories beyond the Blue Nile.[1]

In the second quarter of the nineteenth century, European travellers and missionaries brought information back to the coast about the existence of a number of highly organized despotic monarchies between the Omo and the Didessa. The best known were Limu-Enarea, Gumma, Gomma, Jimma-Kakka and Gera. It is difficult to establish an exact date for the founding of these kingdoms. Rather, their existence was probably the culmination of a process by which the authority of successful war leaders or of traditional office-holders, like the *Abba Dula, Motti,* or *Abba Boku,* was gradually strengthened. By the second half of the eighteenth century the main elective offices among the Mecha Galla of south-western Ethiopia tended to be hereditary. Antoine d'Abbadie, who travelled extensively in Ethiopia between 1838 and 1846 and who was the first European in modern times to reach south-western Ethiopia, wrote that the *Abba Boku,* the 'carrier of the sceptre', is the head of the legislative authority. The *Boku,* a wooden sceptre, is carried in the *Abba Boku*'s belt. It passes into the hands of the son on the father's death and if the *Abba Boku* has no son, his wife holds the sceptre and makes the laws.[2] The *Moti,* or *Abba Dula,* who in the past had been just a war leader during the cycle of his *Gada,*[3] acquired more and more authority until his title came to mean something very close to the Ethiopian *negus.*

[1] Abbadie, F.N.A. 21300, pp. 153, 770; Ibid., 21302, p. 387; Ministère des Affaires Étrangères, Bruxelles, Archives, Dos. 2024, rapport fait en 1843 par M. Blondeel, p. 27.

[2] Abbadie, F.N.A. 21300, p. 569. One of d'Abbadie's informants (F.N.A. 21301, p. 129) calls Bofo 'Abba Bokka' while his son Abba Bagibo is called 'Sultan'. See also: Harris, Vol. III, pp. 53–5; Abbadie, F.N.A. 21300, p. 760; Massaia, G.: *I miei trentacinque anni di missione nell'alta Ethiopia,* Rome, 1925, Vol. III, p. 60. The *Abba Boku* held in each tribe a position similar to that of a magistrate.

[3] Galla tribes are usually divided into five groups called *Gada,* each having special communal and political functions associated with it. After being initiated into the first *Gada,* promotion from one *Gada* to another is done collectively every eight years. Membership in the *Gada* is not according to age. A son is initiated into the first *Gada* only after his father completes a cycle of forty years, having passed through all the classes. *Moti,* d'Abbadie writes (F.N.A. 21300, p. 759), is the executive authority which the Abyssinians called *Negus,* but the Galla *Moti* cannot legislate and his main duty was to lead the army in battle. See also: Massaia, *I miei,* Vol. VI, pp. 5–6. Traditionally, the *Moti* was responsible for the execution of the decisions of

The new monarchies of Enarea, Gumma and Gomma were established, it seems, in the first or possibly second decade of the nineteenth century, while the kingdoms of Gera and Jimma-Kakka were founded later.[1] This process no doubt was affected by the transformation of the Mecha Galla from a nomadic pastoral life to a settled one. It was also influenced by former and still existing Sidama states in the midst of which the Galla lived, as well as by the new kingdom of Showa. But it is also most likely that the revival of Islam in Arabia at the end of the eighteenth century, and the developments in the Red Sea in the first quarter of the nineteenth century, had also influenced the founding of the Galla monarchies of the Gibe.

It is only where the Moslem slave-dealer has successfully commenced the work of conversion to the creed promulgated by the Prophet, that this wild heathen race have been brought to bow the neck to the yoke of kings. Of this Enarea affords a most striking example. . . .[2]

By the second quarter of the nineteenth century many *Ulama* and *Fuqaha* lived in Sakka, Jiren and other trading centres in the midst of a multitude of Muslim merchants, Galla, *Jabarti*, and Arab, who had either settled in the south-west or were staying in the area for a number of years.

It is evident that Islam was carried to the Galla of south-western Ethiopia mostly by way of the trade route from Massawa through Begamder to Gojjam and beyond. The expansion of Christian Showa since the second part of the eighteenth century and especially in the beginning of the nineteenth century had completely disrupted the direct route between the Somali coast and south-western Ethiopia.[3] The Sudan had very little influence

---

the magistrate and of tribal meetings. The *Abba Dula* was elected to lead the tribe in battle.

[1] Regarding the establishment of the monarchy in Enarea and Jimma, see below, pp. 79, 89. Regarding Gumma, Gomma and Gera see: Beke, Dr C. T.: *On the Countries South of Abyssinia*, London, 1843, pp. 6–7; Abbadie, F.N.A. 21300, pp. 751–2; Cecchi, Vol. II, pp. 226–7, 541–2; Massaia, G.: *In Abissinia e fra i Galla*, Florence, 1895, p. 279; Huntingford, G. W. B.: *The Galla of Ethiopia*, London, 1955, p. 20.

[2] Harris, Vol. III, p. 53.

[3] Although some Harari merchants were to be found in Enarea and many more in Jimma about the middle of the nineteenth century. Abbadie, F.N.A. 21303, p. 393, 26.1.1844; Ibid., p. 365, para. 184, 14.11.1843; Lewis, H. S.: *A Galla Monarchy*, Wisconsin, 1965, pp. 41–2.

in south-western Ethiopia until the second half of the nineteenth century. Even the conquest of the Sudan by Muhammad Ali did not change this situation. In the 1840's the Egyptians were still establishing their shaky authority in the Beni Shangul-Boran area bordering on western Ethiopia, through which they hoped to open an avenue to the rich trade of Kaffa and southern Ethiopia.[1] But they were still faced with the hostile negroid, 'Arab' and pagan Galla tribes on the way. Muslim merchants from the Sudan could not penetrate into Wollaga, and although some reached the borders of western and north-western Kaffa, they were not allowed to enter the kingdom.[2] It is true that many Sudanese *Jalaba* traded with Begamder, but for economic or other reasons they were not allowed to go beyond Gondar.[3] But the best evidence that the Sudan had very little to do with the Islamization of the Galla of south-western Ethiopia is the fact that most of the Muslim Galla in the area today belong to the *Shafi'i Madhab*, which is predominant in northern Ethiopia and Harar, and not to the *Maliki Madhab*, which is predominant in the Sudan and has many followers in Egypt.

The kingdom of Limu-Enarea can be considered a prototype for the Galla kingdoms and principalities of the Gibe-Didessa area; it was, however, only its favourable geographical position and its talented king that made it so famous in the second quarter of the nineteenth century, not its size or power.

The ancient kingdom of Enarea was invaded by the Limu-Galla about the beginning of the eighteenth century. The king and some of his followers escaped to Kaffa, but the remaining Sidama population was absorbed by the Limu-Galla who occupied the country.[4] As they became more settled, the power of the

---

[1] Ministère des Affaires Étrangères: Correspondance Politique, Égypte, Alexandrie et le Caire, Vol. 15, pp. 216–17, 24.1.1843; F.O., 78/541, enclosure in No. 16, Campbell, Alex., 19.4.1843. Cerulli's (*Ethiopia Occidentale*, Rome, 1833, Vol. II, p. 190) assumption that the conquest of the Sudan by Egypt has directly helped the spread of Islam in south-western Ethiopia is wrong.

[2] *Athenaeum.* London Literary and Critical Journal, No. 1042 from 1847; Ibid., No. 1105 from 1848.

[3] Katte, pp. 130–1 (1836); M. & D., Vol. 61, p. 404, Lejean, 15.5.1863; Matteucci, p. 270; Combes and Tamisier, Vol. I, pp. 110–11.

[4] Abbadie, F.N.A. 21300, p. 641; Massaia, G.: *In Abissinia e fra i Galla*, Florence, 1895, p. 207; Cecchi, Vol. II, pp. 156–7; Bieber, F. J.: *Kaffa: Ein alt-Kuschitisches Volkstum Inner-Afrika*, Wien, 1923, Vol. I, pp. 78–9; Ibid., Vol. II, pp. 508–10.

Limu chiefs grew until finally a renowned war leader, Bofo, the son of Abba Boku, established the monarchy of Limu-Enarea after strengthening his position by marrying the daughter of the traditional elected political leader. The following oral tradition regarding the establishment of the monarchy of Limu-Enarea was current in Enarea in 1843.[1] Abba Rebu, who was still alive in the 1840's, had in the past been the most important *Soressa*[2] of the Limu tribes, whereas Bofo, the son of Boku, was a poor nobleman, whose land bordered on that of the Nonno Galla. The latter often invaded Limu.[3] From time to time Bofo took part in reprisal raids against Nonno territory riding his war-horse Gomol, and thus he acquired the name Abba Gomol. Being very brave, and always returning with much booty, Bofo became very famous, and Abba Rebu gave him his daughter in marriage. By this wife Bofo had a son, Abba Bagibo—Ibsa, who ruled Enarea from 1825 to 1861. This marriage is represented by another set of oral traditions as a political union between rival clans, Sapera and Sigaro, who, it is claimed, descended from Portuguese settlers who had ruled parts of Enarea in the sixteenth century. It is further claimed that the final blow to the Sigaro clan in the competition between the houses of Sapera and Sigaro was dealt by Abba Gomol (Abba Bagibo's father) in the beginning of the century. Thus Abba Gomol and the Sapera clan were able to establish their authority in the area from Sakka to the south of Sappa, while the northern and eastern provinces of Enarea were annexed in the time of Abba Bagibo. It is of course possible that Bofo represented the Sapera clan while Abba Rebu was a Sigaro, and when Bofo emerged supreme, or even before, a political marriage was arranged between the two clans. To ensure the peace, Bofo later abdicated and Abba Bagibo, who belonged to both clans, came to power.[4] The first tradition recorded by d'Abbadie in 1843 goes

---

[1] Abbadie, 21300, pp. 569–572. One can assume that events as important and as fresh as the founding of the monarchy would still be reported relatively accurately by people who had taken part in the actual event.

[2] Dignitary, chief, leader.

[3] The Nonno Galla were the bitterest enemies of the Limu. They were semi-nomads and lived in the areas north-east of Enarea.

[4] Harris, Vol. III, p. 53; Massaia, *I miei*, Vol. IV, p. 144; Cecchi, Vol. II, p. 157; Bieber, F. J.: *Kaffa: Ein alt-Kuschitisches Volkstum Inner-Afrika*, Wien, 1923, Vol. II, p. 511; Beckingham, lxi.

on to describe at length how Bofo quarrelled with his father-in-law and was disgraced. Meanwhile, relations with the jealous Gumma neighbours rapidly deteriorated and finally the Gumma invaded Enarea. The Limu people led by their chief, Abba Rebu, could not withstand the Gumma attack and they escaped to the *Mogga*.[1] The victorious Gumma who overran the valley of En-area were celebrating their success when Bofo and a few of his friends penetrated into their midst, took them by surprise, and killed many of them. When the battle was over and the Gumma were completely defeated, the Limu people returned to Enarea and fell on their knees before Bofo and said, 'we do not want any other master but you'. Ever after, Abba Rebu was one of Bofo's most devoted subjects.

Bofo abdicated about 1825 in order to ensure the succession of his son Abba Bagibo and then retired to the *Massera* (royal enclosure) of Sappa where he died in 1837.[2] As Abba Bagibo, his son by Abba Rebu's daughter, was twenty-three years old when he came to power[3] around 1825, it is probable that Bofo-Abba Gomol was acknowledged as King of Enarea in the first or perhaps the second decade of the nineteenth century.[4]

Throughout his reign Bofo was a bloodthirsty tyrant and was even cruel to his own flesh and blood. We are told that 'Abba Gumbal (Gomol) sought to destroy his own sons and daughters'.[5] The tyranny of the new king could be explained as having been necessary to suppress rebellion, dispute and civil war in order to establish a new form of government, strange to Galla society. Probably to further establish his authority, Bofo adopted Islam

---

[1] No-man's-land separating each Galla or Sidama territory from its neighbours. See below, p. 81.

[2] Massaia, *I miei*, Vol. IV, p. 144. Massaia, *In Abissinia*, p. 165; Abbadie, F.N.A. 21300, p. 572. It seems more likely that Bofo was deposed by his immediate family. See: Isenberg, p. 14. Abba Bagibo was helped by a council made of his uncles, nephews and sons—Abbadie, F.N.A. 21300, p. 199, November, 1843.

[3] Cecchi, Vol. II, p. 157.

[4] In a letter to Cardinal Franzoni (F.N.A. 23851, p. 34) Abbadie wrote: 'From Lofe we came to Enarea, a country which became a kingdom at the beginning of this century.' In the 1840's Bofo was still remembered as the *Gofta* (patron) of Limu, and not as *Moti* or *Sapera*. Abbadie, F.N.A. 21300, p. 223. See also: Abbadie, F.N.A. 21303, p. 344, para. 166 (from 1843); Cecchi, Vol. II, p. 156; Trimingham, p. 201.

[5] Isenberg, p. 14. See also: L.G., 184, No. 1098, Harris, 7.1.1842.

a short time after coming to power[1] on the advice of Muslim merchants who settled in the country.[2] Soon afterwards, most of the ruling class and a large part of the population followed his example:

This country being the principal place of residence of the Moham-medan merchants of Abyssinia, whose precepts and example have had, and still continue to have, most surprising results in the con-version of the Gallas.[3]

The kingdom of Limu-Enarea was quite small in size and population and very different from the old Sidama kingdom of Enarea, from which it borrowed its name.[4] It would be wrong, however, to accept travellers' descriptions of Enarea in the late 1870's and early 1880's as portraying the Limu-Enarea of the second quarter of the century. During that interval the country underwent two terrible calamities, first a plague which caused a great depopulation of Enarea in the late 1840's, and then the loss of much of its trade as a result of the expansion of Christian Showa, the growth of the sister Galla kingdom of Jimma, and the reopening of an alternative trade route to Kaffa after the death of King Abba Bagibo in 1861.[5] However, even during the golden period of the reign of Abba Bagibo the population of Enarea probably numbered just over 100,000 and its area covered only a few thousand square kilometres.

By the time Abba Bagibo came to power, the people of Enarea were completely settled and led a relatively happy life.[6] Most of the land belonged to individuals but the king owned extensive estates. As in all the Galla areas in southern Ethiopia, there were no villages in Enarea. Small groups of huts belonging to a family

---

[1] Harris, Vol. III, p. 53; Massaia (*In Abissinia*, p. 279) claims that the ruler of Jimma adopted Islam because this religion favours the idea of an absolute monarchy.

[2] Harris, Vol. III, p. 53. 'Gouma, Inarya et Djemma, ont été fondés à la suite de l'islamisme introduit par les marchands étrangères.' Abbadie, Nou-velles annales de voyages, 1845, Vol. III, p. 99. According to Cecchi (Vol. II, p. 160), Islam in Enarea dates to the first years of the century.

[3] Beke, Dr C. T.: *On the Countries South of Abyssinia*, London, 1843, p. 5; Harris, Vol. III, pp. 54–5; Krapf, p. 65. Regarding similar process in Jimma see: Massaia, *I miei*, Vol. VI, p. 10.

[4] Beke, *Southern Abyssinia*, p. 4; Beckingham, chap. 14, p. 149 (sixteenth-century Enarea).

[5] Massaia, *In Abissinia*, p. 282; Massaia, *I miei*, Vol. VI, p. 61.

[6] Massaia, *In Abissinia*, p. 166.

or to an important chief were separated from each other by cultivated fields. Only around some of the royal enclosures (*Massera*)
did anything resembling a village or a small town grow up.[1]
Sakka, the so-called capital of Enarea, was described as a town
of 10,000 to 12,000 people with at least a few hundred Muslim
Ulama. The town was in fact made up of groups of small hamlets, in the centre of which was a market village where merchants
from the north had probably lived since the beginning of the
century. This market village constantly expanded and con-
tracted with the arrival and departure of caravans.[2]

Like every other Galla and Sidama principality in southern
and western Ethiopia, Enarea was surrounded by several lines
of defence. First there was the *Mogga*, a belt of land circum-
scribing the country and left uncultivated, in which roamed
bands of thieves called *Ketto*. The *Mogga* was a battlefield in
which all the wars were fought. The country or the tribe which
was victorious moved its defences into or beyond its *Mogga*, and
turned part of the defeated country into a new *Mogga*.[3] Next
came the lines of defence proper, made up of palisades, ditches,
rivers, swamps and thick forests. Wherever a road from a neighbouring area entered the country, the defences had a gate called
Kella. Each such gate was guarded by a unit of cavalry commanded by an officer called *Abba Kella*. This officer helped a
special representative of the king count all incoming or outgoing
merchants, inspect their merchandise, and collect the customs.
In this way the king had the strictest control over the people
entering his territory, and at the same time could prevent the
many thousands of slaves employed by himself and by his subjects from escaping.[4]

The main duty of the *Abba Kella* was, however, to forestall
unexpected attacks by the enemies of the country. A high plat-
form was constructed beside the *Kella* and a soldier continuously
scrutinized the *Mogga* from it. If anything suspicious was sighted,

[1] Cecchi, Vol. II, p. 255; Massaia, *In Abissinia*, p. 74. Krapf, p. 64.
[2] Abbadie, F.N.A., 21300, p. 205. Abbadie, *Athenaeum*. London Literary
and Critical Journal, No. 1105 of 1848. See also: *Athenaeum*, No. 1042 of
1847; Abbadie, F.N.A. 21303, p. 118, para. 55.
[3] Abbadie, *Athenaeum*, No. 1041 of 1847; Abbadie, Antoine: *Géographie de
l'Éthiopie*, Paris, 1890, p. 40 (preface); Cecchi, Vol. II, p. 162.
[4] Cecchi, Vol. II, p. 228, footnote 1; Abbadie, F.N.A. 21302, pp. 389–90,
411–12; Ibid., 21303, pp. 112–13; Abbadie, *Géographie*, p. 22 (Préface).

the officer of the guard was informed and the alarm was sounded by hitting the *Bideru*, a hollowed tree-trunk suspended from a beam.[1] The sound of the *Bideru* could be heard at a distance of several kilometres. Through a system of *Bideru* placed at appropriate intervals, the news of an approaching enemy could reach the capital in a matter of minutes and every able-bodied man all over the country left the fields and joined the army.

All the free population of Limu-Enarea and her sister kingdoms were liable for military service and could be called upon to fight for the king at any time.[2] When thus summoned, they received no pay and even had to bring their own food, weapons, and war-horses with them. The king had only a small standing army, or bodyguard, consisting of a few hundred professional soldiers. Most of this unit was cavalry, but it also included some infantry, and a handful of matchlockmen. The few matchlocks, which were the pride of Abba Bagibo, were received as a present from *Dejazmatch* Goshu of Gojjam, whom Abba Bagibo courted, and with whom he exchanged presents. As the Galla could not, or did not want to, adapt themselves to firearms, the matchlockmen were Amharan or Tigrean mercenaries.[3]

The king in the Galla kingdoms was an absolute monarch. He had the power of life and death over his subjects and could do what he wished with their property. Abba Bagibo was helped by an advisory council composed of some of his closest relatives and important officials of the court.[4] But this advisory council did not constitute a check on his unlimited power, as he could make or unmake any of the dignitaries who took part in it.[5] The king was also the head of the judicial system. Although every *Abba Korro* and *Abba Ganda*[6] dealt with most of the legal problems that arose in their respective areas, every subject could, at least in theory, apply directly to the king, who regularly held court in the central market of the kingdom while the population looked

[1] Cecchi, Vol. II, p. 327. Compare to practice in Kaffa described by Soleillet, P.: *Voyages en Éthiopie 1882–1884*, Rouen, 1886, p. 187.
[2] Abbadie, F.N.A. 21300, p. 569.
[3] Abbadie, F.N.A. 21300, pp. 797–800, April, 1848; Abbadie, F.N.A. 21303, pp. 393–4, para. 219; Krapf, p. 65; Beke, *Southern Abyssinia*, p. 5.
[4] Abbadie, F.N.A. 21300, p. 199; Cecchi, Vol. II, p. 172; Lewis, H. S.: *A Galla Monarchy*, Wisconsin, 1965, pp. 74, 88.
[5] Cecchi, Vol. II, pp. 151, 270.
[6] See below.

on. Abba Bagibo was said to have been very just, even if he was most severe in his judgment.[1] For minor offences people were put in the *gindo*[2] or sold into slavery. For more serious offences and for murder the culprits were put to death, usually by drowning, and their families were sold into slavery.[3]

The Galla kingdoms were divided into a number of districts called *Koro*. The *Koro* was governed by an official whose title was *Abba Koro* and who held the administrative, judicial and military power in his district.[4] Very often the governor was one of the king's brothers, sons, sons-in-law, or trusted slaves. Each governor had his own estates and *Massera*, or *Massera*s, in which he housed his family, followers and slaves.[5] In time of peace the governor ruled his district, dealt with most of the judicial problems and with the help of an especially appointed administrator collected the taxes from the peasants. In time of war, the governor was the commander of all the able-bodied men in his province, and at the head of his contingent took part in the battles under the command of the king.

The *Abba Koro* had a number of *Abba Ganda*, or village heads, under him. As there were no villages in the Galla areas,[6] the *Abba Ganda* was in fact a parish governor in charge of all the landowners or the heads of families who lived in his parish.

One of the most important officials of the court was the *Abba Mizan*. This official had the combined functions of treasurer and minister for foreign affairs. He supervised the king's treasury, accounts, storehouses, private domains, and royal workshops. He was responsible for relations with foreigners and foreign merchants and he supervised the markets and the merchant villages.[7]

[1] Abbadie, F.N.A. 21300, pp. 218, 572.
[2] A wooden block weighing about sixty kilograms, put around the leg of the offender. Cecchi, Vol. II, p. 162.
[3] Abbadie, F.N.A. 21300, pp. 218, 710, 712. This was the so-called '*Hari*' —legal enslavement. It is possible that the above punishment also helped the wide and sudden Islamization of the population, as a Muslim ruler could not sell Muslim subjects into slavery.
[4] Cecchi, Vol. II, p. 270; Massaia, *I miei*, Vol. IV, p. 146.
[5] Abbadie, F.N.A. 21305, pp. 344–5; Ibid., 21300, pp. 188–9. Lewis, H., pp. 82–3.
[6] Abbadie, F.N.A. 21303, p. 218, para. 55; Ibid., 21300, p. 569; Massaia, *I miei*, Vol. IV, p. 146.
[7] Cecchi, Vol. II, pp. 256, 259, 412–13, 527.

Attached to the court were a number of courtiers called *Dagno*,[1] who carried the royal insignia, usually double-bladed spears, and were known to every official in the country. They were in fact the immigration and customs officials who were entrusted with the inspection and counting of those entering the country, and who accompanied all those permitted to leave the country. The very extensive political life, the intrigue and the negotiation of treaties with the neighbouring countries necessitated a large number of messengers and ambassadors called *Lemi*.[2] The importance of the *Lemi* varied according to the duties they were entrusted with. For minor affairs, the king employed less important personalities, whereas for treaty-making and important messages he would employ a well-known dignitary (*Soressa*) or even an *Abba Koro*. A number of translators of the different languages in use in the surrounding kingdoms were also employed in the court of Abba Bagibo.[3] The services of an interpreter were required whenever embassies arrived from Kaffa or from other countries whose language was not Galliña.

The king had a number of *Massera* all over the country, and when he moved from one to another, depending on the season and on other circumstances,[4] he was accompanied by quite a large retinue which always included his bodyguard and court officials. Abba Bagibo had twelve official wives, hundreds of concubines, and thousands of slaves, of which many lived permanently in each *Massera*. The *Massera* were in fact villages teeming with activity. Merchant villages (*Mander*) resembling small towns also sprang up near the more important *Massera* like Garuka, near Sakka in Enarea, Chala in Gomma, and Jiren in Jimma.[5]

[1] Abbadie, F.N.A. 21302, pp. 411–12; Ibid., 21305, pp. 112–13; Cecchi, Vol. II, p. 228; Soleillet, P.: *Voyages en Éthiopie 1882–1884*, Rouen, 1886, p. 228. See above, p. 81.
[2] Massaia, *In Abissinia*, p. 160; Abbadie, F.N.A. 21303, pp. 323–4; Lewis, H., p. 74.
[3] Abbadie, F.N.A. 21303, p. 323, para. 319; Ibid., p. 378, para. 201; Abbadie, *Géographie*, p. 211. Abba Bagibo had a secretary for Arabic as well. Massaia, *I miei*, Vol. III, p. 49.
[4] Beke, *Southern Abyssinia*, p. 6; Abbadie, *Athenaeum*, No. 1042 of 1847; Abbadie, F.N.A. 21300, pp. 798–9. Massaia, *I miei*, Vol. IV, p. 146. *Massera* means enclosure. When it occurs without the name of the owner it usually means a royal enclosure. Regarding Jimma, see: Lewis, H., p. 41.
[5] Abbadie, F.N.A. 21302, pp. 420, 425; Massaia, *I miei*, Vol. IV, p. 145. Lewis, H., pp. 68–73.

The revenue of Enarea came from three main sources: taxation on the land which was collected by special administrators with the co-operation of each provincial governor, income from the king's domains, cultivated and looked after by slave labour, and the income from trade. The last was by far the most important in the case of Enarea and later on in the case of Jimma-Kakka.

The Gibe Galla kingdoms were all agricultural countries producing mainly cotton, coffee, and cereals. The prosperity of these kingdoms, and above all of Enarea, was derived from the transit trade between northern and south-western Ethiopia. Trade was carried on at Sakka all year round by the resident merchants. But the caravan season lasted only from the end of October to the end of May.[1] Throughout this season, Sakka was a busy commercial centre. Hundreds of small caravans, usually of Galla merchants (*Afkala*), brought to Sakka ivory, precious skins, and incense from as far south as Lake Rudolf, and musk, gold, ivory, and spices from Kaffa and Wollaga.[2] Thousands of Galla, Sidama and negroid (*Shanqalla*) slaves were driven into Enarea from all over the south and south-west. At Sakka, and to a lesser extent in a number of other commercial centres in the neighbouring Galla kingdoms, the merchants from the Galla-Sidama countries were met by merchants from Basso in Gojjam, from Showa, from northern Ethiopia and even from Massawa and Arkiko. The caravans from the north brought to Enarea *amoleh* (salt money), cloth, beads, pepper, cheap metalware and an assortment of metals, particularly copper.[3] The caravans from the north usually stayed in Sakka no more than two months in order to conclude all their business and be able to return to Basso before the rainy season. Some merchants with large quantities of merchandise to be disposed of found it necessary to stay in Sakka for a whole year or even two or three.[4] Others found the country attractive and prosperous and decided to settle in it. Thus a very large *Jabarti* community was to be found in Sakka in the second quarter of the nineteenth century and in their

[1] The heavy rains season lasts from June to October.
[2] Léon des Avanchers (1860). B.S.D.G., Paris, Vol. 12, 1866, p. 171; Beke, *Southern Abyssinia*, p. 6; Borelli, J.: *Éthiopie Méridonale*, Paris, 1890, pp. 344–6; Massaia, *In Abissinia*, pp. 227, 229–30; Cecchi, Vol. II, pp. 364, 516, 559.
[3] Ferret and Galinier, Vol. II, pp. 420–1.
[4] Abbadie, *Athenaeum*, No. 1105 of 1848.

midst lived many *Fuqaha* and *Shuyukh* who came with the caravans to spread the teaching of the prophet.

Coffee of good quality grew wild, or with very little cultivation, in Kaffa, Gera and Enarea. Shortly after the consolidation of the kingdom of Jimma, it was planted in Jimma as well. However, only the less important merchants took part in the coffee trade. Coffee was bulky and difficult to transport, was cheap and brought only small profit.[1] Because in this period the Christian population was still forbidden by the Ethiopian Church to drink coffee,[2] the demand for it existed only in the Muslim areas of northern Ethiopia where it was not grown locally. The great cost of transportation, and the inferior quality of the 'Galla coffee' compared to that of Mokha and Harar, limited its export from south-western Ethiopia.[3] Nevertheless, quantities of coffee were acquired by the many small-scale merchants who traded with the Muslim Galla areas of Wollo and Yejju.

Far more important was the trade in musk. The Muslim population of Kaffa exported sizeable quantities of musk to the Enarea markets. But Enarea was considered by some as the home of the civet cat, and at least as important a producer of musk as Kaffa.[4] The civet cats were captured in the forests of Enarea and Kaffa. Females were released, but males were put into specially constructed cages where they were 'milked' each day by a special process for a few precious drops of civet musk.[5] A *wakia* of musk (about thirty-two grams) sold in Enarea for one-fifth of a thaler, fetched over a thaler in Massawa and two thalers in Cairo. The musk which yielded such high profits was transported in hollowed cattle horns, was not bulky, and could be easily hidden from the inquisitive customs officials and avaricious *goftas* along the road.

The ivory of south-western Ethiopia, called Enarea ivory, was considered the best in Ethiopia, as the elephant tusks were large,

---

[1] Ferret and Galinier, Vol. II, p. 426; M. & D., Vol. 13, p. 126, Lefebvre, 1847.

[2] Beke, *Commerce*, pp. 7, 27.

[3] Ibid., p. 27; M. & D., Vol. 61, p. 93, Lejean, 1863.

[4] L.G., 189, No. 2060G, Harris, 5.1.1842; Harris, Vol. III, p. 56; Plowden, W. C.: *Travels in Abyssinia and the Galla Country*, London, 1868, p. 127; Pearce, Vol. II, pp. 8–9; Cecchi, Vol. II, pp. 513–15.

[5] L.G., 184, No. 1092, Harris, 1.1.1842; Massaia, *In Abissinia*, pp. 229–30; Cecchi, Vol. II, pp. 513–15.

The town of Harar, seat of the Amirate of Harar

The town of Gondar, the permanent seat of the Emperors of Ethiopia since the

soft, and white. The source of this ivory was Kaffa, the far south to Lake Rudolf and the lake district in the eastern Sidama country.[1] The price of ivory in Enarea was one-fourth of a thaler per kilogram, while in Massawa it was sold for one and one-fourth thalers, and in Cairo for two thalers. Although elephants still abounded in parts of south-western Ethiopia, the quantity of ivory reaching the market in the second quarter of the nineteenth century could not have been very great. Elephants were still hunted by primitive methods and the killing of an elephant was considered by the Galla a great feat.[2] Nevertheless, the growing demand for ivory in the nineteenth century hastened the destruction of the elephant herds of Ethiopia and the quantities of ivory reaching the markets grew steadily even before the introduction of firearms.[3] In the 1840's the number of tusks passing annually through the market of Basso alone was, it is claimed, nearly 3,000.[4]

Gold was a royal monopoly in the Galla and Sidama kingdoms, and gold rings were the royal insignia.[5] Gold reached Enarea from Kaffa, from Jimma and, above all, from Wollaga where gold was panned from river beds by slaves.[6] The Wollaga gold was commonly known as 'Galla gold'. It reached the market either in the form of grains or in ingots. The gold trade was carried on in great secrecy, and as it was a royal monopoly the merchants of the Galla areas were compelled to sell their gold to the rulers. The Galla gold was alloyed a number of times on its way to the north and consequently its price was lower than that of gold arriving from other sources.

South-western Ethiopia was famous as a source of high-quality slaves, and slaves were one of the most important items of

---

[1] Cecchi, Vol. II, p. 516; Borelli, J.: *Éthiopie Méridionale*, Paris, 1890, pp. 344–6, 361; Abbadie, F.N.A. 21303, p. 357, para. 178; Ibid., p. 421, para. 277. M. & D., Vol. 61, pp. 232–3, Rochet d'Héricourt.

[2] Pearce, Vol. I, pp. 219–21; Beke, J.R.G.S., Vol. 14, p. 9; Cecchi, Vol. II, p. 331.

[3] C. & C., Massawa, Vol. I, Degoutin, 10.9.1844. Degoutin estimated the quantity of ivory which reached Massawa between 1.6.1843 and 10.9.1844 to be 100,000 kg. In the beginning of the century Valentia (Vol. II, p. 269) estimated the ivory reaching Massawa at one hundred *frazela* of thirty-two and a half lb. each.

[4] Abbadie, F.N.A. 21303, p. 388; Beke, J.R.G.S., Vol. 14, p. 19.

[5] Cecchi, Vol. II, p. 289.

[6] L.G., 189, No. 2060G, Harris, 5.1.1842; Matteucci, pp. 266–7; Cecchi, Vol. II, p. 556.

Enarea's exports.[1] In the second decade of the nineteenth century the Englishman Nathaniel Pearce, a resident of Ethiopia
for a number of years, wrote the following:

The most famous districts for slaves are Yer Angero, Gingaro,
Yamha, Bonja, Lakar, Narria, Sedammar, Nonno, and Goodero. . . .[2]
The Narria slaves are most esteemed; they are in general very fair,
good tempered, and make excellent wives and servants. The men in
those districts are always on the lookout on the borders, whether in
war or not, for the young persons of both sexes . . . whom they steal
and sell to the cofla (caravan).[3]

The slaves, gold, ivory, musk, coffee and other items exported
annually from southern and western Ethiopia fetched on the
coast twice or three times their original cost. As the central and
northern plateau hardly produced any exportable items, it might
be said that the exports of southern and western Ethiopia paid
not only for the imported goods brought to the Galla Sidama
countries, but they also financed to a large extent the imports of
northern Ethiopia, and contributed greatly to Ethiopia's favourable 'balance of trade' with the outside world.

During Bofo's reign Enarea was continuously at war with
Gumma, therefore merchants from Enarea had to go to Kaffa
through Jimma-Badi, which was at this time tributary to Enarea.[4]
Yet even the route through Jimma was very precarious and trade
was sluggish. When Abba Bagibo came to power in 1825 he
abandoned the harsh and in many ways cruel policy of his father
and tried to achieve his aims through politics and intrigues.
Above all he believed in political marriages. He married the
daughters and sisters of many of the neighbouring rulers, and
he gave in marriage to the rulers and important chiefs the
daughters which he had from his many wives and concubines.
Messengers and ambassadors were continually on the road between Enarea and all the countries of southern Ethiopia, and

[1] Beke, F.O.A., Vol. 1841, p. 168.
[2] Most of the names above are corruptions of area names in the south-west,
all of which were kingdoms and principalities around the Omo and Didessa
basins.
[3] Pearce, Vol. II, pp. 8–9. On the slave trade of Ethiopia see Chapter II
above.
[4] Abbadie, F.N.A. 21300, pp. 569–72; Ibid., 21303, p. 231, para. 81;
L.G., 184, No. 1098, Harris, 1.1.1842.

ambassadors from many kings and chiefs visited Abba Bagibo to co-ordinate policies, conclude alliances, declare war or to negotiate peace. Many more Galla, *Jabarti* and Arab merchants were attracted to the country because of the opportunities offered for trade, the security for person and property and the freedom from exactions.[1] Thus although a king of only a small kingdom, Abba Bagibo's name was known all over the Ethiopian highlands and the coast, and Enarea became important out of all proportion to its size.

Two events which occurred just after Abba Bagibo came to power helped to turn Enarea into the trading centre of south-western Ethiopia. A war broke out between Gumma and the principality of Bun-O to the north, closing the direct road to Kaffa through Gumma. Thereafter and until the 1850's the only remaining avenue open for the Kaffa trade was through Jimma-Badi and Enarea.[2] The second event was the pacification of the countries between Enarea and Kaffa and the unification of some of the Jimma tribes by Abba Jifar Sana. The Jimma were under pressure at this time both from Enarea and Kulo which, being disunited, they probably found difficult to resist.[3] However, when about 1830 Abba Jifar Sana became the *Abba Dula* of Hirmata, one of the Jimma principalities south of Enarea, he embarked upon the forceful unification of the Jimma tribes; and within a few years of his coming to power he succeeded in establishing the united kingdom of Jimma, Jimma-Kakka, or Jimma Abba Jifar. To further strengthen his position and to further the unity among his people, Abba Jifar adopted Islam and took the title of *Moti*-king.[4] At first, owing to the stability brought to the Jimma areas to the south, Enarea benefited from this turn of events, as much more of the Kaffa trade reached Sakka by way of Jimma-Badi. Later on, however, some merchants just passed through Enarea on their way to or from Jimma-Kakka. Others

[1] Ferret and Galinier, Vol. II, p. 423; Abbadie, F.N.A. 21303, p. 344, para. 166; Ibid., 21301, p. 66; Ibid., 21301, pp. 797–8; Massaia, *I miei*, Vol. IV, p. 144.
[2] Abbadie, F.N.A. 21300, pp. 197–8, 751–2.
[3] Massaia, *In Abissinia*, p. 279.
[4] The new kingdom included Habatti, Jada, Hirmata, Jimma-Badi and Sadero. In 1847–8 Badi-Folla was annexed as well. Cecchi, Vol. II, p. 540; Abbadie, F.N.A. 21300, p. 797, April, 1848; Abbadie, *Géographie*, pp. 79–80; Massaia, *I miei*, Vol. VI, pp. 3–4; Massaia, *In Abissinia*, p. 279; Soleillet, p. 180. For a slightly different version see: Lewis, H., p. 41.

even tried to avoid Abba Bagibo's taxation and the monopolies he had on certain items by by-passing Enarea altogether. In the mid or late 1830's Abba Bagibo forbade foreign merchants to go beyond Sakka, and the merchants from Gondar, Adowa, Derita, and Dawe were forced to meet their counterparts from Kaffa, Kulo and the south at Sakka only.[1]

It would be wrong to assume that Abba Bagibo's reign was peaceful and undisturbed. Each year Abba Bagibo led a few expeditions against the Nonno Galla in order to secure Enarea's outlet to Gojjam.[2] Those of the enemy who were not killed in battle were enslaved, together with all their women and children. The raided area was turned into a *Mogga* and Limu-Enarea's border was thus slowly expanded in the second quarter of the nineteenth century until it incorporated large parts of the Nonno and Jimma areas. Raids were also carried out against the Agalo and other tribes to the west who were supposedly tributary, but who continuously raided the caravan route to the Soddo markets over which Enarea had some jurisdiction, and the 'coffee route' through Agabja to the Muslim Wollo Galla centres of Warra Himenu north of Showa.[3]

Unfortunately for Abba Bagibo his reign coincided with the expansion of the Amhara kingdom of Showa under Sahle Selassie.[4] The divided Galla and even Limu-Enarea were no match for the vast armies of Showa which were equipped with hundreds of firearms. Showan raids to the west and south-west devastated the area and stopped Limu-Enarea's expansion in this direction. The coffee route to Warra Himenu also fell into Showan hands when the Christian armies conquered Agabja. Moreover, as a result of Showa's southward drive the Galla tribes to the south of Showa came under its sway and Enarea lost its influence over, and even more important its access to, the important Soddo markets.[5] Consequently Enarea was cut off from the Harar,

[1] Ferret and Galinier, Vol. II, p. 423; Isenberg, pp. 13–14.
[2] Abbadie, F.N.A. 21300, pp. 185–7; L.G., 184, No. 1098, Harris, 1.1.1842; Krapf, p. 65.
[3] Massaia, *I miei*, Vol. IV, p. 144; Rochet, *Voyage*, pp. 223–4; Abbadie, *Athenaeum*, No. 1042 of 1847; Ibid., No. 1078; Abbadie, F.N.A. 21303, p. 218. According to Harris (Vol. III, pp. 54–5) his aim was to conquer all the countries as far as the Nile and the Agalo, Yelloo, Betcho, Sudicha, Chera and Nonno were Abba Bagibo's nominal subjects.
[4] See below, Chapter VIII.
[5] Harris, Vol. III, pp. 54–5; Krapf, pp. 64–5.

Zeila and Tajura outlets and became much more dependent on the northern outlet through Gojjam.

Abba Bagibo met with political and military reverses in the south and south-west as well. His advance in this direction was blocked after the 1830's by the rapid rise of Jimma-Kakka. When Jimma-Badi was annexed by the former, Enarea lost its last chance of having a common border with Kaffa, the source of much of the luxury trade going to the coast.

Immediately after the establishment of the united monarchy of the Jimma tribes, it became apparent to Abba Jifar that his interests clashed with those of Enarea. The Jimma-Badi were tributaries of Enarea, and the influence of Abba Bagibo was predominant among the Jimma tribes to the south-east of Enarea. Above all, while the near-monopoly of the trade of the south brought prosperity to Enarea, Jimma enjoyed only the leftovers of this trade. Jimma at this time did not produce any coffee or musk which could attract the traders;[1] on the other hand, it did have direct access to the richest sources of ivory and through it went the only open road to Kaffa. As a result of the security and stability brought to the Jimma area by Abba Jifar, more of the rich trade of Kaffa passed by the Jimma route,[2] but this trade only went through Jimma to Enarea and enriched Abba Bagibo.

Abba Jifar was surrounded by Muslim councillors from among the *Ulama* and many merchants who settled in the *Mander* (traders' village) near his main *Massera*. With war going on intermittently between Jimma and Enarea from the late 1830's, and on the advice of his Muslim councillors, who were themselves involved in commerce, it became one of Abba Jifar's main aims to free himself from his dependence on Enarea's route to the north.[3] Although some merchants defied Abba Bagibo's prohibition and reached Jimma through Liban, Nonno, Agalo and Folla, this route was not very popular, as the merchants had to depend on the good will of many *gofta*s (patrons) and in some parts the route was infested with robbers.[4] As the one practical

---

[1] Abbadie, *Athenaeum*, No. 1042 of 1847; Beke, *Southern Abyssinia*, p. 7.
[2] Abbadie, F.N.A. 21300, p. 364, para. 202; Ibid., 21303, pp. 112–13, para. 162.
[3] Beke, *Southern Abyssinia*, pp. 5–6.
[4] Abbadie, F.N.A. 21300, p. 714; Ibid., 23851, pp. 588–9.

route to the north depended on Abba Bagibo, it became apparent to Abba Jifar that he would either have to conquer Enarea or open a new avenue to the terminal of the trade route of the Harari and Somali coast merchants in the Soddo markets. Abba Bagibo was well aware of the fact that should Jimma obtain an independent route to Soddo, Harar, or Showa, Enarea would lose much of its importance. Therefore he intensified the war against the Agalo and the Nonno, and exerted pressure upon the Badi Folla, who occupied a key position beyond the eastern borders of Enarea.[1] Here again a clash was inevitable between the two Muslim Galla monarchs, as Abba Jifar also wanted to annex the Badi-Folla, who were related to the Jimma-Badi tribes. About 1841, after a few years of war, a peace was negotiated and the daughter of Abba Jifar was given to Abba Dula, the son and heir to Abba Bagibo. Notwithstanding the agreement, Abba Jifar kept up his pressure on the tribes and kingdoms between Jimma and the Soddo markets. By 1843 Jimma's borders reached as far as Botor, and the ancient Sidama kingdom of Janjero, which for a short time during the 1830's was made tributary to Enarea,[2] was attacked a number of times by Jimma. Finally, in 1844 the Janjero were defeated and their king was taken prisoner; but when he regained his freedom in 1847, he immediately renewed the struggle against the Jimma, and the war between the two countries went on until the entire area was annexed to Showa by Menelik in the 1880's.

After a long struggle, Badi Folla was conquered by Jimma in 1847.[3] Abba Bagibo, failing to overcome the resistance of the Agalo and the other tribes to the east, realized that the race was lost and decided to change his tactics. The renewed war against the Jimma was stopped and the Kulo allies of Enarea were called off from the Jimma borders. The prohibition on traders going beyond Sakka was abolished, and all monopolies but the one on gold were done away with.[4] Notwithstanding Abba Bagibo's realistic policy, Enarea began to decline. The death of Abba

[1] Abbadie, *Géographie*, pp. 79–80; Abbadie, F.N.A. 21303, para. 173, October, 1843; Ibid., p. 112, para. 161; Ibid., p. 365, para. 184; Ibid., 21302, p. 141, para. 174.
[2] Harris, Vol. III, pp. 54–5.
[3] Abbadie, *Athenaeum*, No. 1105 of 1848; Abbadie, F.N.A. 21300, p. 797; Abbadie, *Géographie*, pp. 79–80.
[4] Abbadie, F.N.A. 21300, pp. 797–8, April, 1848.

Bagibo in 1861, the rise of his untalented and fanatic Muslim son, the growth of Jimma and the opening of the old route from Kaffa through Gumma to Gojjam hastened this decline. By the beginning of the last quarter of the nineteenth century, just before the great expansion of Showa into southern and south-western Ethiopia, it was quite apparent that Enarea had lost its position in south-western Ethiopia to her sister Galla monarchy, Jimma-Kakka. However, Jimma too had undergone a very serious crisis. Abba Jifar Sana died in 1855 and after a short struggle for power was succeeded by his younger son Abba Rebu. The reign of Abba Rebu was marked by excessive cruelty and tyranny. He succeeded in alienating all the rulers of the Galla monarchies and was finally killed in 1859 in a battle against the united army of Enarea, Gumma and Gera. Upon his death, the government of the greatly weakened Jimma passed into the hands of Abba Boko, Abba Jifar Sana's brother.[1]

CONCLUSION

From the little one knows about the ancient Sidama kingdoms which were submerged by the Galla invasion and about those which still survived until the nineteenth century, as well as from the relatively voluminous material on the Christian kingdom of Showa, it seems that many of the institutions of the Galla monarchies of south-western Ethiopia were probably borrowed either from the Sidama or from the Amhara. One has only to examine the courts of the Galla kings, most aspects of their administrative and judicial system, their military organization and defence system to realize that this was so. Nevertheless, why the Galla monarchies emerged only in a remote corner of Ethiopia and not in the other regions where the Galla settled is puzzling. It is possible, as some writers claim, that this Galla region gave birth to the monarchic system because of the threatening pressure of their Amhara neighbours combined with the influence of Sidama institutions, Islam and commerce. However, the Galla who settled in other parts of the Ethiopian highlands were converted, in some instances, to Islam as early as the seventeenth century. In Showa they were constantly under Amhara pressure

---

[1] Massaia, *I miei*, Vol. VI, p. 6. Massaia passed through Jimma in 1861 when he was deported from Kaffa.

and influence from the eighteenth century onwards; in the Sidama areas they were exposed to the influence of Sidama traditions and institutions for over a century. Nevertheless, in most areas the Galla retained to a large extent their traditional political and social organization, and, at most, developed principalities under hereditary chiefs whose authority depended on their merits and talent.

In the second quarter of the nineteenth century, the Galla monarchies of the Gibe were still small and divided.[1] However, had it not been for the introduction of firearms into the Amhara Christian areas, and for the unification and expansion of Showa, the growth of the monarchic system among the Galla of the south-west at the time when the northern Galla were making their last bid for predominancy combined with the rapid spread of Islam, might have had unforeseeable results on the history of the country. As Cardinal Massaia very ably summed up the situation in Ethiopia at the middle of the nineteenth century: 'were another Ahmad Grañ to arise and unfurl the banner of the prophet, the whole of Abyssinia would become Muhammadan'.[2]

By the 1830's Ethiopia was surrounded on three sides by an aggressive Muslim power. When Egypt began to take a new interest in the area, people in Ethiopia as well as in other countries began to wonder whether Muhammad Ali was not the 'new Grañ'.

[1] To a certain degree one is reminded of the number of weak Muslim commercial kingdoms in the centuries before Grañ.
[2] Massaia, *I miei*, Vol. XI, p. 124.

V

Egypt and Galla-dominated Ethiopia[1*]

The rise of the Wahabia in Arabia and the invasion of Egypt by
Bonaparte opened a new era in the history of the region. Although
by 1818 the Wahabi power was temporarily broken in most of
Arabia, the revival of Islam which the Wahabia initiated affected
many Muslim communities in Asia and Africa throughout the
nineteenth century.

The French action in Egypt finally convinced British official
circles of the need to develop the short route of communication
to India via the Red Sea. Consequently, British interest in the
countries bordering on the Red Sea grew. Boats of the Indian
Navy occasionally visited the ports of Yemen, Hijaz, Egypt and
Ethiopia; and the Factory of the Bombay government in Mokha
and its representative in Jedda, together with the British consul-
general in Egypt, consistently kept an eye on developments.
Moreover, the opening of the Red Sea basin to Europeans
brought to the area a growing number of British, German,
Italian, Austrian and French travellers and missionaries. The
French, especially after the conquest of Aden in 1839, watched
the British activities in the Red Sea basin with jealousy and suspicion and tried to involve their government in the affairs of the
area and to acquire a base on the Ethiopian or Somali coast.

Another outcome of Bonaparte's invasion of Egypt was the
rise of Muhammad Ali to power in Egypt. From the time he had
conquered the Hijaz at the command of the Ottoman Sultan,
Muhammad Ali strove to turn the Red Sea into an Egyptian
Mare nostrum. Had Muhammad Ali come to power in the eighteenth century, it is doubtful whether any considerations other
than his relations with the Ottoman Empire would have influenced his policy and activities in the area. Unfortunately for
Muhammad Ali, his rise to power coincided with the growth of

[1] This chapter is based in parts on my article, 'The Origins of the
Ethiopian-Egyptian Border Problem in the Nineteenth Century', *Journal of
African History*, 1967, Vol. VIII, No. 3.
* Refer to map on page 28 for use in this chapter.

95

British and, to a lesser degree, French interests in the area. Hence his ambitions in the direction of the Red Sea were restrained in order to prevent a clash with the British power which he both respected and feared.[1] The rebellion of the mercenary general Turkchi Bilmas in the Hijaz in 1832 and his escape to the Yemeni coast provided Muhammad Ali with a useful opportunity to implement his ambitions without arousing the opposition of the British, who by this time were watching his activities in the whole region with growing apprehension. Although most of his troops were occupied on the Syrian front, in 1833 Muhammad Ali managed to recapture Massawa from the forces of Turkchi Bilmas, to send an army to fight the Bedouin of Asir, and an expedition to capture the Yemeni coast.[2] By 1835 most of the Red Sea littoral was united under the centralized government of Egypt, although the war with the Asir, between the Hijaz and Yemen, was still going on and the situation in the Yemen was very fluid.[3] The more Muhammad Ali became involved in Arabia and the greater the pressure for reinforcements and funds from his son Ibrahim in Syria, the more he turned his eyes to the Sudan and to *al Habasha* as a source of manpower and revenue.

It is claimed that the two most important motives for the conquest of the Sudan by the Egyptians were the need for manpower for the planned *Nizam I-Jedid*,[4] and Muhammad Ali's desire to tap the legendary gold resources of the south. Some even go further and claim that the final goal of the Egyptian expedition was to conquer Ethiopia in conjunction with the much more ambitious plan, attributed to Muhammad Ali, to dominate the entire area between the Red Sea and the Nile.[5] However,

[1] In 1811, when Muhammad Ali requested permission to buy a number of boats at Bombay for service in the Red Sea, the British government decided to refuse his request on the grounds that 'it would be very dangerous policy to allow the Turkish influence to revive in this part of the world'—F.O., Abyssinia, 1/1, p. 197; Tagher: Mohamad Ali et les Anglais, pp. 452–4; I.O., F.R., Egypt and Red Sea, Vol. 7, dispatches from 1820 to 1825; Range, 385, Vol. 3, No. 1610; Ibid., Vol. 36, No. 4225.

[2] Combes and Tamisier, Vol. I, pp. 93–4. Range, 375, Vol. 50, No. 2968, No. 3167; Range, 387, Vol. 44, No. 1319.

[3] Combes and Tamisier, Vol. IV, pp. 221–2; Range, 388, Vol. 11, No. 205; Ibid., Vol. 13, No. 645, 18.1.1836; Hanotaux, G. A. U.: *Histoire de la nation Égyptienne*, Paris, 1931, Vol. 6, pp. 156–8.

[4] The new army Muhammad Ali was organizing on a European model.

[5] Range, 384, Vol. 14, Salt, 29.4.1816; Sabri, M.: *L'Empire Égyptien sous Mohamed Ali*, Paris, 1930, pp. 66–7; Waddington, G.: *Journal of a Visit to Some Parts of Ethiopia*, London, 1822, p. 91.

Henry Salt, the British Consul-General in Egypt who was an old friend of Ethiopia, fearing the Egyptian intentions, strongly warned Muhammad Ali of the consequences of aggression against Christian Ethiopia.[1] Possibly as a result of Salt's warning, and possibly because he never intended his army to penetrate beyond Sennar, Muhammad Ali instructed the commanders of the expedition against the Sudan to limit their conquests to the kingdom of Dongola, Shendi, Sennar and Kordofan. The gold mines on the borders of Ethiopia were, however, too big a temptation for the Egyptians to overlook, and at the end of 1821 Muhammad Ali's son Ismail penetrated into the Ethiopian mountains to Fazogli and Beni Shangul. Ismail had just gained the borders of the gold-bearing region of Kamamil in western Ethiopia when he received news of growing tension in Sennar and decided to return. After having made himself extremely unpopular with the inhabitants of Sennar and the Nile Valley, Ismail was murdered in the second half of 1822 by Mek Nimr of the Ja'aliyin in Shendi. The consequences of this incident were of great importance to future Egyptian-Ethiopian relations. The rebels, pursued by Muhammad Ali's son-in-law, the *Defterdar*, escaped first to the province of Taka and from there to Sofi on the Setit river. When the *Defterdar* approached the Setit, Nimr made a final escape to the area between the Takkaze river and the Bahr es Salam, in the peripheral area of the Ethiopian province of Wolkait. There he was given protection by *Dejazmatch* Wube, who governed the province in his father's name, and who after the death of the latter in 1826 became the ruler of Semien, Wogera and Wolkait. The *Defterdar* ravaged the area of Taka, Sofi and Gallabat but retreated without leaving behind either a permanent post or administration.[2]

Until 1828 Muhammad Ali was far too occupied with the Greek rebellion and with disturbances in the Hijaz to be able

---

[1] Halls, *Salt*, Vol. II, p. 68. Already in June 1818 Salt wrote to Nathaniel Pearce: 'The Pasha here talks of conquering Abyssinia some day or other, but that will never do, for though bad Christians that is better than being Mussulmans.' Ibid., p. 108.

[2] Robinson, E. A.: Nimr, the Last King of Shendi, *Sudan Notes and Records*, Vol. VIII, p. 113; Cumming, D. C.: The History of Kassala and the Province of Taka, *Sudan Notes and Records*, Vol. XX, p. 11; Deherain, H: *Le Soudan égyptien sous Mehemed Ali*, Paris, 1898, p. 107; Morié, L. J.: *Histoire de l'Éthiopie*, Paris, 1904, pp. 442–3.

to devote any attention to the Sudan and to Ethiopia. Consequently his hold over the areas south of Dongola became extremely shaky and a vast no-man's-land existed between the most forward position of the Egyptians and the areas controlled by the Ethiopian border governors.

In 1827, after Massawa was evacuated by the Egyptians, *Dejazmatch* Seb'agadis, the ruler of Tigre, who was aspiring to the guardianship of the King of Kings, despatched Coffin with a letter to King George IV.[1] What was simply a new stage in Seb'agadis's struggle against the Galla lords of northern Ethiopia was misrepresented in Britain by Lord Valentia as a complaint against Egyptian Muslim pressure on Christian Ethiopia, though nothing could have been further from the mind of the ruler of Tigre in 1827. In fact, at the time that he was applying to Britain for help, he also sent a delegation to Muhammad Ali to express his friendship to him, to ask his help in solving some theological problems which pestered northern Ethiopia, and above all, to obtain an *Abuna* whom he wanted to use in his approaching campaign against his Galla rivals.[2] Using Seb'agadis's letter to the British foreign office, Lord Valentia, who took it upon himself to involve England in the affairs of Ethiopia, so distorted the situation that he has misled a number of historians. Moreover, he finally persuaded the British government to request the East India Company to present Seb'agadis with a few thousand matchlocks. This decision was taken by the Foreign Office because:

In view of our future attempts to establish expeditious communications with India, it might be an object of national interest to conciliate a friendly feeling among a people whose country borders on the Red Sea.[3]

Had the shipment of matchlocks reached Seb'agadis in time they might have changed the whole history of Ethiopia. As it was,

[1] See above, pp. 34–5.
[2] Messages had been exchanged between the two rulers in the past as well. See: Tagher, Mohamad Ali et les Anglais, pp. 471–3; Cadalvene and Breuvey, Vol. II, p. 446; Amin Sami: *Taqwim al-Nil*, Cairo, 1927, Vol. II, p. 315.
[3] F.O., Abyssinia, 1/2, 19.11.1829, pp. 38–9. Also draft letter to Treasury, 28.12.1830, p. 40; F.O., Abyssinia, 1/2, p. 85. For samples of Valentia's letters to F.O. see: F.O., Abyssinia, 1/2, pp. 38–40, November, 1829.

Ethiopia and Sennar to come to a complete standstill. At the
end of 1834, Nimr raided Egyptian-held territory as far as
Sennar and in retaliation the Egyptians raided Wolkait.[1] By that
time Muhammad Ali was anxious to get his hands on Nimr at all
costs. A reward was offered for his head but to no avail. Finally
negotiations were opened with Nimr's protector, *Dejazmatch*
Wube of Semien and Tigre, for the surrender of the former.
Wube, who was already thinking of usurping *Ras* Ali's authority
as guardian of the King of Kings,[2] was not beyond betraying
Nimr for a price. In the middle of 1835 he despatched to Egypt
the Armenian merchant Betlehem, who was known to all European
travellers in Ethiopia in the 1830's, to try to get an *Abuna*.
Ethiopia had not had an *Abuna* since the death of *Abuna* Kerilos
about 1829, and Wube planned to make use of the new *Abuna*
against *Ras* Ali and his Muslim supporters. At the same time,
he instructed Betlehem to negotiate with the British Consul-
General in Egypt for a present of firearms, or at least to get the
British to consent to transferring to him the matchlocks that
were originally sent to Seb'agadis and were still in Massawa.
Failing to get the British interested, Betlehem was instructed to
negotiate with the Egyptians for the purpose. It seems, however,
that Betlehem failed in his mission and the Egyptian troops were
ordered to step up their raids on Wube's territory.[3] At the end
of September, 1835, while Khurshid Pasha was slave-raiding
between the two Niles, a Nimrab force descended upon Dar al-
Atish. Ahmad Kashef, the governor of Gedaref, quickly advanced
to the area, defeated the invaders and captured their leader.
With a large force he then proceeded to raid Wolkait. His army
sacked the province, burnt churches, and took many prisoners.
On his way back, probably in December, 1835, Ahmad Kashef
was ambushed by Wube's armies and, according to one of Wube's
soldiers, lost a few hundred men and a quantity of firearms and
equipment. Nevertheless, Ahmad Kashef managed to escape
with hundreds of slaves who were taken to Khartoum.[4]

[1] Robinson, Nimr, p. 114; Combes and Tamisier, Vol. III, p. 346.
[2] Combes and Tamisier, Vol. I, pp. 251–2; Ibid., Vol. III, pp. 159–60, 162.
[3] F.O., 78/343, Isenberg to Campbell, p. 279; Cambes, *Égypte*, Vol. II,
p. 176; Combes and Tamisier, Vol. I, pp. 251–2; Ibid., Vol. IV, p. 231.
[4] Combes and Tamisier, Vol. III, p. 346; *T'arikh Muluk*, pp. 30–31;
Robinson, Nimr, p. 114; Robinson, E. A.: "The Egyptian-Abyssinian War of

At the beginning of 1837 a small Egyptian unit was sent to collect tribute from the area of Gallabat. This commercially important area had partially submitted to Khurshid in 1832 and again in 1834, but was still claimed by the Ethiopians. The Egyptians had just arrived at Metemma when they heard that a large Ethiopian force was advancing to Gallabat for the same purpose and decided to retreat. A few months later, in May, 1837, a much larger Egyptian force entered Metemma accompanied by Sheikh Miri, the Sheikh of Gallabat. Reinforced by part of the Muslim population, the Egyptians started to advance in the direction of Gondar, burning and pillaging the land they crossed.[1] Gondar was thrown into a panic, since it was believed that the Egyptians intended to sack the town. However, *Dejazmatch* Kinfu, *Dejazmatch* Maru's nephew, who in 1831 was given the estates of his uncle and whose province Dembya was directly affected by the Egyptian aggression, quickly gathered an army[2] and moved down to attack the Egyptians, who by this time had returned to the area of Gallabat. Faced with a superior Ethiopian force, the Egyptians started to retreat in the direction of the military post at Doka. But at a place called Kalnabu near Rashid, in an open area most unsuitable for defence against the Ethiopian cavalry, they were forced to give battle. Although part of the irregular Egyptian cavalry managed to escape, most of the regular forces, and Sheikh Miri of Gallabat, were killed or taken prisoner. After punishing the population of Metemma for cooperating with the Egyptians, Kinfu returned to Dembya and declared that he did not think very highly of Egyptian regulars. He boisterously informed Khurshid by messengers that if the Egyptians again dared enter Ethiopian territory, he would descend upon them with an army of 60,000 soldiers. Khurshid Pasha quickly took up Kinfu's challenge, especially since it was also rumoured that the border 'Arab' tribes were plotting with the Ethiopians to put an end to Egyptian rule in the Sudan.[3]

1874–1876', *Journal of the African Society*, Vol. XXVI, 1926–7, p. 246. Robinson mistakenly claims that Gondar was attacked; Wallis Budge, E. A.: *The Egyptian Sudan*, etc., London, 1907, Vol. II, p. 213.

[1] Robinson, Nimr, p. 115; F.O., 78/320, extract from a report of the Vice-Consulate in Cairo, 21.9.1837; Mengin, F.: *Histoire sommaire d'Égypte*, etc., Paris, 1838, p. 97.

[2] Estimates ranged between 6,000 and 20,000 men.

[3] *Douze ans*, p. 312; Mengin, F.: *Histoire sommaire d'Égypte*, etc., Paris,

After sending to Egypt for reinforcements, he advanced in the latter half of 1837 with 6,000 regulars and irregulars beyond Metemma as far as Wekhni, a Muslim centre on the caravan route three or four days' march from Gondar. Ethiopian resistance was nominal, Kinfu was sick, *Ras* Ali was helpless or not willing to act, and it seemed as if the Egyptians would take Gondar without much effort. However, although the Egyptian forces continued their activity along the Ethiopian border between Wekhni and Fazogli until the first months of 1838, they did not advance beyond Wekhni in the direction of Gondar. Meanwhile, a strong corps was organized comprising a number of irregular units, an infantry regiment and a cavalry regiment. In September, 1837, this corps was sent from Egypt to the Sudan under the command of Ahmad Pasha, the ex-minister of war, who was also Muhammad Ali's son-in-law.[1] To the European consuls in Egypt the situation along the Ethiopian border seemed to be extremely explosive. Some even predicted that this was the beginning of the conquest of Ethiopia.[2] The British Consul-General in Alexandria, disturbed by such a possibility, reminded the Egyptians in September of England's attitude regarding 'Christian' Ethiopia. In the last months of 1837, pressed by his government, which was already very suspicious of Muhammad Ali's policy and intentions in the Near East and Arabia, the British Consul, repeatedly urged Muhammad Ali to clarify his intentions regarding Ethiopia. Under the persistent British and French pressure, Muhammad Ali reaffirmed his previous intention of not conquering Ethiopia; but he made it quite clear that he was determined to establish his authority in those peripheral areas inhabited by Muslim tribes who, in Muhammad Ali's

---

1838, pp. 97–8; T'arikh Muluk, p. 31; F.O., Abyssinia, 1/3, pp. 13–15; F.O., 78/320, 2.10.1837; *Royal Chronicles*, p. 490.

[1] Tagher, Mohammed Ali et les Anglais, p. 477, footnote 3, Consul Cochelet, 6.11.1837; F.O., 78/320, enclosure to Campbell's despatch, 2.10.1837; Robinson, Nimr, p. 115. According to Mengin (*Histoire sommaire*, p. 98) Ahmad Pasha was given the means to organize another regiment in the Sudan, thus bringing his corps to 8,000, excluding artillery men.

[2] *T'arikh Muluk*, p. 32, footnote 1; F.O., 78/320, extract of report of Vice-Consulate in Cairo, 21.9.1837; Robinson, Nimr, p. 115; Bowring, J.: *Report on Egypt and Candia*, London, 1840, p. 88; A.E.B., Dos. 2024, rapport de Blondeel, Annexe 1, Alex., 6.4.1839.

words, were the 'enemies of the Christian tribes of the interior'.[1]

By the beginning of 1838 the Egyptian army in the Sudan consisted of five regular infantry regiments and a number of regular and irregular cavalry units, about 20,000 soldiers in all. In the face of the advance and build-up of the Egyptian army in the Sudan, which they thought was intended to conquer their country, the rulers of northern Ethiopia became increasingly alarmed.

In the first days of January, 1838, the Protestant missionaries in Adowa were approached by one of *Dejazmatch* Wube's lieutenants, who told them that Wube 'being afraid of Muhammad Ali's troops, wished to contract friendship with the British government in order that the latter should prevent the Egyptians from entering Abyssinia'. A few days later the missionaries were told by Wube that he intended sending an embassy to the British government to negotiate the treaty of friendship and to obtain British assistance against the Egyptians.[2] Similar overtures were made simultaneously to a number of Frenchmen who were in Tigre at the time, in order to get help from the French as well. Immediately after, Wube left the area of Adowa on his way to attack Seb'agadis's son, *Dejazmatch* Kassai, the governor of Agame,[3] who after a number of abortive revolutions again rebelled against Wube. After chasing Kassai over the mountains of Temben, Wube returned to Adowa at the end of February, but nothing more was mentioned regarding the embassy to England. The missionaries were advised by friends not to press the matter. It seems that meanwhile Wube had rethought the whole matter and come to the conclusion that an Egyptian attack on Ali's territories might be to his benefit. Furthermore, the Protestant missionaries were at this time so disliked in Tigre that Wube may have decided not to have any ties with them. None the less, the missionaries and the French travellers brought the matter to the attention of their respective governments. The French traveller Antoine d'Abbadie, who was in Gondar in May, 1838,

[1] A.E., Corr. Pol., Égy., Alexandrie et le Caire, Vol. VI, 1837–8, 7.10.1837, p. 140; F.O., Abyssinia, 1/3, p. 7, Alexandria, 3.10.1837.
[2] Isenberg, F.O., 78/343, p. 275–7. Soon after, Isenberg and his friends were ordered to leave the country.
[3] Combes and Tamisier, Vol. IV, p. 132; Gobat, pp. 307–11.

with his brother Arnauld, was requested by the puppet Emperor and the nobility of Gondar to deliver letters to Queen Victoria and the government of France pleading for their prompt intervention against the Egyptian aggression.[1] This request seems strange in view of the fact that by May the crisis was apparently over. It is of course possible that d'Abbadie himself pressed the idea of calling upon the Powers in order to enhance his importance in Europe and in Ethiopia. However, considering the power and the influence of the Muslim elements around *Ras* Ali and the acknowledged Islamic tendencies of Ali himself,[2] one would expect that so grave a decision as to apply for help from the Christian *Ferenji* powers against the Muslim government of Muhammad Ali was not easily reached. In fact, according to Antoine d'Abbadie,[3] *Dejazmatch* Ahmade of Warra Himenu, *Ras* Ali's Muslim uncle, was known to have been in correspondence with Muhammad Ali and to have invited him to join him in conquering Ethiopia.[4] It seems that the influence of the Christian lords, the fear of the Church, and the common sense of Mennen, Ali's mother, finally prevailed and when rumours still persisted that the Egyptians intended to pillage Gondar, it was decided to send the letters to the European Powers.[5] Ironically, a few months later, while the strongest Christian lord in the region, *Dejazmatch* Kinfu, was on his death-bed, the town was pillaged by *Ras* Ali's supporters.[6]

In March, 1838, Khurshid Pasha was recalled to Egypt and Ahmad Pasha, Muhammad Ali's son-in-law, was appointed governor-general of the Sudan. Most of the Egyptian army was withdrawn from the sector facing Gondar and sent to pacify the area of Fazogli which Muhammad Ali intended to inspect. Throughout the rest of 1838 and the beginning of 1839 the new governor-general was completely preoccupied with the aged Viceroy's visit to the Sudan.

[1] F.O., Abyssinia, 1/3, p. 29; *Douze ans*, p. 553.
[2] Rochet, *Voyage*, p. 148; Soleillet, p. 272.
[3] Abbadie, F.N.A. 21301, p. 46, para. 130.
[4] *Dejazmatch* Ahmade and *Dejazmatch* Bashir, Ali's uncles, led the Muslim Wollo against the Christian Amhara in the 1830's—Combes and Tamisier, Vol. II, p. 293.
[5] Duchesne, A.: *Le Consul Blondéel en Abyssinie*, Bruxelles, 1953, p. 137. *Douze ans*, pp. 402-3, 553. *Royal Chronicles*, p. 490.
[6] *Royal Chronicles*, pp. 490-1.

One tends to regard with suspicion the Egyptian claim in the notes to the British Foreign Office that the 1837 incident was spontaneous and that the Egyptian forces were attacked without provocation by the Ethiopians within territories 'under the Pasha' quite a distance from the Ethiopian border.[1] The 1837 incident was probably the climax of the policy which was initiated as early as 1833 by Khurshid Pasha in his first year as governor-general of the Sudan. The Egyptian army in the Sudan grew between 1833 and 1836 from one regular regiment to three,[2] during a period when Muhammad Ali needed every unit he had for Syria and Arabia. Of course the Egyptian military build-up in the Sudan could be explained as an effort to obtain the much-needed manpower for the new regiments of Sudanese slaves. A number of such regiments had already been sent to Arabia in 1835 and 1836, and recruiting officers from the Hijaz were waiting at Berber (Sudan) for thousands of slaves captured in the slave hunts which were conducted simultaneously in a number of areas in the Sudan.[3] However, it is more likely that the Egyptian actions in 1837 were aimed mainly at establishing Egyptian authority in the presumably mineral-rich border provinces.

Even after receiving a disappointing report from his son Ismail in 1822 regarding the minerals in the areas of Fazogli and Beni Shangul, Muhammad Ali did not despair of his dream of El Dorado. An Italian mineralogist was sent into the Sudan to examine the area of Fazogli as early as 1825, but unfortunately he died in Khartoum; and because Muhammad Ali became pre-occupied with more pressing matters, the plans to exploit the legendary minerals were temporarily shelved. In 1836 Khurshid received from the Egyptian officers responsible for the expansion of Egyptian authority in the direction of Ethiopia reports of the existence of rich mineral deposits, mainly gold and silver, in the mountainous area between Fazogli and the upper reaches of the Atbara. By the end of 1836 these reports were passed on

[1] F.O., 78/320, No. 55, Campbell to Palmerston, 2.10.1837.
[2] Umar Tusan: *Al-Jaysh al-Misri al-Barri wa'l-Bahri*, Cairo, 1946, p. 60; F.O., 78/214, Barker, 21.7.1832; F.O., 78/231, Barker, 18.2.1833; Duc de Raguse: *Voyage*, Paris, 1835, Vol. IV, p. 229. See also growth of slave raiding in this period—Ruppell, Vol. I, pp. 30–1.
[3] F.O., 78/285, Sloane, Alexandria, 22.3.1836; Bowring, J.: *Report on Egypt and Candia*, London, 1840, p. 83.

to Muhammad Ali.[1] The resources of Egypt were at this time stretched to their limits as a result of the rebellion against the Egyptians in Palestine and in the different parts of Syria, and of the unending war against the Asir in Arabia. Muhammad Ali was under constant pressure from his son Ibrahim for funds, supplies, and reinforcements in order to prepare for the inevitable struggle with the Ottoman sultan. The commanders in Arabia, after a number of disastrous defeats, also pressed for funds and reinforcements which could hardly be spared in view of the more urgent needs in Syria. Muhammad Ali, therefore, ordered his governors in the Sudan to organize wide-scale slave hunts in the different parts of the country, including some peripheral areas of Ethiopia, but above all he was determined to get his hands on the minerals of the Sudan in order to solve his financial problems.[2] In January, 1837, a number of mining engineers under the direction of the Austrian Rossiger were already on their way to the Sudan, and an Italian mining engineer, Boreani, who was in Muhammad Ali's service, was also despatched post-haste to the area. By the middle of 1837 reports reached Egypt that gold had been found in the mountains between Atbara and Fazogli, and this news was a source of much jubilation in the court of the Viceroy. While battles were still raging on the Ethiopian borders, the Egyptians detached a sizeable force to accompany Rossiger and Boreani in their surveys in hostile areas.[3] The fact is impressive that at the end of 1838, in a time of crisis in Syria and Arabia, and against the advice of his doctors, the aged Muhammad Ali rushed to Fazogli to see for himself the truth regarding the minerals in the area. It is therefore likely that because of the heavy demands upon the Egyptian resources, which were at this time stretched to their limits, Muhammad Ali was ready to gamble the resources in manpower and funds which he still had in Egypt, in order to capture the legendary treasures of the Ethiopian frontier provinces.

[1] F.O., 78/319, No. 17, Campbell, 10.4.1837.
[2] F.O., 78/319, No. 17, Campbell, 10.4.1837; Sammarco, A.: *Il viaggio di Mohammed Ali al Sudan*, Cairo, 1929, Introduction, I–V.
[3] F.O., 78/319, No. 17, Campbell, 10.4.1837; F.O., 78/320, No. 44, Campbell to Palmerston, Alexandria, 5.8.1837; Hamont, P. N.: *Égypte sous Mehemet Ali*, Paris, 1834, p. 539; Sammarco: *Il viaggio di Mohammed Ali al Sudan*, Cairo, 1929, p. 30.

When he arrived in the Fazogli district, Muhammad Ali found that the Rossiger report was greatly exaggerated. Moreover, to his surprise and frustration he realized that the most promising mineral area between Fazogli and Beni Shangul was only nominally subdued (if it was subdued at all) by his armies. Many of the sheikhs of the so-called Arab tribes inhabiting the area had to be coerced to come and meet 'their ruler', while others were bribed by presents and promises.[1]

Before his departure from Sennar at the beginning of 1839, Muhammad Ali instructed Ahmad Pasha to consolidate the Egyptian possessions in the Sudan and to intensify the slave raids in order to supply the much-needed manpower for the army. But even more important, he instructed him to open, by force, if necessary, the caravan routes leading to the lucrative Ethiopian trade, which in the past had brought a steady revenue to Egypt.[2] This trade had been interrupted in the late 1830's and early 1840's by the activities of desperadoes like Nimr, and by Ethiopian *shifta* (highwaymen), whose ranks the future Emperor Kassa-Teodros was about to join.[3] Muhammad Ali's instructions could be flexibly interpreted, especially in the light of internal developments in Ethiopia.[4] In fact, at the end of 1839, just before the departure of an expedition to conquer the rich province of Taka, Ahmad Pasha, who was to lead the expedition, told Ferdinand Werne, an Austrian adventurer, of his intention to conquer *Habasha*.[5]

By the second half of 1838 it was an open secret that *Dejazmatch* Wube was actively plotting to overthrow *Ras* Ali. Although Wube was forming alliances with *Dejazmatch* Goshu of Gojjam and Damot, who was trying to hold on to the estates of the dead Kinfu contrary to the instructions of Ali, he was not yet ready

---

[1] Werne, F.: *Expedition to Discover the Sources of the White Nile*, London, 1849, Vol. I, p. 43; A.E., Corr. Pol., Égy., Alexandrie et le Caire, Vol. VIII, 1839, 16.2.1839.
[2] Werne, *African Wanderings*, Vol. II, p. 261; Corr. Pol., Égy., Alexandrie et le Caire, Vol. XV, p. 92, Alexandrie, 23.5.1842; A.E.B., Dos. 2024, Annex 1, Blondeel report, Alexandrie, 6.1.1839, p. 7.
[3] Robinson, Nimr, p. 116; Duchesne, A.: *Le Consul Blondéel en Abyssinie*, Bruxelles, 1953, p. 166; Lejean, G.: *Théodor II*, Paris, 1865, p. 21; Stern, H. A.: *Wanderings among the Falashas*, London, 1862, p. 65; Parkyns, Vol. II, p. 318.
[4] See below.
[5] Werne, *African Wanderings*, Vol. I, p. 8; Ibid., Vol. II, p. 261.

for an overt clash with Ali, as the situation in Tigre was still uncertain. In fact, when Wube rushed from Tigre across the Takkaze to Semien in September, in expectation of an attack by Ali, Seb'agadis's son, *Dejazmatch* Kassai, rebelled again and succeeded in making himself the master of most of Tigre. Wube quickly recrossed the Takkaze, and having succeeded by deceit in getting Kassai into his camp, put him in irons and appointed *Dejazmatch* Merso (Wube's half-brother) as governor of Temben in place of Kassai.[1] Before coming out into the open, Wube wanted more firearms to offset the superiority of the Galla cavalry in the field, and he wanted an *Abuna* to unite the Christians of Ethiopia behind him. Under the influence of a number of Frenchmen, particularly Théophile Lefebvre, he sent an embassy to Louis Philippe offering the French the Bay of Amphila in return for firearms and French support in his ambitions along the coast. However, Amphila was clearly out of Wube's jurisdiction and it was later discovered that Wube's presumed embassy was made up of minor chiefs and of Lefebvre's servants. A few months later, Wube, together with a number of other Ethiopian rulers, sent an embassy to Egypt to get an *Abuna*.[2] Finally, about the middle of 1841, he despatched Coffin, who still lived in Tigre, with a letter to Queen Victoria soliciting the help and friendship of the British and asking their help in facilitating the passage of the new *Abuna* to Ethiopia.[3]

After his defeat by *Ras* Ali at the beginning of 1839, *Dejazmatch* Goshu of Gojjam swore allegiance to the *Ras* and was reinstated in his position. But the provinces of *Dejazmatch* Kinfu to the west and north of Lake Tana were taken away from him

---

[1] Lefebvre, Vol. I, p. 92; F.O., 78/343, p. 283, Isenberg; Isenberg, p. 500; *Douze ans*, p. 188; L.G., 189, No. 2031, para. 14, Harris, 10.11.1841. Kassai applied to Ali for help—Parkyns, Vol. II, p. 119.

[2] M. & D., Vol. 61, p. 21, May, 1850. Wube asked the French priest Jacobis to accompany the embassy. Jacobis agreed on condition that he would be allowed to take the embassy from Alexandria to Rome. Although some of the members of the embassy actually went with him to Rome, his plan backfired and *Abuna* Salama sent by the Coptic Church of Egypt was strongly anti-Catholic. Coulbeaux, J. B.: *Un martyr abyssin*, Paris, 1902, pp. 62–3. See also: A.E.B., Dos. 2024, Annexe 22, Blondeel, Massawa, 17.2.1841; *Bulletin de l'Académie Royale des Sciences Coloniales*, Vol. 1959. Roeykens: Les préoccupations missionnaires du Consul Belge Éduard Blondéel, pp. 1138–9.

[3] L.G., 164, No. 2153, Willoughby, 5.7.1841; F.O., Abyssinia, 1/3, pp. 122, 149, Alexandria, 19.9.1841.

and were given to Mennen, Ali's mother. Goshu's ambitious son, Birru Goshu, who was dissatisfied with his father's submissiveness, remained in open rebellion and was finally forced to fight his own father, whom he defeated. Consequently, he was unsuccessfully pursued by *Ras* Ali from the end of the rainy season of 1840 till finally Ali gave up and turned against a number of rebellious chiefs of the Wollo and Tuloma on the borders of Showa, but again he was unsuccessful. The situation in Begamder and the whole north had by this time become so explosive that Ali was forced to return to help his mother Mennen, who was faced with a rebellion in Agawmeder and growing tension in Dembya and Wogera, where *shifta* leaders, the most important of whom was Kassa-Teodros, were defying her authority.[1] Far more serious was the widening coalition formed by Wube, Birru Goshu and Faris Aligaz of Lasta which succeeded in subverting the loyalty of many Amhara rulers of Begamder and Amhara by accusing Ali of becoming a Muslim. Similar subversive tactics were used to win over Sahle Selassie, the king of Showa, who was seriously troubled by the agitation of the followers of the *Sost Lidet*, especially *Ichege* Gebre Mariam[2] of Gondar, a close friend of Mennen and a supporter of *Ras* Ali. However, Sahle Selassie, who at the time gave in to the pressure of Gondar and *Ras* Ali and openly supported the party of the *Sost Lidet*, decided to remain neutral in the impending struggle between the northern rulers.[3]

Even Wube was not free from trouble at home. His half-brother Merso, the governor of Temben, rebelled against him and after devastating part of Lasta, which was under Wube's ally Faris Aligaz, threatened Temben and Enderta. However, when faced by the army of his brother, he retreated into the Yejju country to the south of Lasta. Another rebel, *Dejazmatch* Gwan-

[1] Isenberg, p. 335; F.O., 78/508, Harris, 24.8.1841, para. 54; A.E.B., Dos. 2024, Annexe 38, p. 8, Blondeel, Dembya, 6.8.1841; Ibid., Dos. 2024 II, Rapport, 30.9.1843, pp. 15–20; *Douze ans*, pp. 387, 390, 404.

[2] *Douze ans*, pp. 402–3. See also above, p. 41. Gebre Mariam is called by some sources Mahsantu.

[3] L.G., 190, No. 2004, Krapf, 6.6.1842; F.O., 78/511, Harris, 28.8.1841, para. 7; Ibid., Harris, 5.1.1842, para. 79; *Douze ans*, pp. 174–5; Harris, Vol. III, p. 190; L.G., 159, No. 1486B, Krapf, 5.12.1840, 17.12.1840; F.O., 78/468, Krapf to Harris, 20.4.1841; L.G., 190, No. 2060A, Harris, 14.10.1841, para. 43; Ibid., No. 2060B, 29.10.1841, para. 7; Ferret and Galinier, Vol. II, p. 469; Parkyns, Vol. II, pp. 125–6.

gul of Agame, a son of Seb'agadis, was also defeated in the second half of 1841 and had to escape to the Taltals.[1]

By the middle of 1841 Lefebvre arrived in Tigre with a small quantity of firearms, a present from the French king, and a number of artisans who were immediately put to work repairing the cannon of *Ras* Wolde Selassie and to producing war materials. Wube's camp was teeming by this time with messengers from his allies; and after hearing that a new *Abuna* was on his way to Ethiopia, Wube lost all discretion, and messengers of *Ras* Ali who had come to Wube offering him the title of *Ras* and other concessions were treated with contempt and were sent back to their master with abusive messages. Wube openly announced that he intended to attack *Ras* Ali, who he claimed was a Muslim at heart. He also proclaimed that he would install the lawful descendant of the line of Solomon, King of Kings Tekle Giorgis, who was at the time in his camp, on the imperial throne in Gondar.[2]

When *Abuna* Salama arrived in Ethiopia in the last months of 1841 he was escorted to Wube's camp and soon won over by the party of the two births of Christ (the *Wold Qib*), and was convinced by Wube of the Islamic tendencies of *Ras* Ali. He therefore excommunicated the *Ras* and proclaimed the *Ichege* a heretic.[3] At the end of 1841 Wube advanced into Begamder and soon after, together with Birru Goshu, captured Gondar. The united army of Wube and Birru Goshu then proceeded to attack Ali's army, and on 6th February, 1842, the two armies met near Debra Tabor. *Ras* Ali's army, numbering nearly 30,000 soldiers, was composed mainly of Galla contingents and was supported by *Dejazmatch* Merso and strangely enough by Birru Aligaz, who according to one source joined *Ras* Ali at the last minute.[4] The battle of Debra Tabor was clearly a battle between the

---

[1] Faris Aligaz was the brother of Birru Aligaz, governor of Wadela, and, as claimed by some sources, of Hirut Aligaz, Merso's mother. Lefebvre, Vol. I, pp. 77, 187, 233; A.E.B., Dos. 2024, Annexe 38, p. 8, Dembya, 6.8.1841.

[2] Lefebvre, Vol. I, pp. 293, 356; F.O., 78/508, Harris, 24.8.1841; Plowden, *Travels*, p. 386; L.G., 164, No. 2153, Willoughby, 5.7.1841.

[3] L.G., 186, No. 1470, Christopher, 18.1.1842.

[4] See note 1, above; also *Bulletin de l'Académie*, pp. 1142–3; A.E.B., Dos. 2024, Document 120, No. 9, Blondeel, Khartoum, 20.6.1842; Ibid., Annexe 43, Gondar, 25.1.1842; Ibid., rapport fait en 1843 par M. Blondeel, p. 26; Lefebvre, Vol. II, pp. 256–7; Ferret and Galinier, Vol. II, pp. 458–65; Parkyns, Vol. II, p. 134.

Christian Amhara and Tigrean elements and the Galla, fighting desperately to preserve their predominant position in northern Ethiopia. The contesting armies were nearly equal in size but the overwhelming superiority in firearms of Wube's army tipped the scale in favour of the Amhara and Tigreans. The battle was won by Wube and Birru Goshu, but during their subsequent celebrations, the victors were surprised by a small Galla army led by Birru Aligaz. Wube and his son were taken prisoners, but Birru Goshu managed to escape across the Abbay into Gojjam. *Ras* Ali, who escaped after his defeat with a number of his followers, then returned to Debra Tabor and grudgingly rewarded the true victor, Birru Aligaz, with the governorship of Daunt, a district to the south of Amhara bordering on the Wollo country, while Merso was given all of Wube's territories.[1]

Despite this Pyrrhic victory *Ras* Ali's position was far from secure. His enemies were still active in Gojjam, Damot, Dembya and Lasta. Most of the clergy were against him and the Christian population of Begamder and Amhara were further alienated from him by the propaganda of Wube and his allies. In such circumstances Ali desperately needed the support of the *Abuna* and was therefore willing to accept *Abuna* Salama's advice to liberate Wube and return his estates to him for nominal compensation and an oath of allegiance. However, the aftermath of the Debra Tabor battle further complicated Ali's position. *Dejazmatch* Merso, who had reached Semien in the meantime, refused to give up his brother's governorship and Ali was forced to march with his former enemy against his loyal ally. Moreover, the Muslim rulers of Wollo, who had always supported Ali, were greatly worried at the turn of events; they especially objected to the grant of a governorship on their natural avenue of expansion to Birru Aligaz, who was a Christian Yejju Galla, and who was supported by his brother Faris Aligaz, an old enemy of some of the most important Muslim Wollo chiefs.[2]

Throughout this uneasy period in 1841 and 1842 there was a general belief that Muhammad Ali, having concentrated large

[1] Isenberg, pp. 352, 358; A.E.B., Dos. 2024, Document 120, No. 9, Blondeel, Khartoum, 20.6.1842; Ferret and Galinier, Vol. II, p. 469.
[2] L.G., 190, No. 2404, Krapf, 6.6.1842; Plowden, *Travels*, p. 388; Ferret and Galinier, Vol. II, pp. 470–1. Combes and Tamisier, Vol. III, pp. 158–9; Isenberg, pp. 330, 352, 358, 362, 450.

forces not very far from Gondar, intended to invade Ethiopia. 'It is generally supposed that Mohammad Ali contemplates the conquest of Abyssinia', reported Captain Harris. When Consul Blondeel passed through Arkiko in April, 1841, the *Na'ib* of Arkiko told him of an Egyptian plan to conquer Ethiopia, in which the *Na'ib* was supposed to participate.[1] Moreover, ever since 1838 rumours had persisted that the leaders of the Muslim population of northern Ethiopia, together with a number of Muslim Galla lords, had conspired with the Egyptians, if not actually invited them to conquer Christian Ethiopia. The historian Coulbeaux,[2] basing his statement on Catholic missionary sources, says the following about Muhammad Ali's plans concerning Ethiopia after 1838:

Ses espérances dans ces contrées étaient fondées sur de secrètes ententes que lui avaient ménagées, auprès des Galla parents du Ras Ali, ses agents déguisés en commerçants musulmans et répandus dans toute l'Éthiopie. Tels le bacha Zeinou négadras d'Adoua, et son frère, le négadras de Gonder, auxquelles leur charge lucrative avaient acquis une influence considérable. La maison du Ras Ali demandait l'alliance de l'Égypte....

That Pasha Zainu, the leading Muslim figure in Tigre, was in the service of the Egyptians was rumoured as early as the time of Seb'agadis. In fact, the accusations against Zainu were so strong that in 1834 Wube ordered an investigation of the matter.[3] Tekruri and other Muslim merchants from the Hijaz and from the Sudan actively propagated Islam in the courts of many Galla nobles in Begamder, Amhara, and Wollo, and had they not feared the Church and the reaction of the Christian population, these nobles would have come out openly in favour of Islam. The Muslim party among the lords of northern Ethiopia and especially in the court of *Ras* Ali was so strong that, because of its influence, it was claimed, Ethiopia was left without an *Abuna* for ten years.[4] The leaders of this Muslim party were *Ras* Ali's

[1] L.G., 189, No. 2031, para. 22, October, 1841. A.E.B., Dos. 2024, Blondeel report, Annexe 1, Alexandrie, 6.1.1839; Ibid., Annexe 26, Arkiko, 5.4.1841, pp. 3–4. See also: L.G., Vol. 189, No. 1846B, Krapf, 3.10.1841; Ibid., Vol. 190, No. 2327, Christopher, 6.7.1842; Ibid., Vol. 196, Christopher, 2.10.1842; L.F.A., Vol. 1843, p. 23, Cruttenden, 28.12.1842; Corr. Pol., Égy., Alexandrie et le Caire, Vol. XV, p. 114, Alexandrie, 7.8.1842.
[2] Coulbeaux, J. B.: *Histoire politique et religieuse d'Abyssinie*, Paris, 1929, p. 397.
[3] F.O., 78/434, p. 299, Isenberg to Campbell, 1838–9.
[4] *Bayna al-Habasha*, pp. 199–201; *Royal Chronicles*, p. 488. *Douze ans*, p. 402.

uncles *Dejazmatch* Beshir and *Dejazmatch* Ahmade of Warra Himenu. The latter was accused in 1838, a short time before his death, of having secretly invited Muhammad Ali to conquer Ethiopia jointly with himself.[1] On leaving Ethiopia at the end of 1839, Arnauld d'Abbadie met an Arab notable called Muhammad al-Basrawi in the house of the governor of Massawa. This notable was on a mission to *Ras* Ali and *Dejazmatch* Wube from the Pasha of Mecca;[2] but it is not known whether this mission was political, religious, or economic. In October, 1841, the missionary Krapf, who was in Showa, wrote the following:

If Mohammed Ali will capture Abyssinia he would be able to recruit large forces for the army, especially by taking and organizing . . . the Galla people, who will furnish him with men and horses.[3]

The Belgian Consul in Egypt, Blondeel, arrived at Gondar towards the middle of 1841 on a secret mission to Ethiopia. After meeting *Ras* Ali, he reported his conversation with him and wrote, among other things:

aussi avait-il (Ras Ali) député au Pacha d'Égypte un de ses hommes de confiance chargé de lui déclarer, 'Je suis musulman comme vous, mais j'ai peur de prêtres et de mes généraux, soyons amis, et la foi de Mohammed dominera les Abyssins'.[4]

Blondeel further reported that about the time he met *Ras* Ali a messenger came to the latter from Muhammad Ali carrying the following message signed with the seal of the Pasha: '*Ne craignez rien, vos amis seront mes amis, et vos ennemies seront mes ennemies'*.[5] That Muhammad Ali's agents were freely circulating in Gondar is clear from the fact that a number of Muslim Ethiopians in the service of Ahmad Pasha, the governor of the Sudan, were sent to Gondar to accompany Blondeel out of Ethiopia.[6] Last but not least, in August, 1842, when Muhammad Ali discussed the Harris Mission to Showa with the French

---

[1] Abbadie, 21301, p. 46, para. 130. Ahmade died in 1838–9 but his son *Imam* Liban was just as fanatically a Muslim as his father.
[2] *Douze ans*, p. 558; Soleillet, p. 272.
[3] L.G., Vol. 189, No. 1846B.
[4] A.E.B., Dos. 2024, Annexe 37, 23.7.1841.
[5] Ibid.
[6] A.E.B., Dos. 2024, Document 120, No. 9, Khartoum, 20.6.1842.

Consul, he boasted that he could provide the French with all the influence they might wish to have in Ethiopia.[1]

It is possible, and even probable, that Muslim merchants and notables as well as the Galla rulers of northern Ethiopia, were actually in contact with Muhammad Ali after the conquest of the Sudan, but there is no evidence that their overtures were taken seriously by Muhammad Ali until about 1840. It is doubtful if the plans for the conquest of '*Habesch*' which Ahmad Pasha discussed in 1839–40 with the Austrian adventurer Werne actually had the sanction of Muhammad Ali, other than to consolidate Egyptian authority along the border with Ethiopia and to try to reopen, by force[2] if necessary, the caravan trade between Ethiopia and the Sudan.

It seems that when threatened on all sides in 1841, Ali and his mother Mennen succumbed to the pressure of the Muslim party, whose support they badly needed. It is more than likely that they appealed to Ahmad Pasha for help, using Islamic affinity as an incentive. At the end of January, 1842, just before the battle of Debra Tabor, Captain Harris, who was still in Showa, reported that '*the latter (Ras Ali)* in consequence of the defeat . . . has embraced the Mahammedan faith, and solicited military aid from the Egyptian governor of the Sennar'.[3] On his way out of Ethiopia at the end of March, 1842, Blondeel claims that a messenger from Goshu, who had meanwhile made it up with his son Birru Goshu, asked him in the name of his master to try to dissuade Ahmad Pasha from accepting the offer of alliance sent by *Ras* Ali and to convince him to form an alliance with Goshu instead.

Probably as a result of these approaches, and probably also to take advantage of the difficult situation in which the Ethiopians found themselves, the Egyptian army was despatched to Wekhni to watch the situation from that vantage point and also to quell a rebellion which had spread all over the province of Metemma–Gallabat. As soon as *Ras* Ali's troubles were over, the Egyptians withdrew most of their army from the Gondar

[1] Corr. Pol., Égy., Alexandrie et le Caire, Vol. XV, p. 114.
[2] Robinson, Nimr, p. 116; Duchesne, *Blondéel*, p. 166; Lejean, G.: *Théodor II*, Paris, 1865, p. 21; Stern, H. A.: *Wanderings Among the Falashas*, London, 1862, p. 65.
[3] L.G., Vol. 190, No. 2060I, Harris, 31.1.1842.

sector, and when Blondeel reached Khartoum about the middle of 1842, he found that Ahmad Pasha was fighting in the vicinity of Taka, north of Wolkait.[1] In May, 1842, Muhammad Ali already told the French Consul-General in Egypt that Ahmad Pasha was about to sign a peace treaty with the 'northern provinces of Abyssinia'. He added that the hostilities between the population of Ethiopia and the Egyptians were never serious, but as they greatly disturbed the caravan trade, the governor of the Sudan had been sent to the border to reopen the route.[2] By the end of 1842 the Egyptians were so absorbed with their expansion along the Nile that the talk of conquering Gondar completely subsided. As a result of the second geographic expedition sent by Muhammad Ali along the Nile, everyone in Cairo was discussing the richness of the areas of the south and a further expedition that would open an avenue to the rich trade of Kaffa, Enarea and western Ethiopia.

CONCLUSIONS

Ethiopian notions of borders and of the delimitation of areas in the nineteenth century were very different from those of the Egyptians, who were already influenced by European thought. They never considered the boundaries of their territories a fixed line, but rather an undetermined area, stretching into the land of their neighbours. Even when the Ethiopians spoke of their empire in the nineteenth century, their definition of its area was extremely vague. The borders of Ethiopia were not surrounded by the classical *Mogga* of the Sidama and Galla of southern and south-western Ethiopia;[3] nor was this the situation along those Ethiopian boundaries which became the common frontier with the Egyptians. Even the areas stretching as far as the lowlands and the plains of the Sudan, which were not under direct rule of the Ethiopian lords, were still considered as belonging to Ethiopia.[4] They would be penetrated from time to time when a

---

[1] A.E.B., Dos. 2024, Document 120, No. 9, Khartoum, 20.6.1842; Ibid., Blondeel report, Annexe 43, Gondar, 25.1.1842.

[2] Corr. Pol., Égy., Alexandrie et le Caire, Vol. XV, p. 92, 23.5.1842. Corr. Pol., Égy., Massouah, 1840–53, p. 94. At the end of 1841 Consul Blondeel reported that the whole area of Gallabat was in rebellion—A.E.B., Dos. 2024, Document 120, No. 9, Khartoum, 20.6.1842.

[3] See above p. 81. See also: *Douze ans*, p. 89; Parkyns, Vol. II, pp. 224–5.

[4] Dufton, H.: *Narrative of a Journey Through Abyssinia in 1862–1863*,

provincial governor could disengage himself from the unceasing internal struggle for power, and the inhabitants would be forced to pay tribute.[1] Thus the 'Arab' tribes, the *Shanqalla* negroids and the Hamitic nomadic and semi-nomadic people of northern Ethiopia were considered by different Ethiopian rulers as their subjects although an Ethiopian might not have been seen within these areas for decades.

Muhammad Ali, who accepted the European concept of a border, never agreed that the vast areas lying along the slopes of the Ethiopian plateau and beyond, inhabited by what he considered non-Ethiopian people, many of them Muslim, and not actually governed by the Ethiopians, belonged to Ethiopia. This was especially true because these areas became the refuge of bands of robbers and tribes who wanted to avoid taxation, and because he thought they contained the minerals for which, among other things, he had invaded the Sudan. Even when he was warned by the European Powers against conquering Christian Ethiopia, and he agreed not to interfere in that country, it seemed that he sincerely thought that this agreement did not include the peripheral areas. Muhammad Ali was in fact using the principle of 'effective occupation' which later became the yardstick in the division of Africa, and his actions were aimed at establishing a permanent and logical border along what he considered to be the provinces of Ethiopia proper.

Muhammad Ali greatly valued the good opinion of the European Powers and went to great lengths not to annoy them. Above all he tried not to bring upon himself the wrath of the British, whom he admired and feared. The Egyptian ruler and his governors in the Sudan might have, from time to time, toyed with the idea of taking advantage of the anarchy in Ethiopia, especially when entreated to do so by the Muslim chiefs of the country; but after being repeatedly warned, Muhammad Ali realized that an outright military conquest of Christian Ethiopia at that time would mean a confrontation with Great Britain and possibly France. Muhammad Ali was nevertheless a gambler; he hoped that as long as he refrained from attacking Ethiopia proper the

---

London, 1867, p. 46; Rassam, H.: *Narrative of the British Mission to Theodore King of Abyssinia*, London, 1869, Vol. I, p. 251.
[1] See above, p. 32.

Powers would close their eyes to the establishment of Egyptian authority in the border regions which he thought were rich in minerals, and through which went most of Ethiopia's trade. Often when it was thought that Muhammad Ali's actions were leading to the conquest of Ethiopia, the Egyptian ruler had in fact only a limited objective, and was all the while keeping an eye on the reaction of the Great Powers. Still, the Egyptian presence and activities on the verges of Ethiopia contributed to the spread of Islam in that area and were a boon to the efforts of the Galla to retain their predominant position in most of the country.

VI

The collapse of Galla predominance
Ethiopia and Egypt - second stage

In accordance with the agreement between Muhammad Ali and the Porte, the Egyptian forces were withdrawn from the Ethiopian coast in 1841, and Massawa was garrisoned by a handful of Ottoman soldiers under a *Kaimakam*.[1] However, the real authority on the coast in this transitional period rested with the *Na'ib* of Arkiko.

When the news of Wube's defeat at Debra Tabor reached the coast, the *Na'ib*, with the help of some rebellious chiefs who had recently been converted to Islam, started encroaching upon Wube's territories in Hamasen. Wube's dominions were at this time in a chaotic state; in Semien *Dejazmatch* Merso openly rebelled against the decision of *Ras* Ali to reinstate his brother; and in Tigre the situation was similar to that which had existed after the death of *Ras* Wolde Selassie. Many pretenders fought for dominance in the different provinces. *Balgada* Araya, governor of the salt-producing district of Arho, a great-nephew of Wolde Selassie and also a nephew of Seb'agadis, called himself *Dejazmatch* Araya Selassie, ruler of Tigre, and camped with his army in the region of Adowa. But most of the smaller chiefs simply refused to obey anyone and waited to see which way the wind would blow.[2]

Throughout 1842 and the first half of 1843, Wube slowly re-established his authority on both sides of the Takkaze. *Ras* Ali, who at the beginning fought beside him, was soon afterwards forced to march back to his own domains to suppress the many rebellions in Gojjam, Wollo, Yejju, and Dembya. Nevertheless, Wube succeeded in defeating his brother Merso, who later

[1] Equivalent to a colonel in the army, but in the Egyptian-Turkish administration and irregular units, equivalent to a petty chief.
[2] L.G., 190, No. 2404, Krapf, 6.6.1842; L.G., 191, No. 2602; L.G., 196, No. 3489, Harris, 7.4.1842; L.F.A., Vol. 28, Christopher, 15.12.1843; Parkyns, Vol. I, pp. 129–33.

escaped to the sanctuary of *Ichege Beit*, the quarter of the *Ichege* in Gondar. After engaging in a number of battles with Araya Selassie, Wube forced the latter to flee to the Raya Galla south of Tigre,[1] after which he was free to deal with the situation in Hamasen.

Although he had temporarily given up his imperial aspirations, Wube was desperately anxious to replace the firearms which he had lost in the battle of Debra Tabor; and mainly for this reason he adopted Seb'agadis's policy of fostering relations with the European Powers. Greatly encouraged by French travellers and Catholic missionaries, he decided to get a foothold on the coast in order to facilitate the free flow of firearms and trade to the highlands.[2] At the end of 1843, Wube despatched his army to the mountains overlooking the plains of Samhar; at the same time a message was sent to the *Na'ib* of Arkiko to the effect that the coast would be attacked unless he returned what he had looted from the highlands, and handed over Coffin and the matchlocks sent by the British to Seb'agadis in 1832. It was clear that Wube's impossible demands[3] were only a pretext to conquer the coast or part of it.

In December of 1843 Wube's army descended upon the coast and looted the nomadic population of the Samhar; but as the people of Arkiko were determined to defend their village with the help of the Turks, the Ethiopians returned to Hamasen after receiving partial compensation from the *Na'ib*. During the first months of 1844, while some of Wube's generals were raiding Bogos, the Bani Amir and the Habab, the bulk of Wube's army remained in Hamasen.[4] The continuous presence of a large Ethiopian army, in addition to a number of incidents between the people of the highlands and the coastal Muslims, caused an

[1] Parkyns, Vol. I, pp. 132–3; Archives of Church Missionary Society (London), East African Mission, CA/5/013, Journals of Isenberg 1842–3, 29.3.1843, 28.7.1843; Ibid., No. 21, Isenberg, 27.7.1843.

[2] Corr. Pol., Égypte, Massouah, p. 96, Jacobis, Adowa, 11.10.1843; Ibid., p. 101, 14.4.1843.

[3] Especially the demand to hand over Coffin, who refused to return to Wube after the failure of his mission, and who was protected by the British. Corr. Pol., Égypte, Massouah, pp. 95–6, 99, 101, 109; L.F.A., Vol. 28, p. 60, Christopher, 16.3.1844.

[4] Corr. Pol., Égypte, Massouah, pp. 112–13; Parkyns, Vol. II, p. 292; L.F.A., Vol. 28, p. 56, Christopher, 18.3.1844.

uneasy feeling in Massawa and Arkiko, and another raid into the coastal area was expected.[1]

In September, 1844, *Na'ib* Yihye of Arkiko died and his brother Hassan was appointed by the Pasha of Jedda to succeed him. The sons of Yihye, who objected to this appointment, collected their supporters and blockaded the island of Massawa. As Massawa was completely dependent on Arkiko for its water supply, money was collected by the authorities from the merchants, and the sons of the dead *Na'ib* were paid to give up their claim. During this time, Wube was busy raiding the *Shanqalla* areas of Barea and Kunama. In October he returned to Hamasen with many slaves and much loot, and upon hearing of the appointment of Hassan, he invited the latter to the border to confirm his appointment and thereby establish his authority over him. The *Na'ib*, however, fearing Wube's intentions, refused to meet him without the permission of the Pasha of Jedda, who he declared was his master and ally. Wube again threatened to descend to the coast. However, this time he was faced with far more serious opposition than the *Na'ib* and the Turkish *Kaimakam*.[2]

Since 1842 the Egyptians in the Sudan had been concentrating their efforts on opening new areas along the Nile and on consolidating their hold on the area of Taka, the Bani Amir and Habab.[3] Apparently at the invitation of the governor of Massawa, and incensed by Wube's raids on peoples whom they considered under Egyptian rule, a corps made up of 5,000 infantry and 1,000 cavalry under the command of Amin Bey advanced through the country of the Habab, and after receiving tribute from the Habab, reached the borders of the Christian areas. As a result of the Egyptian advance, and of the urgent request from the governor of Massawa for reinforcements, a Turkish battalion

[1] Corr. Pol., Égy., Massouah, pp. 113, 123; L.F.A., Vol. 28, p. 168, Haines, 15.8.1844; Lejean, G.: *Voyage en Abyssinie, executé de 1862 à 1864*, Paris, 1868, pp. 55–6.
[2] Corr. Pol., Égy., Massouah, p. 125, Degoutin, 1.10.1844; Ibid., p. 128, 16.11.1844; Ibid., p. 130; Lejean, G.: *Voyage en Abyssinie, executé de 1862 à 1864*, Paris, 1868, p. 56; Parkyns, Vol. I, pp. 344–5, 350–1; Tekla Haimanot, p. 65.
[3] Lepsius, R.: *Letters from Egypt, Ethiopia, and the Peninsula of Sinai*, London, 1853, p. 196; Parkyns, Vol. II, pp. 332–4; Deherain, H.: *Le Soudan égyptien sous Mehemed Ali*, Paris, 1898, p. 110; T'arikh Muluk, pp. 33–4; Werne, *Expedition*, Vol. I, p. 54.

reached the island from the Hijaz. Wube was greatly alarmed, and after making the empty gesture of unilaterally appointing Muhammad, the son of the deceased *Na'ib* Yihye, to replace Hassan, he retreated inland.[1]

Faced with the new situation which frustrated his plans, Wube applied to France for protection and assistance, on the advice of the Catholic missionaries in Tigre. In a letter to the French government he complained that the 'Turks', having surrounded Christian Ethiopia, were now planning to conquer the country from the coast, and by way of Sennar. He also accused the Egyptian ruler of encouraging his (Wube's) Muslim subjects to keep up political relations with him through the Pasha of Khartoum. Finally Wube claimed that, being the ruler of Tigre, he was the legal master of the coast and asked the French to intervene with the Porte to give up its claim to the Samhar.[2] In exchange for French support Wube was ready to cede to the French the coast of Arkiko or the province of Bogos and to permit them to trade freely with the highlands. However, the French government, with an eye on its relations with Muhammad Ali, was not duped by Wube's offer of territories which he did not possess. France declined his proposals and cautiously instructed its ambassadors in Constantinople and Egypt to prevent an unjustified aggression against Abyssinian territories inhabited by Christians, which did not belong to the Ottomans.[3]

For a short time there was peace at Massawa, but when the *Na'ib* and the Belaus did not receive their stipend they again rebelled. In order to neutralize the Belaus, the governor of Massawa tried to come to an understanding with Wube, but to no avail, as Wube insisted that the coast belonged to him. In order to appease Wube the governor of Massawa replaced *Na'ib* Hassan with Wube's favourite, Muhammad, the son of Yihye. Soon afterwards, suspecting that Muhammad was purposely delaying

[1] Corr. Pol., Égy., Massouah, p. 128, 16.11.1844; Ibid., p. 130, 20.2.1845; Ibid., p. 132, Degoutin, 15.4.1845; Ibid., p. 209, Schimper; Lejean, *Voyage*, p. 58; Parkyns, Vol. I, p. 86.
[2] Corr. Pol., Égy., Massouah, p. 138, Wube, 5.5.1845; Ibid., p. 141, Wube, 24.5.1845; Ibid., pp. 141–3, Jacobis, 1.6.1845; M. & D., Vol. 61, p. 21.
[3] Corr. Pol., Égy., Massouah, p. 148, Affaires Étrangères to Degoutin, 9.10.1845. In fact the missionary Jacobis was rebuked for 'excès de zèle', Ibid., p. 148, Affaires Étrangères to Degoutin, 15.11.1845; Ibid., p. 155, Degoutin, 5.3.1846; Corr. Pol., Égy., Alexandrie et le Caire, Vol. XVII, p. 122, Alexandrie, 18.9.1845; Ibid., p. 203, 14.9.1845.

the customary payment made at each appointment, the governor marched upon Arkiko with his small unit of Turkish troops. Faced with this threat, the two branches of the *Na'ib* family united to repel the Ottoman attack upon their territory and drove the Turkish forces back to Massawa. Massawa was again blockaded and the Belaus were appeased only at the beginning of 1846 after a new governor arrived from the Hijaz with a *firman* confirming the appointment of Muhammad. But the Belaus, encouraged by their success, completely disregarded the Ottoman governor.[1]

During 1846, Ottoman authority in the Hijaz and the Red Sea was on the verge of collapse. The Egyptians for their part wanted the Ethiopian coast mainly for economic reasons. The Porte was by now completely reconciled with Muhammad Ali and it badly needed his support. Thus when Muhammad Ali offered to farm the Abyssinian coast against an annual payment of 20,000 thalers, his offer was accepted, and by the end of 1846 the Ethiopian coast was again under Egyptian authority.[2] At this time Wube's troops were removed from Tigre to meet the threat of an attack by *Ras* Ali, with whom relations had deteriorated. Nevertheless, letters were dispatched to the *diwan* of Massawa and to the French Consul Degoutin demanding the surrender of the Samhar. To coerce the authorities of Massawa and the nomads of the plain, a free hand was given to the rulers of Hamasen to raid the coast.[3]

After his return from Semien in 1842 *Ras* Ali became involved in an unending chase of Birru Goshu in Gojjam. *Dejazmatch* Merso, who was again taken into the service of the *Ras*, was dispatched with an army to fight Faris Aligaz and the victor of the battle of Debra Tabor, Birru Aligaz, who were defying Ali's authority in Yejju and Lasta.[4] In the meantime *Abuna* Salama succeeded in reconciling *Dejazmatch* Goshu and his son Birru

[1] Corr. Pol., Égy., Massouah, p. 132, 15.4.1845; Ibid., p. 144, 25.7.1845; Ibid., p. 146, 2.9.1845; Ibid., p. 149, 10.12.1845; Ibid., p. 151, December, 1845; Ibid., 24.2.1846; Lejean, *Voyage*, p. 56.
[2] Corr. Pol., Égy., Massouah, p. 144, 25.7.1845; Ibid., p. 156, 24.12.1846; Sabri, M.: *L'empire égyptien sous Ismail*, Paris, 1933, pp. 389–90.
[3] L.F.A., Vol. 29, Lt. Aden, 17.12.1846; M. & D., Vol. 61, p. 26, Degoutin, 20.4.1847; Corr. Pol., Égy., Massouah, p. 176, Degoutin, 23.4.1847.
[4] *Nuovi documenti*, pp. 381–2. He and his brother were captured by Merso and handed over to Wube. Lefebvre, Vol. II, pp. 123–31.

Goshu; but *Ras* Ali, who could not forgive Birru Goshu for having taken his wife before the battle of Debra Tabor, was far from pleased. At the end of the rainy season of 1843 he directed his army and that of Mennen against Goshu and his son. Goshu was taken prisoner by Mennen in March, 1844, but Birru Goshu succeeded in eluding his enemies and remained at large. Merso, who returned from Lasta, was left as governor of Gojjam but was soon defeated by Birru Goshu, who again became the master of most of Gojjam and Damot in the *Ras's* absence. At the end of 1844, after the *Abuna* interceded in favour of Goshu and Birru Goshu, it seemed as if Ali was ready for a reconciliation. *Dejazmatch* Goshu was released from his chains[1] and Birru Goshu and Ali exchanged messages and presents. However, Ali was only playing for time. Before taking the field against Birru Goshu, he wanted to collect taxes from his estates and to deal with the situation in Yejju and Lasta which, it was rumoured, were again in rebellion.[2] Once Ali was ready, the war with Birru Goshu was renewed.

Throughout 1845 and the beginning of 1846 Ali's army was continually engaged in the suppression of rebellions in the Yejju and Wollo areas and in a fruitless chase of Birru Goshu. The latter, though forced to escape beyond the Abbay or into the Wollo country, always evaded capture, and in the beginning of 1845 even managed to penetrate Begamder and burn Debra Tabor, the capital of the *Ras*. Goshu, who at first co-operated with Ali against his son, again joined forces with Birru Goshu, and once Ali left Gojjam in June, 1846, they managed to defeat the governors whom he had left behind.[3] Although Goshu was finally reconciled with Ali at the beginning of 1849, Birru Goshu remained a thorn in *Ras* Ali's side until the defeat of the *Ras* in the battle (Ayshal) with Kassa-Teodros in 1853.

Another source of continuous trouble for the *Ras* was *Abuna*

---

[1] His other son, *Fitaurari* Tesemma, was imprisoned in the Wollo area as a guarantee for his good behaviour.

[2] *Nuovi documenti*, pp. 382–3; Corr. Pol., Égy., Massouah, p. 123, Degoutin, 4.9.1844; L.F.A., Vol. 28, pp. 50–1, Christopher, 15.12.1843.

[3] The strong chief of the Borana Galla south of the Wollo on both sides of the Abbay, Ali Wadajo, was friendly to Goshu and his son and always gave them shelter. *Nuovi documenti*, pp. 382–5, 388; Hotten, J. C.: *Abyssinia and Its People*, London, 1868, p. 203; Tubiana, pp. 30, 32, 53–4, 64–5, 84–5; Plowden, *Travels*, p. 208.

Salama. The *Abuna*, who had been kept by *Ras* Ali in Gondar since 1842, proved to be a liability rather than an asset. Still a supporter of the *Hulet Lidet*, he was openly at war with the *Ichege* and with the majority of the clergy of Gondar. Displeased by Wube's friendship with the Catholic missionaries, he threatened him with excommunication unless they were banished from his territories. He also instructed *Negus* Sahle Selassie to reinstate the clergy which the latter had dismissed on the recommendation of the *Ichege* and *Ras* Ali,[1] and threatened the *Negus* as well with excommunication unless he complied. His relations with Mennen were also extremely strained because Mennen supported the *Ichege* and refused to give up the estates of the *Abuna* within her territories. At the end of 1844 or the beginning of 1845 the *Abuna* even left Gondar for a short period because of his differences with Mennen and the *Ichege*. However, after a time he returned to the town and for a few months it seemed as if he was reconciled with Mennen and even with the *Ichege*.[2]

In 1845 Ali succeeded in capturing his cousin, *Imam* Liban, son of *Dejazmatch* Ahmade (died 1838/9), who was now the chief of the Warra Himenu Wollo and who had led a number of rebellions against him since 1842. *Imam* Liban, however, broke out of his prison; and although he was a Muslim, he was given asylum in the quarter of the *Abuna* in Gondar, which traditionally served as a sanctuary. Although *Ras* Ali promised not to harm him, he was later arrested and was again imprisoned. This was the beginning of the estrangement between *Ras* Ali and the *Abuna*, but the final break between the two resulted from the *Abuna* having excommunicated Sahle Selassie, the ruler of Showa, for supporting the *Sost Lidet*, and for his having dismissed and banished a number of ecclesiastics who were not ready to comply with the doctrines of Gondar.[3] At the end of 1845 an embassy of Showan clergy, carrying many presents from Sahle Selassie to Ali and Mennen, reached Gondar to plead the case of Sahle Selassie. The *Ichege* and his followers,

---

[1] See below, pp. 157–8.
[2] Archives of Church Missionary Society (London), East African Mission, C.A./5/016, Krapf Letters, No. 2, Ankober, 28.1.1842; Coulbeaux, *Histoire*, Vol. II, pp. 392–3; Tubiana, pp. 48, 67; *Nuovi documenti*, pp. 383–5; Tekla Haimanot, p. 79.
[3] See below, pp. 158–9.

who strongly opposed the *Abuna*'s doctrines, added their pressure in support of the Showan case. At first Ali and Mennen implored the *Abuna* to reconsider the excommunication of Sahle Selassie. But finally, because of his categoric refusal to comply, the *Abuna* was given a choice of either giving Sahle Selassie absolution or of leaving the territories of the *Ras*. At the beginning of 1846 when Salama still refused to reconsider the excommunication, he was arrested by Mennen's soldiers and abused by the followers of the *Ichege*. After excommunicating Mennen, her son, and the followers of the *Ichege*, he was escorted to the territories of Wube, where he was received with full honours and was accompanied to the *Abuna*'s traditional estates in the district of Addi Abuna in Tigre.[1]

After the abortive attempt of *Dejazmatch* Goshu in 1839–40 to gain control over the territories of *Dejazmatch* Kinfu, the provinces to the west and to the north of Lake Tana were placed under the Empress Mennen. The peripheral areas of those provinces were infested with bands of *Shifta* who raided the trade routes between Ethiopia and the Sudan, and were in turn often raided by 'Arab' and Tekruri bands from Egyptian-held territories. By 1845 one of the *Shifta* leaders, Kassa, who was related to *Dejazmatch* Kinfu, had gained such power and fame that Ali and Mennen wanted to have him on their side. He was therefore promised that if he would declare his loyalty to the *Ras* and join his followers he would be given Ali's daughter and the governorship of his birthplace, the district of Qwara. Kassa accepted the offer, but after being kept for some time in Mennen's court he found out that the position he was to be given in Qwara was subordinate to that of one of Mennen's Muslim generals. At the end of 1845 Kassa was asked to guide the military commander of Qwara and his army into the lowlands. This expedition may have been prompted by a Tekruri raid upon Dembya.[2] However, the humility which Kassa had shown in the presence of Mennen had just been a pretence, and

[1] *Nuovi documenti*, pp. 385–8; F.O., 78/551, Beke, 9.12.1843; L.F.A., Vol. 28, Christopher, 15.12.1843; Plowden, *Travels*, p. 38; L.F.A., Vol. 29, p.28, Lt. Aden, 17.12.1846; Corr. Pol., Égy., Massouah, p. 123, 4.9.1844; Hotten, *Plowden*, p. 162; Tekla Haimanot, pp. 69, 74; Coulbeaux, *Histoire*, Vol. II, p. 393; Tubiana, p. 69; CA/5/016, Krapf Letters, No. 113, Massawa, 2.3.1855.
[2] Robinson, *Journal of the African Society*, Vol. 26, 1926–7, p. 50.

once in the border areas Kassa started to incite the population against the new governor. At first he raided the Sudan and attacked isolated posts of Mennen's troops; but by the beginning of 1846 he was in open revolt, after having ravaged the district of Chelega. Consequently, at the end of the rainy season (about September) Mennen marched with her army to Chelega, but Kassa avoided battle with the main army of the Empress and retreated. He nevertheless managed to defeat a number of units which were sent after him into the more inaccessible border areas. Mennen was furious and wanted to revenge this humiliation; but in the meantime the relations between Ali and Wube had so deteriorated that another major contest between the two was expected momentarily, and Mennen was forced to leave Chelega in order to support her son in the approaching crisis. While Mennen marched to join *Ras* Ali in Wogera, Kassa, never lacking audacity, took advantage of the opportunity, ravaged Dembya and entered Gondar in January, 1847. He demanded and received tribute and appointed his own officials in the town.[1]

During the rainy season of 1846, Ali, who was preparing for his annual expedition against Birru Goshu, called upon his tributary *Dejazmatch* Wube to send him funds and soldiers for the coming campaign. Wube, who was himself pestered with rebellions in Tigre and who was closely watching developments on the coast, used all kinds of pretexts in order not to comply with the commands of his master. The *Ras*, who had distrusted Wube since the battle of Debra Tabor and who was already in Gojjam, recrossed the Abbay at the end of 1846 and advanced into Wogera. At the news of the approaching attack, Wube mobilized his armies and rushed from Tigre to Semien. When he reached Semien, he dispatched a number of units to Wogera to delay Ali's advance, and having fortified the mountain passes he waited there with the bulk of his army.

Once Wube was again at war with Ali, the situation in Tigre

---

[1] *Nuovi documenti*, pp. 389–90; Morié, L. G.: *Histoire de l'Éthiopie*, Paris, 1904, Vol. II, p. 362; Stern, *Falashas*, pp. 6–7; Dufton, H.: *Narrative of a Journey Through Abyssinia in 1862*, London, 1867, p. 123; Fusella, L.: *La cronaca dell'Emperatore Theodoro II di Etiopia*, Rome, 1957 (author unknown), pp. 11–12; Rubenson, S.: *King of Kings Tewodros of Ethiopia*, Addis Ababa, 1966, pp. 36–7. I am greatly indebted to Prof. Rubenson's monograph for some of the more important sources on the period of Teodros.

reverted to what it had been in 1842. Rebellion broke out in different provinces and *Balgada* Araya (*Dejazmatch* Araya Sel-assie), who for some years had been conducting guerrilla warfare against Wube, appeared in the area of Adowa and declared himself ruler of Tigre. Moreover, in the interim period before the arrival of the governor of Muhammad Ali in Massawa, the *Na'ib* assumed full authority on the coast and began raiding the Christian areas of Hamasen in the name of Muhammad Ali.[1]

By the first months of 1847 it became evident that both Ali and Wube were avoiding a major clash. Ali contented himself with ravaging the plains of Wogera, which were admirably suit-able for cavalry, while Wube remained in the mountains of Semien and waited for Ali to advance into the mountain defiles which were heavily guarded by matchlockmen. In fact, both leaders were eager to find a way out of the deadlock. Ali was anxious to terminate the hostilities because Birru Goshu had once again made himself the master of Gojjam, because the Ali-gaz brothers, freed by Wube at the end of 1846, were again inciting the Yejju and the Wollo, and because of Kassa's con-quest of Gondar. Wube, to say the least, was as interested as Ali in reconciliation. The situation in Tigre was fast deteriorating because the *Abuna*, it seems, was intriguing with *Balgada* Araya and inciting the population against Wube for giving refuge to the Catholic missionaries. No less alarming was the news which reached Wube at the end of March of Egyptian forces landing in Massawa. Thus, about the middle of 1847, without even coming to grips with Ali, Wube submitted, paid tribute, and was recon-firmed as governor of Wogera, Semien, Wolkait and Tigre.[2] Once the hostilities were over Mennen quickly returned to Gon-dar and soon afterwards followed the retreating army of Kassa in the direction of the northern shores of Lake Tana. On 18th June the two armies met and, although she personally led the attack, Mennen was completely defeated and was taken prisoner

---

[1] M. & D., Vol. 61, Rochet d'Héricourt, pp. 301–2; Corr. Pol., Égy., Massouah, p. 172, Degoutin, 15.3.1847; Tekla Haimanot, pp. 77–81; Massaia, *I miei*, Vol. I, p. 87; Parkyns, Vol. I, pp. 193–4; Plowden, *Travels*, pp. 383, 391; L.F.A., Vol. 29, pp. 28–9, Lt. Aden, 17.12.1846.

[2] Massaia, *I miei*, Vol. I, p. 58; Plowden, *Travels*, p. 389; Tekla Haimanot, p. 79.

together with her husband, the Emperor Yohannes. Ali, who was on his way to Lasta, quickly marched to Gondar to revenge the shame brought upon him by Kassa. When he reached Gondar, common sense prevailed and he agreed to give Kassa all the territories of *Dejazmatch* Kinfu as well as the title *Dejazmatch* in exchange for his mother.[1]

At the end of the rainy season of 1847, *Ras* Ali led his armies against Birru Aligaz in Lasta. While the *Ras* was away, *Dejazmatch* Goshu and his son Birru Goshu invaded Begamder, and at the end of 1847 entered Gondar.[2] Being a follower of the *Hulet Lidet* and deeply religious, he strongly resented the treatment which the clergy and the population of Gondar had given *Abuna* Salama. He therefore allowed the town to be sacked; and the *Ichege*, the arch-enemy of the *Abuna*, was put in irons and was taken to Gojjam by the retreating army of Goshu.[3]

Dejazmatch Kassa, the supposed defender of Gondar, for reasons of his own did not interfere with the activities of the army of Gojjam and retreated to the lowlands. In retaliation for a number of Egyptian raids into his territories he descended upon Metemma in the beginning of 1848, defeated its small garrison and looted its market. Encouraged by his easy success and having collected an army of about 16,000 men, Kassa began to advance towards Sennar, possibly with the idea of reconquering the areas which he considered to have been part of his governorship before the Egyptian aggression. The Egyptians rushed reinforcements to the border and in March, 1848, at a place called Dabarki, between the Rahad and the Dindar rivers, Kassa came upon a fortified Egyptian camp with about 800 regulars, and two cannons. Unfortunately for the Ethiopians, Kassa probably inherited the contempt of *Dejazmatch* Kinfu for the Egyptian troops, and he led a frontal attack on the fortified Egyptian positions. The well-entrenched infantry opened fire at close quarters and the Ethiopians were cut to pieces by the accurate fire of the muskets and the two cannons. Kassa, himself slightly

---

[1] *Nuovi documenti*, p. 389; Lejean, *Theodore*, pp. 16–17; Massaia, *I miei*, Vol. I, p. 58; L.F.A., Vol. 29, p. 524, Lt. Rennie, 17.8.1847; Tekla Haimanot, p. 88; Coulbeaux, *Histoire*, Vol. II, pp. 413–15.

[2] *Nuovi documenti*, pp. 394–5—according to this source, Goshu received the title of *Ras* from Emperor Yohannes, who was in Gondar at the time.

[3] *Nuovi documenti*, pp. 394–5; Tubiana, p. 51; Coulbeaux, *Histoire*, Vol. II, p. 393.

wounded, led the remnants of his army back to the security of the Dembya mountains.[1]

When Kassa recovered from his wounds, he was in a most difficult situation. Many of his soldiers had deserted his camp and even the remnants of his army were in a rebellious mood. After having overcome this last problem by punishing the rebels in a most cruel manner, he was faced with an even more serious challenge. *Ras* Ali, who had in the meantime returned from Lasta after accepting the submission of Birru Aligaz, summoned him to appear in Debra Tabor. Kassa realized that compliance with his master's order could mean imprisonment in retaliation for the shame inflicted upon Mennen in the past. For some time he delayed his answer and at the end of June informed the *Ras* that he was unable to obey his order because the rainy season had commenced. He then took advantage of this to rebuild his army, mainly from the rabble of Dembya and the many deserters from the armies of other nobles, who were attracted to his camp by the prospect of loot. When Rochet d'Héricourt, on a mission from the French Ministry of Commerce, reached Gondar in September, 1848, Kassa had under his command from 6,000 to 7,000 soldiers, who were camped a short distance from Gondar.[2]

With the end of the rainy season the inevitable messengers from *Ras* Ali arrived in Kassa's camp and brought a new summons to appear before the *Ras* in Debra Tabor. This time Kassa flatly refused, and in anticipation of an attack, he marched southwards to the north-eastern corner of Lake Tana.[3] When Rochet d'Héricourt reached Debra Tabor at the end of October, he was told by *Ras* that he (the *Ras*) intended attacking Kassa very soon. However, shortly afterwards a Gondarine dignitary appeared at Ali's camp in an effort to intercede for the rebellious *Dejazmatch*.[4] Notwithstanding this and other efforts to reach a peaceful solu-

---

[1] Tremaux, P.: *Égypte et Éthiopie*, Paris, 1861, Vol. II, pp. 19, 97–9; Stern, H.: *The Captive Missionary*, London, 1869, pp. 8–9; Blanc, H.: *A Narrative of Captivity in Abyssinia*, London, 1868, p. 3; Lejean, *Theodore*, p. 24; Rassam, H.: *Narrative of the British Mission to Theodore King of Abyssinia*, London, 1869, Vol. I, p. 251; Dufton, pp. 123–4.

[2] Rochet d'Héricourt, M. & D., Vol. 61, pp. 61, 330–1.

[3] Ibid., pp. 329, 330–1. Rochet, who met the *Ras*'s messengers in the beginning of October, was under the impression that they brought Kassa instructions to send Rochet himself to the *Ras*.

[4] Ibid., pp. 314, 349.

tion, Ali's army marched on Dembya in January, 1849.[1] Dembya was once again ravaged, and facing an army far superior to his own, Kassa surrendered, appeared before the *Ras* and asked for forgiveness.[2] Strangely enough, he was forgiven and confirmed in his governorship and later joined the *Ras* in a new campaign against Goshu and Birru Goshu. Until 1852 Kassa served the *Ras* faithfully and joined his campaigns whenever called upon to do so.

When faced by the armies of most of the rulers of northern Ethiopia, *Dejazmatch* Goshu, who was tired of the perpetual wars which ravaged his territories, surrendered immediately and was confirmed in his governorship. But his turbulent son, well acquainted with Ali's hate for him and expecting no mercy should he surrender, preferred to escape to his mountain fortress where he was besieged until the fall of the *Ras* in 1853.[3]

Between 1849 and 1852 most of northern Ethiopia enjoyed a period of relative stability and internal peace, the like of which it had not known since the times of *Ras* Gugsa, but this was just a lull before the big storm which was to bring the *Zamana Masafint* to an end, and which was to change the history of the country.

Although the coast of *al Habasha* was farmed by Muhammad Ali at the end of 1846, an Egyptian governor (Ismail Hakki) arrived at Massawa with a few attendants only about the middle of March, 1847. The worried mercantile population of the island, which had suffered from the oppression of the *Na'ib* and the Belaus from the beginning of 1846, was told that Egyptian troops would reach Massawa by land from Sennar. This might have been in line with the policy formulated by Ibrahim Pasha, who became the regent of Egypt at the end of 1846, to connect Taka

[1] A Catholic missionary wrote from Gondar on 10th January that a big battle was expected in the area of Gondar any minute. The missionary was probably Father Philipini, mentioned by Rochet d'Héricourt. Ibid., p. 322; Coulbeaux, *Histoire*, Vol. II, p. 416; see also L.F.A., Vol. 30, p. 546, Adams, enclosure in Haines, 13.6.1849; Plowden, *Travels*, p. 396.

[2] It is even possible that contingents from the armies of Wube and Birru Aligaz took part in the expedition against Kassa and later against Birru Goshu. L.F.A., Vol. 30, p. 546, Adams, enclosure in Haines, 13.6.1849; Plowden, *Travels*, p. 422; *Nuovi documenti*, p. 397; Deftera Zeneb: *The Chronicle of King Theodore* (*Yetewodros Tarik*), ed. Enno Littman, Princeton, 1902, p. 14.

[3] Plowden, *Travels*, pp. 417, 422; Massaia, *I miei*, Vol. I, p. 90; *Nuovi documenti*, p. 397; Rassam, Vol. I, pp. 282–3.

with Massawa and to provide a better outlet for the trade of his landlocked possessions in the Sudan. Nevertheless, it seems that the execution of such a plan, if it existed at all, was left to the future. An advance party of Egyptian troops reached Massawa by sea at the end of March, and soon afterwards a regular battalion of infantry landed on the coast of Arkiko.[1]

The Egyptian governor now felt that he was strong enough to break the power of the *Na'ibs*, who had usurped the authority of the Massawa government since the beginning of 1846. The ex-*Na'ib* Hassan, who was at the head of the opposition to the Ottoman authority, was called to Massawa and arrested on arrival. At the same time the Egyptian forces attacked Arkiko and burnt the village. Most of the Sahos and their Belau rulers left Arkiko and the surrounding area, and escaped into the mountains. To guard the water sources of Massawa, the Egyptians built a mud fort in Arkiko and garrisoned it with 500 soldiers while Monkollo, another Belau village not far from Arkiko, was garrisoned by one hundred soldiers. *Na'ib* Muhammad was again confirmed as chief of the Belaus but he was stripped of all authority and became in fact a puppet of the Egyptian governor.[2]

In the middle of 1847 letters from the governor of Massawa were dispatched to all the coastal rulers as far as Berbera, calling upon them to come to Massawa and submit to the government of Muhammad Ali. A few months earlier the commander of the Egyptian troops had claimed openly that he was ordered by the Viceroy to '*reconnaître le côte Africaine de la Mer Rouge jusqu'au détroit de Bab il Mandab*'.[3] The governor of Massawa still bragged that he expected 6,000 soldiers to reach Massawa from Taka. Consequently rumours began circulating freely that Egyptian troops were about to land at different places along the coast. The British authorities in Aden, who were extremely sensitive to political changes in the Red Sea littoral and the Gulf of Aden, and who were always apprehensive of the aggressive policy of Muhammad Ali, warned their government of the pos-

[1] Corr. Pol., Égy., Massouah, p. 172, Degoutin, 15.3.1847; Ibid., p. 175, 1.4.1847.
[2] L.F.A., Vol. 29, Lt. Aden, 17.12.1846; Corr. Pol., Égy., Massouah, p. 172, Degoutin, 15.3.1847; Ibid., p. 178, 20.5.1847; Ibid., p. 179, 17.6.1847; F.O., Abyssinia, 1/5, pp. 216–17, Plowden, 16.8.1848; L.G., 258, No. 939, 4.9.1848.
[3] Corr. Pol., Égy., Massouah, p. 175, Degoutin, 1.4.1847.

sible consequences of the new developments to their still shaky hold over Aden.[1]

Towards the end of 1847 European newspapers published the news that the Egyptian forces had conquered, or were about to conquer, the salt mines which supplied most of Ethiopia with *amoleh*.[2] Walter Chrichele Plowden, who travelled extensively in Ethiopia in the 1840's and in 1846 was entrusted with presents and a message of friendship from *Ras* Ali to Queen Victoria, was about to depart for Ethiopia to negotiate a treaty of friendship and commerce with *Ras* Ali and to establish a British consulate in Massawa. Hearing of the Egyptian activities, he wrote an urgent letter to the British Foreign Office warning them of the consequences of the Egyptian action. Among other things he said:

On the first distraction of a European war, the troops of Egypt, on the one side occupying the coast of the Red Sea, on the other 'Sennaar' to within ninety miles from Gondar, will pour upon the fertile provinces of Abyssinia . . . by superior discipline they will perhaps succeed in realizing one of the favourite schemes of their present master by consolidating his African dominions into one vast realm from 'Cairo' to 'Enarea' and from the Red Sea to the deserts of Central Africa.[3]

Lord Palmerston, who by this time had a pathological dislike of Muhammad Ali, reacted instantaneously and wrote to the British ambassador in Constantinople:

I heard that Mohammed Ali wants the appointment for Sawakin and Massawa. Mohammed Ali's meddling with those places, although he has the appointment of the Porte, was an encroachment on his part on Abyssinia, a country with which Great Britain is endeavouring to establish relations of trade. Inform the authorities of our opposition to this appointment.[4]

---

[1] L.F.A., Vol. 29, p. 529, 17.8.1847; Ibid., p. 563, 25.10.1847; Ibid., p. 599, 24.11.1847; Corr. Pol., Égy., Massouah, p. 183, Degoutin, 15.10.1847; Plowden, *Travels*, p. 2. In April, 1847, Lt. Cruttenden was instructed to investigate a rumour that Seyyid Said, the Sultan of Zanzibar, was trying to assert his authority in Berbera. L.F.A., Vol. 29, p. 385, Cruttenden, 20.4.1847.

[2] See above, pp. 49–50.

[3] F.O., Abyssinia, 1/4, p. 126, Plowden, 17.11.1847; see also: F.O., Abyssinia, 1/4, p. 13, 15.10.1847; Ibid., p. 120, 18.11.1847; L.F.A., Vol. 29, p. 316, 13.1.1847.

[4] F.O., 78/3185, 6.12.1847.

The ambitious governor of Massawa, Ismail Hakki, was dismissed in the beginning of 1848 because of his high-handedness and because of his unauthorized actions.[1] Moreover, the much-talked-about reinforcements to the garrison of Massawa never materialized. Nevertheless, Consul Plowden, who reached Massawa in the first months of 1848, and who was well informed of the official policy regarding Muhammad Ali, continued to accuse Egypt of preparing for the conquest of Ethiopia. Even as late as September, 1848, Plowden still reported to Palmerston that 'Egyptian reinforcements are expected for further conquest'.[2] However, by this time it should have been quite evident that if anyone was about to commit aggression, it was not the Egyptians but Wube, who was again trying to establish his authority on the coast, and whom Plowden tried to befriend.[3]

After submitting to Ali in June, 1847, Wube was immobilized in Semien by the rainy season. Only around September, when the Takkaze became traversable, did he dispatch his son, *Dejazmatch* Chettu, and some of his generals to put down the rebellion in Tigre. Wube himself marched against *Balgada* Araya at the end of 1847; and having driven the *Balgada* from Enderta, he sent his officers on punitive expeditions against *Balgada* Araya's supporters.[4] The *Abuna*, who was accused of having supported Wube's enemies, found it prudent to retire to the monastery of Debra Damo. From there he excommunicated Wube because he heard that the latter wanted to arrest him, and because he (Wube) protected the Catholic missionaries in Tigre. In retaliation Wube confiscated the *Abuna*'s estates at the beginning of 1848 and then, having decided to rid himself of the rebellious chiefs of Tigre, he began to replace them with his own generals and followers.[5] Much as Wube wanted to preserve his relations with the French and much as he might have liked the head of the Catholic mission, de Jacobis, who had served his cause most

---

[1] Palmerston's letter, dispatched only in December, 1847, had nothing to do with his dismissal.

[2] F.O., Abyssinia, 1/5, p. 229, 17.9.1848; see also: Ibid., p. 218, 16.8.1848; Plowden, *Travels*, p. 356; similar accusations were made by the authorities of Aden. L.F.A., Vol. 30, p. 383, Haines, 13.9.1848.

[3] L.F.A., Vol. 30, p. 386, Adams, 4.9.1848; Plowden, *Travels*, p. 360; Massaia, *I miei*, Vol. I, p. 74.

[4] Tekla Haimanot, pp. 85–8.

[5] CA/5/016, Krapf Letters, No. 113, Massawa, 2.3.1855; Tekla Haimanot, pp. 80, 86, 88–9, 92–5.

loyally since 1840, he was finally convinced by his chief advisers that he could not hope to establish his government in Tigre as long as he antagonized the Orthodox Church[1] and fought the traditional aristocracy at the same time. Thus in the last months of 1848 Wube went to Debra Damo to make his peace with the *Abuna*, which he only succeeded in doing after agreeing to banish all the Catholics from his territories.[2]

While Wube was at Debra Damo, his army, commanded by his two sons and his chief generals, had moved into the provinces of Akalaguzai and Hamasen facing the Samhar and begun to raid the Muslim areas.[3] In December, a force of 10,000 of Wube's soldiers descended upon the Samhar. The greatly outnumbered Egyptians abandoned Monkollo, but entrenched themselves in Arkiko. In the first days of 1849 Wube's army was still looting the Samhar, and only when a large indemnity was paid to Wube's generals did they retreat to the mountains.[4] Back in Hamasen, Wube's army advanced upon the Habab and the Barea, pillaged the entire area and took many slaves. Wube's army retreated only when its commanders heard that a large Egyptian force had been dispatched to the area south-east of Kassala.[5] Consul Plowden, who was at the time in Adowa, reported the following to Palmerston:

The forces of Djaj Oobeay have made a descent upon the coast, declaring that the Turkish troops, by occupying the mainland, had trespassed upon the ancient dominions of Abyssinia, and had, by crushing the Naib, prevented that chief from paying to Oobeay his accustomed tribute . . . it is probable that succours will be sent from Egypt . . . for further conquest.[6]

When this dispatch was written, Ibrahim Pasha was already dead, and soon afterwards, with the reins of the Egyptian government (still in the name of Muhammad Ali) in the hand of

---

[1] Most of Tigre followed the *Hulet Lidet* in its *Wold Qib* (*Karra Haymanot*) interpretation.
[2] Tekla Haimanot, pp. 95–6; M. & D., Vol. 61, p. 30; *Nuovi documenti*, pp. 397–8; CA/5/016, Krapf Letters, No. 113, Massawa, 2.3.1855; Corr. Pol., Egy., Massouah, Degoutin, 10.11.1848.
[3] L.F.A., Vol. 30, p. 386, Adams, 4.9.1848; Plowden, *Travels*, p. 360; *Nuovi documenti*, pp. 397–8.
[4] Corr. Pol., Egy., Massouah, p. 205, Degoutin, 6.1.1849; L.F.A., Vol. 30, p. 433, Haines, 28.1.1849.
[5] Corr. Pol., Egy., Massouah, p. 245, 9.2.1849.
[6] F.O., Abyssinia, 1/5, p. 285, Plowden, 27.1.1849.

Abbas, the Egyptians gave up their concession on the Ethiopian coast, and an Ottoman governor was sent to Massawa.[1]

Wube continued his campaign for mastery of the coast and the peripheral provinces of northern Ethiopia until his final defeat in 1855. He tried to get European diplomatic support, but in any event was determined to re-establish Ethiopian authority in those areas. Throughout this time the inhabitants of the coastal plain, the Habab, the people of Bogos and Barea lived under the perpetual threat of raids by Wube's army.[2]

CONCLUSION

The Ottoman conception of the province of *al Habasha* included the whole Ethiopian and Somali coast as far as Cape Guardafui.[3] Thus what was probably intended by Ibrahim Pasha to be a relatively peaceful occupation of *al Habasha* was exaggerated out of all proportion by the British authorities in the Red Sea area. The Egyptian garrison in Massawa during 1847–8 was never larger than one battalion and a few score engineers and artillerymen. The Egyptians tried to bring all the petty chiefs along the coast as far as Berbera to recognize their authority, but they hoped to achieve this mainly by peaceful means. It is even doubtful whether the Egyptians actually conquered the salt mines of the Taltal, as reported by Plowden at the end of 1847. Only Arkiko and the neighbouring village of Monkollo were actually taken by force, probably because they guarded the water supply of Massawa.

It is difficult to comprehend how the few hundred soldiers in Massawa and the three depleted and mutinous regiments, thinly spread between Sennar and Takka, could conquer Christian Ethiopia.[4] It is far more likely that, as in the period between 1837 and 1842, the Egyptians had a limited objective before them. This time their efforts were aimed at controlling the whole

[1] F.O., Abyssinia, 1/5, p. 273, Murray to Palmerston, 18.3.1849; L.F.A., Vol. 30, p. 256, Adams, enclosure in Haines, 13.6.1849.
[2] Lejean, *Voyage*, pp. 57–9; Plowden, *Travels*, p. 471; Robinson, Nimr, p. 116; M. & D., Vol. 61, pp. 25–8.
[3] F.O., Abyssinia, 1/5, p. 218, Plowden, 16.8.1848. This fact is also proved by events in the 1870's. See: Sabry, M.: *L'empire Égyptien sous Ismail*, Paris, 1933, pp. 391–5.
[4] Corr. Pol., Égy., Alexandrie et le Caire, Vol. XVIII, p. 19; Lepsius, pp. 190–2; T'arikh Muluk, pp. 34–5; Werne, *Expedition*, Vol. I, p. 54; Deherain, *Soudan*, p. 110.

coast of Ethiopia and connecting the rich agricultural area of Taka with its natural outlet, Massawa.[1] However, indirectly the Egyptian activities added to the unrest in the highlands and, as in the past, further provided for the spread of Islam.

The French, whom Wube continuously courted, viewed the situation without emotion, and because of their friendship with Muhammad Ali were careful not to take the claims of Wube supported by the Catholic missionaries at face value. The British, on the other hand, being hostile to the ambitions of Muhammad Ali in the Red Sea because they clashed with their own interests in the area, might have become allies *par excellence* of Wube, had it not been for the fact that Wube was surrounded by Frenchmen and by Catholic missionaries. The British therefore preferred that the coast remain in the hands of petty chiefs, or possibly be taken by a weak European country.[2]

By the middle of the nineteenth century the impoverished and long-suffering population of Ethiopia was completely exhausted by the perpetual wars. It was evident that the Galla nobility was not able to bring peace and unity to the country. The Galla were far too disunited among themselves and too deeply hated by the Amhara and Tigreans to be able to take advantage of their temporary dominance. The Church, torn by controversy, only added to the confusion and instability of the country and could not provide the much-needed guidance and unity. The ground was prepared for the appearance of the long-awaited Ethiopian 'Messiah', Teodros, who, as tradition predicted, would reunite the Christians, conquer Jerusalem, Mecca and Medina, put an end to Islam, punish the Galla and bring the kingdom of peace.[3]

---

[1] Sabri, M.: *L'Empire Égyptien sous Ismail*, Paris, 1933, p. 389; F.O., Abyssinia, 1/5, p. 274, Murray to Palmerston, 18.3.1849.

[2] In 1844 the British, it is claimed, had no objection to the establishment of a Belgian colony on the coast of Ethiopia. See letters of Belgian ambassador in London regarding his discussions with Lord Stanley and Lord Aberdeen. A.E.B., AF 4, No. 197, 198, 5.7.1844; Ibid., No. 270, 7.9.1844.

[3] Bruce, Vol. III, p. 94 (ed. 1805); Isenberg, pp. 496–7; Harris, Vol. II, pp. 34–5; CA/5/016, Krapf Journals, January–July, 1855, p. 52, April, 1855; Ibid., Krapf Letters, pp. 13–14, Letter to Gobat, Cairo, 1.8.1855; Stern, H.: *The Captive Missionary*, London, 1869, p. 6.

VII

Teodros

By the beginning of 1852 Kassa was tired of being used as the tool
of a master whom he secretly despised and who consistently kept
him in the more remote provinces. So, when he was summoned
again with his army for the annual expedition to Gojjam, Kassa
ignored his master's command. *Ras* Ali, who by 1852 succeeded
through tireless campaigning in bringing to submission most of
the rebellious nobles of northern Ethiopia, was not slow to react.
A strong army was dispatched to Agawmeder to chase the rebel,[1]
but for a number of months Kassa managed to avoid battle and
he spent the rainy season of 1852 among his kinsmen of Qwara,
where he was always welcome. As in the past, he used the rainy
season to reorganize his army and strengthen it with the riff-
raff of the border areas. Moreover, this time Kassa was able to
recruit into his service a number of deserters from the Egyptian army with whose help he was probably able to discipline
his followers and strengthen the firepower of his army.[2] In
contrast to Ali's troops who ravaged the countryside un-
hindered, Kassa dealt fairly with the population of the lowlands
and Dembya, and being a native of the area, easily won their
support.[3]

At the end of the rainy season of 1852, about September,
when he renewed the campaign against Birru Goshu, Ali ordered
his own troops back to Begamder and commanded *Dejazmatch*
Goshu to march against Kassa. It seems as if he wished to pit
the two chiefs for whom he did not much care against each other
and did not mind very much which would win the battle, as long
as at least one would be destroyed. For some time the two
generals manœuvred in Dembya until at the end of November,
1852, they finally met on the plains of Gur Amba. The victory

---

[1] *Nuovi documenti*, p. 401; A.E.B., Dos. 2024, Document B 2232, letter
from Jacobis attached to Athens, 4.5.1852; Dufton, p. 126.

[2] Lejean, *Theodore*, pp. 29–30; Hotten, *Plowden*, pp. 151, 191; CA/5/016,
Krapf Letters, No. 113, Massawa, 2.3.1855.

[3] *Nuovi documenti*, pp. 401–3; Dimotheos, p. 97; Dufton, p. 126.

fell to Kassa, Goshu was killed, and his army dispersed. The Gojjamites, who blamed Ali for sending their beloved *Dejaz-match* to his death in order to inherit his provinces, were saying the following: 'Goshu is like Uriya (the Hittite), Ali is like David. There is no difference but for the mode in which he (Goshu) was sent to his death.'[1]

The victory at Gur Amba was the first of a number of successive victories which made Kassa the master of Ethiopia; but at the end of 1852 Kassa did not yet feel strong enough to challenge Ali, and in an effort to appease the *Ras* blamed Mennen for all their misunderstandings. Although he still solicited peace, Ali was beyond forgiving him. In the first months of 1853 a sizeable army was collected in Begamder including units from Wollo, Gojjam, and Yejju, as well as a strong contingent from Wube's army under one of his leading generals. This formidable army was put under Birru Aligaz, the victor of Debra Tabor, and sent into Dembya. In April the two armies met at Taqusa and the whole of Ethiopia was dumbfounded when it became known that Kassa was the victor and that two of the most famous followers of *Ras* Ali, *Dejazmatch* Birru Aligaz and *Dejazmatch* Balaw, were killed.[2] Finally Kassa was able to come out from behind his mask of submissiveness and openly declare his aim to defeat Ali and reunite Ethiopia under his rule.

A short time after the battle of Taqusa, Kassa marched southwards to Debra Tabor, but in the meantime Ali had moved down to the plains of Ayshal, which were particularly suitable for the employment of his unbeatable Galla cavalry. After burning Debra Tabor, Kassa followed Ali to Qwarata and on 29th June the two armies clashed at Ayshal in one of the bloodiest battles of the *Zamana Masafint*. The charges of the Galla cavalry were

---

[1] Mondon Vidailhet: *Chronique de Theodros II, Roi des Rois d'Éthiopie*, Paris (no date), pp. 3–4; see also: *Nuovi documenti*, p. 404; Deftera Zeneb: *The Chronicle of King Theodore* (Yeterwodros Tarik), ed. Enno Littmann, Princeton, 1902, p. 14; Dufton, pp. 126–7; Coulbeaux, *Histoire*, Vol. II, p. 417; Rubenson, S.: *King of Kings Tewodros of Ethiopia*, Addis Ababa, 1966, p. 42.

[2] Lejean, Theodore, pp. 30–1; Fusella, L.: *La cronaca dell'Emperatore Theodore II di Etiopia*, Rome, 1957 (author unknown), p. 13; The Chronicle of Fussela is so confused in its facts and sequence of events that it should be used with many reservations. Mondon Vidailhet, p. 5; Dufton, pp. 127–8; Rassam, Vol. I, p. 283, according to Plowden report, June, 1855.

only smashed because of Kassa's personal bravery and because of the devotion of his Amhara followers. When it became apparent that Kassa was about to win the day, *Ras* Ali was among the first to flee from the battlefield. He took asylum in the sanctuary of Mahadera Maryam (not far from Debra Tabor) but remained there only a short time, for at the approach of Kassa, he fled to his kinsmen, the Yejju, closely pursued by units from Kassa's army. He was, however, never apprehended.[1] The battle of Ayshal dealt the death blow to the Galla aspirations, brought to an end the Yejju dynasty of Begamder, and in a way brought to a close the *Zamana Masafint*.

The only remaining serious challenge to Kassa's authority in northern Ethiopia was *Dejazmatch* Wube, who was completely unprepared for Kassa's successive victories and was caught with most of his army in Tigre. He was jealous of Kassa, who managed to achieve in a few years with neither firearms nor an opening to the sea what he himself had been trying to do for the past twenty years; but the ruler of Semien and Tigre was by that time an old man, and realized that situations were rapidly changing and that he was not yet sufficiently prepared to challenge Kassa. He therefore decided to try to come to terms with him and to that end sent his son Gwangul and his general Kokabi with many presents to the victor. Kassa, on his part, wanted to secure his rear by doing away with Birru Goshu, who, wishing to revenge his father, had collected a large army from among his Gojjamite followers and the remnants of Ali's army. Consequently Kassa welcomed Wube's emissaries and only demanded that *Abuña* Salama, who was most essential for his plans to unify the country, be sent to him and that Wube recognize him as *Ras* Ali's successor.

Having consolidated his position in Begamder, Kassa crossed the Abbay into Gojjam in the beginning of 1854. Meanwhile, confident of success because of his large and devoted army, Birru Goshu left his invincible mountain fortress, Jebeli. In March Kassa came upon Birru Goshu's army and decisively defeated it. Birru then tried to use the same evasive tactics

[1] Mondon Vidailhet, pp. 5–7; *Nuovi documenti*, p. 407; Plowden, *Travels*, p. 421; Dufton, p. 128; Lejean, *Theodore*, pp. 32–3; Rassam, Vol. I, p. 283, according to Plowden report, June, 1855; Zeneb, p. 15.

against Kassa that he had successfully used against Ali; however, despite his being an inspiring and able leader, his army
lost heart. His Gojjamites were no longer fighting the hated
Galla who had continuously ravaged their country, but a successful Amhara leader who was able to crush the much-disliked
Yejju dynasty. Moreover, Kassa was also the idol of the soldiers
and his personal bravery became legendary. Therefore, when
Kassa caught up with Birru Goshu in May, Birru's army
disintegrated and Birru Goshu was taken prisoner and sent in
chains to Issar Amba.[1]

After settling the affairs of Gojjam, Kassa marched against
Faris Aligaz in Lasta. He won an easy victory and at the beginning of the rainy season of 1854, around July, he returned to the
area of Gondar.[2]

In the meantime, because Bishop de Jacobis had installed
himself in Gondar in March of 1854 with the *Ichege*'s consent,
the *Abuna* refused to enter the town. Only after de Jacobis,
together with the other Catholic missionaries, was escorted out
of the country at Kassa's orders did *Abuna* Salama triumphantly
enter Gondar.[3]

During the rainy season of 1854, an alliance developed between Kassa and the *Abuna*. Both the spiritual leader and the
temporal one came to the conclusion that they ought to work in
harmony. The *Abuna*'s plans to unify the Church under his
leadership and to stop the controversy within it by edict needed
Kassa's support; at the same time this fitted the latter's plan
to unify the country politically, a plan for which he needed
the support of the *Abuna*. Kassa therefore decreed that the
Hulet Lidet in its *Karra Haymanot* (*Wold Qib*) interpretation should be accepted by the clergy and by the population,
and threatened to punish whoever would not comply or whoever would oppose the *Abuna* in spiritual matters. The *Ichege*
was coerced into denouncing the *Sost Lidet* and was further

---

[1] Lejean, *Theodore*, pp. 33–4; Mondon Vidailhet, p. 6; *Nuovi documenti*,
p. 408; Rassam, Vol. I, p. 284; Blanc, *A Narrative*, p. 3; Zeneb, p. 16.
[2] Tekla Haimanot, pp. 126–7, 137; *Nuovi documenti*, p. 408; Rubenson,
pp. 43–4.
[3] CA/5/016, Krapf Letters, No. 113, Massawa, 2.3.1855; Ibid., Krapf
Journals, No. 51, 19.4.1855; Lejean, *Theodore*, pp. 44–5; Rassam, Vol. I,
pp. 283–4, according to Plowden report of June, 1855; *Nuovi documenti*, pp.
407–8.

humiliated by being forced to be reconciled with the *Abuna*. From then on there was an understanding between Kassa and Salama that the Church would refrain from interfering in politics, and the State would leave spiritual matters to the Church.[1]

Although Wube had temporarily recognized the overlordship of Kassa, it was evident to both sides that it was only a matter of time before the final struggle would come. While Kassa was consolidating his position by lining up the Church and the people of his newly acquired territories behind him, Wube was desperately trying to get a foothold on the coast, to collect more firearms, and to strengthen his government in Tigre. In a last effort to maintain peace, or in order to deceive his enemy, Kassa encouraged the *Abuna* and the *Ichege* to mediate between Wube and himself and offered the latter the title of *Ras*, which Wube much coveted, he himself having already taken the title of *Negus*, king, with the blessing of the *Abuna*.[2]

In January the peace efforts were given up and Kassa marched through Wogera into Semien. Wube came hurriedly from Tigre at the head of the united armies of Tigre and Semien and the two armies met on 9th February in Deresge in Semien. The great number of firearms on Wube's side were as poorly employed as in the time of Seb'agadis. Moreover, the Tigreans did not exert themselves for a master they disliked, and although Wube's sons fought bravely, the battle was won by Kassa, and Wube was taken prisoner and put in chains. On 11th February, in the church of Doresgo Maryam, the *Abuna* crowned and anointed Kassa as Teodros, King of Kings of Ethiopia.[3]

Emperor Teodros did not rest very long on his laurels. Shortly after the battle of Deresge, he made public his intention once and for all to break the Galla threat, suppress Islam, abolish slavery and, above all, reunite Ethiopia as a Christian empire.[4]

---

[1] CA/5/016, Krapf Journals, pp. 45, 46, 20.4.1855; Zeneb, pp. 3–4; Tekle Tsadiq Makuria: *Ye Itiopia Tarik Ke Atse Teodros Iske Qedamawi Haile Selassie*, Addis Ababa, 4th ed., 1946 (E.C.), p. 22; *Ye Galla Tarik* (History of the Galla), a manuscript by Ato Asmye, written about 1907, p. 49.

[2] *Nuovi documenti*, p. 408; Rubenson, p. 44.

[3] *Nuovi documenti*, p. 410; Zeneb, p. 18; Lejean, *Theodore*, pp. 48–50; Mondon Vidailhet, pp. 6–7; Rubenson, pp. 44–55.

[4] CA/5/016, Krapf Journals, 29.3.1855, 19.4.1855; Ibid., Krapf Letters, No. 113, Massawa, 4.3.1855.

After the defeat of Wube, the only serious obstacle remaining in Kassa's path to the unification of Christian Ethiopia was Haile Melekot, the ruler of the kingdom of Showa. In April, 1855, Kassa's army was already advancing to the Wollo country on its way to Showa.

VIII

The rise of the Kingdom of Showa
and the new Christian Empire

Having been overrun by the forces of Grañ and separated from the main body of the Ethiopian empire by the Galla advance in the sixteenth century, Showa disintegrated into a number of Christian Amhara principalities surrounded by areas conquered by the Galla and the Muslims. Each of these Amhara principalities was governed by a local dynasty which was directly tributary to the Emperor in Gondar and each vied for his favour. The Galla, who continued their pressure upon the divided Amhara, succeeded in the first decades of the seventeenth century in penetrating the province of Tegulet, and thereby drove a wedge through the heart of the Christian areas in the direction of Yifat.[1]

Because of the isolation of this part of Ethiopia and because of its relative unimportance in the seventeenth and eighteenth centuries, very little is known of the origins and early history of the new dynasty of Showa. Fortunately, a number of oral traditions were collected by European visitors in the nineteenth century, and by adding these to the more recent indigenous chronicles, a picture of sorts can be reconstructed.

According to tradition, the new dynasty of Showa began with Negassie, who was the offspring of a union between a woman of imperial descent and a rich landowner from the parish of Aganche in the district of Gera in the province of Menz.[2] After fight-

---

[1] Rochet, *Voyage*, p. 210; Coulbeaux, *Histoire*, Vol. II, p. 201; Cecchi, Vol. I, p. 235; M. & D., Vol. 61, p. 87, Gilbert, 28.8.1861. Tegulet was the heart of the Empire in the sixteenth century and the town of Debra Berhan had been one of its provisional capitals.

[2] One set of traditions collected about 1840 claims that Negassie's mother was the daughter of *Ras* Faris, who with many other followers of Emperor Susenyos escaped into Menz. Later traditions, however, claim that Negassie was a descendant of Yaqob, a son of Emperor Libna Dengel, who remained in Showa. Harris, Vol. III, pp. 7–8; Isenberg, pp. 308, 312; Rochet, *Voyage*, pp. 210–11. This last source is of special interest because Rochet's information came from Serta Wold, who held a position similar to that of minister for foreign affairs in the court of Sahle Selassie in the 1830's and 1840's. See

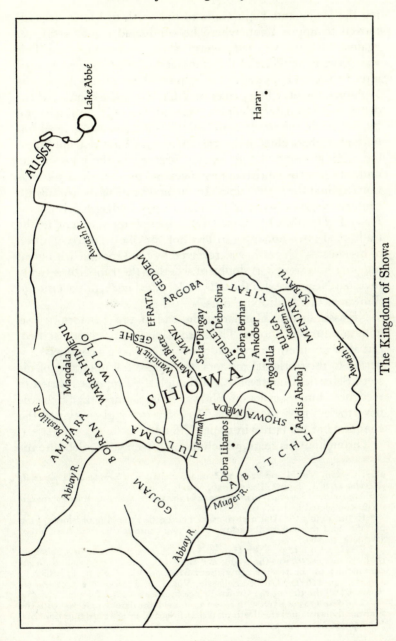

The Kingdom of Showa

ing the Wolle and Yejju Galla to the north of Menz Negassie moved to upper Yifat, where he conducted a successful war against the Galla who had penetrated this ancient kingdom. This was presumably done at the command of the Emperor Iyasu I after an urgent application for help had been received from the Walasma, the hereditary ruler of Yifat.[1] Negassie conquered the districts of Debdabo, Mengist, Makfud, Doqaqit, Asandabe and by the end of the seventeenth century emerged as the most important Amhara chief in the area. After this, Yifat, and not Menz, the original home of the dynasty,[2] served as the base for the unification of the Christian provinces and for the military operations against the Galla tribes. In the first years of the eighteenth century Negassie went to Gondar to pay homage to Emperor Iyasu I. He probably hoped for imperial appointment to the traditional governorship of the whole of Showa in recognition of his success. Negassie was received by the Emperor with great honour; however, it is doubtful whether the Emperor actually invested Negassie with the title of *Meridazmatch*, or governor of Showa, as one tradition claims.[3]

Negassie died in Gondar at the end of 1703[4] before he was able to return to Showa. The succession was not easily settled, but after an interim in which many of Negassie's conquests reverted to their original masters, the choice fell upon one of his sons, Sebastie (Sebastyanos). Although the Emperor refused to recognize him as ruler of Showa, it is claimed that Sebastie nevertheless took the title of *Meridazmatch* and continued the conquests of his father in upper Yifat.[5]

Throughout his reign, which lasted fifteen years, Sebastie re-

---

also: Cecchi, Vol. I, pp. 235–7; Guebre Sellassie, *Chronique du règne de Menelik II*, Éd. Coppet, Paris, 1930, Vol. I, p. 56.

[1] Ato Asmye, *Yegalla Tarik* (History of the Gallas), an unpublished manuscript completed in 1907, p. 56.

[2] In the 1830's the Afar and the Galla still called the king of Showa, king of Yifat, and the bulk of the army of the king came at this time from Yifat. Isenberg, p. 289.

[3] Cecchi, Vol. I, p. 238; Harris, Vol. III, pp. 7–8; Guebre Sellassie, ibid. *Meridazmatch* was the traditional title of the ruler of Showa and meant commander of the reserve army. See: Mondon Vidailhet, p. 17; Rochet, *Voyage*, pp. 210–11; Guebre Sellassie, Vol. I, p. 93, footnote 3. *Meridazmatch* is still the title of the Crown Prince in present-day Ethiopia.

[4] The date 1703 is given with reservation as all the dates connected with the Showan dynasty until the death of Wossen Segged in 1813 are questionable.

[5] Asmye, MS., pp. 57–8.

fused to go to Gondar to submit to the Emperor.[1] Consequently, when his son Abbiye came to power in the first quarter of the eighteenth century, he was confronted with an attack by the army of Iyasu II. Through friends in the imperial camp and also because the emperor's army was badly needed elsewhere, Abbiye was able to negotiate an agreement by which he was officially invested with the title *Meridazmatch* after declaring his loyalty and paying tribute.[2]

Having dealt with the threat from the north and having received the imperial appointment, Abbiye was free to deal with his neighbours. He succeeded in defeating the rulers of a number of Christian provinces, including Menz, and made them his tributaries. Then, taking advantage of the Galla pressure upon the Muslim rulers of lower Yifat, he conquered that kingdom and put an end to its independence, which it had managed to preserve since the time of Grañ.[3]

After a reign of about twenty-five years, Abbiye died in the 1740's fighting the Karayu to the south of Yifat. He was buried in his capital, Har Amba, and was succeeded by his son Ammehayes.[4] It was during the reign of Ammehayes that the reconquest of the territories held by the Galla in Showa really seriously began.

Having imported a number of firearms from the north, Ammehayes succeeded in asserting his authority over a number of Christian principalities, including Tegulet, Menz, Efrata and Bulga. From his capital Doqaqit not far from Debra Sina in northern Yifat he raided the Afar and conquered the valleys of Geddem leading into the Afar country. He renewed the war with

[1] Cecchi, Vol. I, p. 236; Guebre Sellassie, Vol. I, p. 56; Harris (Vol. III, pp. 7–9) claims that he ruled for twenty-five years and Rochet (*Voyage*, pp. 211–12) thirty-three years.

[2] Cecchi, Vol. I, p. 239; Coulbeaux, *Histoire* (Vol. II, p. 372) and Guebre Sellassie's (Vol. I, p. 56) claim that Abbiye defeated the imperial army with the help of the armies of the neighbouring Amhara provinces seems doubtful. For further details on early rulers of Showa based on more recent Ethiopian chroniclers see: Levin, D.: *Wax and Gold*, Chicago, 1965, pp. 31–5.

[3] Cecchi, Vol. I, p. 239; Rochet, *Voyage*, pp. 210–11; Isenberg, p. 299; Harris, Vol. II, pp. 341–2. On the Walasma dynasty of Yifat see: Cerruli, E.: *Documenti arabi per la storia del Ethiopia*, Rome, 1931, p. 40.

[4] Guebre Sellassie, Vol. I, p. 58; Cecchi, Vol. I, p. 239; Harris (Vol. II, pp. 341–2) claims that he ruled Showa for fifteen years; Coulbeaux (*Histoire*, Vol. II, p. 372) claims that he reigned from 1725 until 1750. According to Rochet (*Voyage*, p. 241) he ruled for sixty years and was buried at Qundi. See also: Morié, Vol. II, p. 410.

the Karayu, but was far more successful in his attacks on the Abitchu Galla. He conquered the area of Ankober as far as the river Chia Chia near Angolalla and made a number of Abitchu tribes his tributaries. Though presumably not on his specific orders, his generals later massacred the Galla population in the area between Ankober and Debra Berhan. This part of Tegulet which had previously been conquered by the Galla was then resettled by Amhara farmers.[1]

Ammehayes was the initiator of a policy, later taken up by the other rulers of the Showan dynasty, of encouraging the separation of Showa from northern Ethiopia and concentrating on expansion to the south and to the west. He intentionally left the district of Wallaka between the rivers Geshen and Samba to the Wollo Galla in order to have them as a buffer between Showa and northern Ethiopia. Likewise, the removal of the capital from Doqaqit to Ankober, although the royal family nevertheless remained in Har Amba, was also indicative of the new southern-oriented policy. When he, or more likely his son, visited the Emperor in Gondar in 1771, he was received more like an honoured ally than a vassal. Although Ammehayes brought with him presents for the Emperor, the traveller Bruce, who was present at the Emperor's court at the time, states clearly that he managed to make himself *de facto* independent in his province.[2]

On the death of Ammehayes he was succeeded by his son Asfa Wossen.[3] During his long reign, from the 1770's until about 1808, the tributary principalities of Geshe, Antziokia, Efrata, Moret and Marra Biete were more firmly annexed to Showa. But this process seems to have been rather difficult and Asfa Wossen, on the advice of his father confessor, was even ready to become the follower of the *Sost Lidet* in order to get the support of the Church in his efforts to absorb Marra Biete, which held a key position among the semi-autonomous Christian principali-

[1] Guebre Sellassie, Vol. I, pp. 58–9; Coulbeaux, *Histoire*, Vol. II, p. 373; Rochet, *Voyage*, p. 212.
[2] Bruce, Vol. III, p. 255; Ibid., Vol. IV, pp. 93–6, 108. See also: Cecchi, Vol. I, pp. 239–40; Harris, Vol. II, pp. 46, 308; Ibid., Vol. III, pp. 8–9; Guebre Sellassie, Vol. I, pp. 58–9; Coulbeaux, *Histoire*, Vol. II, p. 373; Rochet, *Voyage*, p. 21.
[3] One of his forty-eight offspring—Harris, Vol. III, p. 9.

ties.[1] Once he had partially succeeded in his efforts to integrate the Christian Amhara provinces, the united army was turned against the plains of Showa (Showa Meda), and their Galla inhabitants were put to the sword in a most treacherous manner. After them came the turn of the Tuloma and Mogher, who lived as far away as the Abbay, and finally the Abitchu, as far as the sources of the Awash, and the Woberi and Gallan Galla to the mountains of Garra Korfu.[2]

Asfa Wossen was far more of an administrator than a war leader, and he left the expansion of his kingdom to his generals while he occupied himself with the organization of the administration of Showa. The greatly enlarged kingdom was divided by him into four major provinces and thirty-nine districts.[3] A light system of taxation on each village was introduced and many new laws were made. It is evident that the administrative innovations introduced by Asfa Wossen were not readily accepted by the population and were unpopular, to say the least. Many of the new laws, especially those regarding the royal monopolies introduced by the ruler, were considered cruel and despotic; they enraged the population and caused a number of rebellions.[4]

The situation was especially serious on two occasions when the rebellions were led by successful generals who got the support of the feudal rulers. The latter were glad to make the best of the opportunity to subvert Asfa Wossen's authority. However, when the need arose, Asfa Wossen proved himself to be as brave and talented a warrior as he was a good administrator, and having defeated the rebels he strengthened his authority over the vassal principalities. Just as it seemed that he had succeeded to some extent in consolidating his authority, the imperial armies of Emperor Tekla Giorgios I (1779–84) appeared in

---

[1] See above, p. 40. Also: Isenberg, p. 315; Harris, Vol. III, p. 36; Ibid., Vol. II, p. 340; L.G., 175, No. 3970, para. 14, Harris, 8.10.1841; Guebre Sellassie, Vol. I, pp. 60–2; Cecchi, Vol. I, p. 241; Coulbeaux, *Histoire*, p. 373.

[2] Guebre Sellassie, Vol. I, pp. 63–4; Morié, Vol. II, p. 411; Cecchi, Vol. I, p. 241. According to Paulitschke, P. (*Ethnographie Nordest-Afrikas*, Berlin, 1896, Vol. II, p. 242) this occurred in 1807 in the time of Wossen Segged. See also: L.G., 175, No. 3970, para. 14, Harris, 8.10.1841; Harris, Vol. II, pp. 46, 148, 340; Isenberg, p. 298.

[3] Morié, Vol. II, pp. 411–12.

[4] Cecchi, Vol. I, pp. 240–1; Harris, Vol. III, p. 9; Rochet, *Second voyage*, p. 243.

Wollo and camped in a peripheral district of Showa called Chaffa in the province of Geshe. The Emperor resented the growing independence of Showa and the power and wealth of its ruler and was therefore ready to wage war upon Asfa Wossen. However, through friends in the imperial camp, the Showan ruler expressed his willingness to submit and pay tribute; but at the same time he made it very clear that if forced to fight he would fight to the end. Moreover, he pointed out to the Emperor that he had only expanded his territories to the south and to the west of Showa and at the expense of the common enemy, the Galla. Under pressure from some of his generals and especially Wolde Selassie of Enderta, the Emperor was forced to make peace, and after receiving tribute from Asfa Wossen the imperial army left Showa to itself.[1] Until 1855 this was the last time that tribute was exacted from Showa.

In his youth, Asfa Wossen had a son by a woman related to the imperial house. Later on, following his policy of consolidating his hold over the Christian principalities, especially Menz, the home of his dynasty, Asfa Wossen married a woman from the Menz aristocracy and by her had a number of further children. His elder son, Wossen Segged, who had already proved himself an able general, feared that his Menz relatives would tip the scales in favour of his brother by Asfa Wossen's Menz wife. He therefore rebelled against his father, but lacking support he was defeated and taken prisoner.[2] The ageing Asfa Wossen was, however, soon reconciled with his son, and Wossen Segged was released from imprisonment, was appointed his father's heir and was dispatched as governor of the northern provinces. In the area of Antziokia this turbulent prince continuously fought the Muslim Wollo and Yejju neighbours of his country. In one of the battles he was taken prisoner by the Yejju chief Guji, the grandson of Gwangul, the father of the Yejju family which became the guardians of the Emperor in Gondar. According to tradition, the chief of the Showan Church disguised himself as

[1] This was probably the beginning of the friendship between the rulers of Showa and *Ras* Wolde Selassie. See: Pearce, Vol. I, pp. 83, 97; Salt, p. 133; Cecchi, Vol. I, p. 242; Harris, Vol. III, p. 9; Coulbeaux, *Histoire*, Vol. II, p. 373.

[2] Soleillet, p. 270; Guebre Sellassie, Vol. I, p. 65; Cecchi, Vol. I, p. 242; Harris, Vol. III, p. 9.

a Muslim sheikh, penetrated into the Galla country and ransomed Wossen Segged.[1]

In the last years of his reign Asfa Wossen became totally blind and underwent a period of suffering and many mishaps. On his death, about 1808, he was buried in his capital Ankober, and was succeeded by Wossen Segged, who was immediately faced with a rebellion of his Galla subjects. By the beginning of the nineteenth century Showa was still far from united and its population far from homogeneous. The quick territorial expansion was given up and from then on the rulers concentrated mainly on consolidation. While at the end of the eighteenth century Asfa Wossen had turned to the Church for support in integrating the Christian provinces,[2] the main problem faced by Wossen Segged was how to integrate the vast masses of Muslims and Galla who by then constituted the majority of his subjects. Following the policy of his father, he continued to strengthen and centralize the administration but at the same time he formulated a policy of complete tolerance for Islam, and a slow Amharization and christianization of his pagan Galla subjects. The Galla tribes who were willing to be integrated into Showa were given full privileges; and their chiefs, together with the Muslim aristocracy of Yifat, Fatigar and Moret, were employed in the administration of the country, especially of the Galla and Muslim areas.

Il comprit que sa principale force devait résider dans l'union de ses sujets; et, quoique les populations auxquelles il commandait fussent divisées par trois cultes différents, il accorda indistinctement ses faveurs aux musulmans, aux païens et aux chrétiens. Il donna plusieurs gouvernements à des musulmans dans la province d'Éfate et il éleva des Gallas aux fonctions de kachefs.[3]

Wossen Segged was fiercely proud of his imperial origin and of his power, and after giving himself the title of *Ras* he even challenged the authority of the Emperor in Gondar and of his Galla regent Gugsa. In co-operation with *Ras* Wolde Selassie of Tigre he began to raid the Wollo and Yejju Galla territories and

---

[1] Guebre Sellassie, Vol. I, p. 60; Cecchi, Vol. I, p. 242; Harris, Vol. II, p. 340.
[2] See above, p. 40.
[3] Rochet, *Second voyage*, p. 243. See also: Rochet, *Voyage*, pp. 212, 217.

was preparing an expedition against Gugsa.[1] His new policy and high-handedness aroused the resentment and opposition of many, including the clergy, who were dissatisfied with his tolerance of his Muslim subjects. After a short but exceedingly active rule of four-and-a-half years, he was murdered in 1813 by one of his slaves in his capital Qundi (north of Ankober).[2]

On the death of Wossen Segged, messengers were sent to bring the news to his sons ruling the outlying provinces. In the meantime, the Galla, hearing of Wossen Segged's death, rose in rebellion, as did some of the tributary rulers of the Amhara provinces. Thus Becureje, Wossen Segged's eldest son, who was the governor (*Abegaz*) of Marra Biete,[3] was forced to fight the Galla rebels and was prevented from reaching his late father's capital Qundi. The younger brother, Sahle Selassie (clemency of the trinity), who was in his teens, profited from the situation; he hurried from the monastery near Sala Dingai in Menz, where he was being educated and presented himself before the elders and chiefs of the country who had assembled in Qundi, and probably with the support of his mother's Menzian kinsmen was proclaimed the *Ras* of Showa.[4] When Becureje finally succeeded in cutting his way through the Galla rebels and approached Qundi, he was defeated and imprisoned in the state prison in Gonchu together with his other brothers and some of his main supporters.[5]

Even after he disposed of his elder brother, Sahle Selassie was still faced with a most threatening situation. Some of the hereditary rulers of the Amhara provinces of Showa, who had mean-

---

[1] Guebre Sellassie, Vol. I, pp. 68–9; Coulbeaux, *Histoire*, Vol. II, p. 374; Range, 383, Vol. 52, pp. 2912–14, Pearce, Adowa, 15.2.1814; Cecchi, Vol. I, p. 243; Salt, p. 337; F.O., Abyssinia, 1/1, p. 215, Pearce, Antalo, 29.12.1810; Combes and Tamisier, Vol. II, p. 293; Pearce, Vol. I, pp. 83, 97.

[2] Rochet, *Voyage*, p. 212; Rochet, *Second voyage*, p. 244; Cecchi, Vol. I, pp. 243–4; Guebre Sellassie, Vol. I, p. 69; Harris, Vol. III, pp. 11–12; L.G., 175, No. 3970, para. 4, Harris, 8.10.1841. This murder was reported by Nathaniel Pearce and is therefore the first certain date in the history of the Showan dynasty. See: Range, 383, Vol. 52, pp. 2912–14, Adowa, 15.2.1814.

[3] Asmye, MS., p. 62; Harris, Vol. III, p. 37; Cecchi, Vol. I, p. 244.

[4] Cecchi (Vol. I, p. 244) and Coulbeaux (*Histoire*, Vol. III, p. 374) claim that he was eighteen when he came to power. Isenberg (p. 47) and Harris (Vol. III, p. 11) claim that he was only twelve years old. See also: Isenberg, p. 290.

[5] Cecchi, Vol. I, p. 244; Harris, Vol. III, p. 14; Isenberg, p. 87. According to Asmye (MS., p. 62) the name of the eldest son was Bekru and he was killed by the Galla while on his way to Qundi.

while succeeded in acquiring a number of firearms, reasserted their independence.[1] The Abitchu Galla erupted into Tegulet and burned Debra Berhan, and the Tuloma, who were to some degree subdued by Sahle Selassie's forefathers, renounced their dependence on the Showan rulers and began advancing southwards. In those dark days in Showan history, the young Sahle Selassie proved himself to be a most gifted leader. Having consolidated his authority in Yifat and in some of the Christian principalities, he slowly began to re-establish his government among the Galla, more through diplomacy than by the sword. First to submit were the Abitchu who were hard pressed by the Tuloma and who badly needed Sahle Selassie's military support. With the help of some of their chiefs, Sahle Selassie's authority was re-established among the southern Galla. He also managed to defeat the Tuloma and in the course of the 1820's regained Showa Meda.[2] Sahle Selassie rebuilt Debra Berhan and a number of other towns which were burnt by the Galla; and to consolidate the Amhara's hold over the area beyond the Baresa river he erected a number of fortified villages, including the town of Angolalla in the heart of the Abitchu country. To the south-east, the young ruler tried to re-establish his authority in Bulga and among the Karayu. And although in the beginning he was driven back because he was poorly provided with old firearms, he later succeeded in conquering Bulga and the Karayu country as far as the Arussi Galla after getting possession of more firearms.[3]

While the eastern border of Showa was protected by the loyal governor of lower Yifat and Argobba and was relatively safe from incursion of the weak and divided Afar, the north-eastern and northern borders of Showa were a source of constant worry to Sahle Selassie. Just after coming to power he was forced to fight some of the Wollo and Yejju principalities. But his campaigning in this direction was mostly defensive and he preferred the use of intrigue when dealing with the Wollo and Yejju lords. To gain friends among those powerful chiefs he handed over a

[1] Harris, Vol. III, p. 37; Isenberg, p. 300.
[2] Cecchi, Vol. I, pp. 244–5; Beke, F.O.A., Vol. 2, p. 172, 15.12.1841; Rochet, *Voyage*, p. 213; Coulbeaux, *Histoire*, Vol. II, p. 374; Harris, Vol. II, p. 350; Gobat, p. 341; Harris, Vol. III, p. 37.
[3] L.G., 193, No. 2917, para. 6, Harris, 7.4.1841; Harris, Vol. III, pp. 253, 258; Cecchi, Vol. I, pp. 244–5; Rochet, *Voyage*, p. 213.

number of districts to an important Wollo ruler, and even consented to the marriage of a princess of royal blood to the chief of the Yejju who had been converted to Christianity for the third time just for that occasion.[1] The restraint which Sahle Selassie had shown along his northern border was no doubt motivated by his fear of the combined power of *Ras* Ali and his Muslim Wollo and Yejju kinsmen.[2] It was also essential to keep open the trade routes of Showa to Tigre and Gondar through which a small number of firearms and quantities of foreign products reached Showa every year.[3] Above all, Sahle Selassie was interested in the continued existence of the Galla barrier, which the Showan rulers from the time of Ammehayes had intentionally imposed upon their country to isolate it from northern Ethiopia. This barrier saved the greatly weakened Showa from the constant wars which brought ruin and devastation in the north and allowed Sahle Selassie to consolidate his hold over his country,

fortunate it is for His Majesty as well as for his dominions, that the surrounding Galla tribes, united with natural defences, should have so completely shut him out from participation in the intestine disturbances which have ravaged and laid waste every other province.[4]

The efforts of the Showan rulers from the last decades of the eighteenth century were concentrated in the direction of the south-west and the south and aimed at creating a large kingdom that would bring the borders of Showa to its legendary boundaries in the past. In the diary which he kept while travelling through Showa in 1842 the missionary Krapf had written the following:

The Shoan monarchs are going on towards the south and centre of Africa and this is a matter which we must keep in mind in talking of Shoa. The Shoan politics are directed towards the south regarding

[1] Pearce, Vol. I, pp. 46–7; Isenberg, pp. 106–7, 320–21; J.R.G.S., Vol. 10, Krapf, p. 475, July, 1839; Harris, Vol. III, p. 38; L.G., 193, No. 2918A, para. 7, Harris, 8.5.1842; Ferret and Galinier, Vol. II, p. 330; L.G., 190, No. 2060I, para. 2, Harris, 31.1.1842; L.G., 196, No. 3489, Harris, 4.7.1842.
[2] Guebre Sellassie, Vol. I, pp. 72–3; Ferret and Galinier, Vol. II, p. 330; J.R.G.S., Vol. 10, p. 475, Krapf, July, 1839; Krapf, p. 91; Isenberg, p. 316; Abbadie, F.N.A. 21303, pp. 478–82.
[3] L.G., 185, No. 1440, paras. 18, 22, 24, Barker, 7.1.1842; Combes and Tamisier, Vol. II, chapters VII–IX; Isenberg, p. 316; Krapf, p. 61; C. & C., Massawa, Degoutin, 13.1.1843; Abbadie, F.N.A. 21301, p. 107, para. 324, J.R.G.S., Vol. 12, p. 94, Beke; Harris, Vol. II, p. 33.
[4] Harris, Vol. III, p. 34.

conquests. This appears to be the reason why the kings of Shoa do not meddle with the affairs of northern Abyssinia . . . .[1]

Sahle Selassie most probably harboured secret hopes of becoming the emperor of the united Ethiopian empire.[2] However, his first target before attempting anything so ambitious was

to resume the lost possessions of his ancestors—to wield the sceptre as they did, three hundred miles south of his present limits—and to reunite the scattered remnants of Christian population.[3]

No doubt the expansion to the south and south-west was also preferred because this was the direction of least resistance, as the Galla of those areas were disunited and possessed no fire-arms. At the same time the south and south-west promised a much richer reward than the north or the east. Therefore, the first objective of Sahle Selassie was to capture the belt of land from Gurage to the sources of the Awash and from there in a north-westerly direction to the Abbay. This belt was one of the most important areas in Ethiopia from a commercial point of view, as it was crossed by some of the major caravan routes of Ethiopia. In it were many famous markets such as Roggi, Mogher, Imelel, Anduwodi and Chakka, which served as meeting points between the merchants of the south and their counterparts from northern Ethiopia and the coast. In the beginning of 1842 Major Harris reported from Showa that

the influence of the king properly directed, will have the effect of drawing thither (to Showa) all the rich kafilas from Enarea, Caffa, Godjam, Damot and other unexplored regions, which laden with coffee, civet, myrrh, frankincense, ivory, gold dust and costly peltries, at present leave the dominions of Sahle Sellassie to the eastward, on their way to the sea port of Massawa.[4]

---

[1] CA/5/013, Krapf Journals, 1842, p. 17. The unedited original text was crossed out. See also: Soleillet, p. 133; Harris, Vol. II, p. 162; L.G., 175, No. 3970, para. 16, Harris, 8.10.1841; Rochet, *Voyage*, pp. 223–4; Rochet, *Second voyage*, pp. 174–5; Harris, Vol. III, pp. 36–7.

[2] F.O., 78/590, Johnston, 8.8.1844; L.G., 175, No. 3970, para. 73, Harris, 8.10.1841; Coulbeaux, *Histoire*, Vol. II, p. 375; F.O., 78/343, Isenberg, pp. 288–9.

[3] L.G., 190, No. 2060B, para. 50, Harris, 29.10.1841.

[4] L.G., 189, No. 2060G, para. 23, Harris, 5.1.1842. See also: Ibid., para. 24 and para. 6; Cecchi, Vol. II, pp. 15, 57; Bianchi, G.: *Alla terra dei Galla (1879–1880)*, Milan, 1886, pp. 288–9; Cecchi, Vol. I, pp. 486–8. See also: Abbadie, F.N.A. 21302, p. 25, para. 38, 30.12.1840; Ibid., 21303, p. 350, para. 173, October, 1843.

By 1830 Sahle Selassie had succeeded in overcoming most of the traditional rulers of Showa, in establishing his authority over the Galla tribes who had been subjugated by his forefathers and even succeeded in further expanding the borders of Showa to the south and to the west. While the rulers of northern Ethiopia were locked in a deadly struggle for predominance which was followed by the regency of a minor, *Ras* Ali, Sahle Selassie gained enough confidence through his successes to take the title of king (*Negus*) of Showa, Yifat, the Galla people and Gurage.[1] Just when Sahle Selassie seemed to have attained security, stability and success he was confronted by a series of exceedingly serious challenges. In the early 1830's Showa was stricken by cholera which had passed through the Horn of Africa like wild-fire and ravaged the whole area.[2] Soon afterwards a very serious rebellion threatened Showa in consequence of Sahle Selassie's refusal to give one of his daughters in marriage to a general, Medoko, who was responsible for many of the Showan victories in the south. This general and his followers, among whom were a number of matchlockmen, deserted to the Galla and were the cementing factor in a coalition of Galla tribes which threatened the existence of Showa. When the royal town of Angolalla was attacked, the situation seemed so serious that Sahle Selassie applied to his Menz kinsmen for help in the following words: 'my brothers, my relations, come and help me'.[3] When he finally succeeded in putting down the rebellion in 1834 or 1835, Showa was again hit, this time by the terrible drought which lasted for two consecutive years, which brought the people to the verge of starvation and which killed off most of the domestic animals. In this difficult period Sahle Selassie endeared himself

---

[1] L.G., 141, No. 4781, Haines, 25.9.1840. The title of *Negus*, which Sahle Selassie had taken himself was never recognized by the nobility and clergy of Gondar. In 1838 d'Abbadie wrote (M. & D., Vol. 13, pp. 9–10) that the *Meridazmatch* Sahle Selassie who is in fact the independent master of Showa took the title of king, but this is not recognized by the clergy and nobles of Gondar. The unknown chronicler of *Nuovi documenti* (p. 394), who presumably lived in Gondar, called Sahle Selassie *Meridazmatch* even in 1847. See also: Combes and Tamisier, Vol. III, pp. 17–18; Morié, Vol. II, p. 415. The claim of Soleillet (p. 272) after the rise of Menelik, that the title of *Negus* was adopted by Sahle Selassie at the suggestion of the clergy of Gondar who were worried about the Islamic tendencies of *Ras* Ali, is very dubious.

[2] Isenberg, p. 398; Johnston, Vol. II, pp. 158–9.

[3] Isenberg, p. 301. See also: Harris, Vol. II, pp. 99–142; Cecchi, Vol. I, p. 245.

to his subjects by opening the well-stocked royal stores to the needy, and by distributing seed and oxen to facilitate the ploughing and sowing. When the famine was over in 1836 or 1837 Medoko rebelled again. Even though this rebellion was crushed soon after it started, Sahle Selassie was faced with the possibility of civil war as a result of ecclesiastical controversies fermented in Showa by the clergy of Gondar and Tigre.[1]

The Church in Showa had been an important instrument in the ascendancy of the new dynasty of that country. It exercised tremendous influence on the Christian population of Showa, and the rulers always favoured the clergy. They never embarked upon any action without first consulting the leaders of the Church, and priests and *tabot*[2] always accompanied them into battle. The king nevertheless preserved close control of the Church and appointed its heads from among the local ecclesiastics after consulting with the leading clergymen.[3]

The *Abuna*, who lived in northern Ethiopia, had never exerted much influence on Showa because they were far too much occupied with the affairs of the north to face the difficulties entailed in visiting Showa. Therefore the Showan Church had always enjoyed some degree of spiritual independence, which well suited the Showan rulers' policy of furthering their political independence from Gondar.[4] During the period of the disgrace of *Abuna* Kerilos and after his death, an Armenian ecclesiastic whose title or name was Muallem (learned man) was recognized to some extent in Showa in the capacity of an *Abuna*. It was even said that he ordained a number of deacons, which in the Ethiopian Church was a prerogative of the *Abuna*.[5] After the death of Muallem about 1837 or 1838, to further strengthen his independence of Gondar and his control over the Showan Church, Sahle Selassie appointed from among his faithful soldiers a new

---

[1] Guebre Sellassie, Vol. I, pp. 70–1; Harris, Vol. III, p. 33; Cecchi, Vol. I, p. 245; Isenberg, p. 398; Johnston, Vol. II, pp. 158–9. Although the events are corroborated by a number of sources and all the sources agree that they occurred in the 1830's the same sources cannot agree on the exact dates.

[2] The ark which every church in Ethiopia has.

[3] L.G., 175, No. 3970, para. 28, Harris, 8.10.1841; L.G., 185, No. 1440, 20.3.1842; Rochet, *Voyage*, pp. 163, 188, 279–80; Rochet, *Second voyage*, pp. 221–3; Harris, Vol. II, pp. 19, 27; Ibid., Vol. III, pp. 25, 27, 141.

[4] CA/5/016, Krapf Letters, No. 8, Cairo, 3.10.1842.

[5] Rochet, *Second voyage*, p. 221.

head to the Church of Showa and a new *Alaka*[1] to the monastery of Debra Libanos. The Showan ruler thus violated the established custom of the past, because he did not consult the leaders of the clergy and because the new appointees were laymen and ex-soldiers. This action was opposed by a number of monks of Debra Libanos, who after getting the support of the *Ichege* felt confident enough to challenge the action of the king by accusing the new appointees of adhering to the theory of the *Wold Qib*.[2] The controversy soon spread in Showa and divided the country into two camps. The old resistance to the *Sost Lidet* (three births) in most parts of Christian Showa again broke into the open. The king, though supporting his appointees, made it quite clear that he would not tolerate opposition to the *Sost Lidet*. Notwithstanding this, the *Ichege*, under the influence of his supporters in Debra Libanos, denounced Sahle Selassie for appointing laymen whom he suspected of having leanings to the *Hulet Lidet* party to the highest position in the Church of Showa. Sahle Selassie was especially incensed by a message from *Ras* Ali which 'informed the king by way of command to resign himself to the judgment of the Ichege'. The king declared that he was a sovereign and not a vassal of Gondar. He nevertheless sent an ambassador to Gondar carrying presents to the *Ichege* and to Mennen to explain his position. By the end of 1840 it was felt that unless the matter was settled, war would break out between Showa and some of the rulers of northern Ethiopia.[3] The presence of *Ras* Ali in Wollo further complicated matters and strengthened the fears of the king. Finally, under the threat of excommunication, Sahle Selassie gave in to the pressure and replaced his two appointees, whose main fault had been that they, together with many of the Showan clergy, had not been ready to accept the theory adopted by Gondar that the human soul has knowledge, fasts, and worships in the womb.[4] However, the king's submission did not end the controversy.

---

[1] The financial and administrative chief of each monastery had the title of *Alaka* and was not necessarily a clergyman.

[2] See above, p. 40; see above p. 41.

[3] L.G., 159, No. 1486B, Krapf, 5.12.1840; Ibid., 17.12.1840.

[4] Ibid., F.O., 78/468, Krapf, 20.4.1841; L.G., 190, No. 2060A, para. 43, Harris, 14.10.1841; Ibid., No. 2060B, para. 7, Harris, 29.10.1841; Ibid., No. 2060F, Harris, 31.12.1841; Harris, Vol. III, pp. 190–1; Isenberg, p. 273; CA/5/016, Krapf Letters, No. 1, Ankober, 11.12.1841.

The dismissed heads of the Showan Church and of the monastery of Debra Libanos had widespread support among the clergy of Menz, Marra Biete and other provinces of Showa who not only rejected the new theory of Gondar but had never accepted the *Sost Lidet*. The situation became so dangerous that Sahle Selassie's position was threatened and he anxiously awaited the arrival of the firearms promised by the British through the missionary, Krapf, and of those he had commissioned Rochet d'Héricourt to acquire for him in France. He went to the extreme of banishing from the country all the clergy who were not ready to accept the new theory of Gondar, including the head of the church of Menz, a close friend of his mother. And in the hope of bringing an end to the dissension and controversy, it was proclaimed that whoever else would not accept the *Sost Lidet* in its Gondarine interpretation would also be banished from the country and his property confiscated. Just at this point, when Sahle Selassie hoped that peace and quiet would return to his country, the new *Abuna* (Salama) arrived in Gondar. The *Abuna*, being a staunch supporter of the *Wold Qib* and a strong opponent of the *Ichege* and his party, threatened Sahle Selassie with excommunication unless the banished clergy were reinstated. Sahle Selassie, who was caught between the different ecclesiastical parties, did his best to appease the haughty *Abuna*, though not to the extent of denouncing the *Sost Lidet*.[1] After the failure of the numerous embassies sent to negotiate with the *Abuna*, and after an edict of excommunication had been pronounced against him by the *Abuna* at the end of 1845, Sahle Selassie sent Ali presents and applied for his intervention. *Ras* Ali tried all means of conciliation but, as he did not succeed, he was finally forced to arrest the *Abuna* in 1846 and banish him from Gondar. By this time Sahle Selassie was very sick and could not enjoy the relative tranquillity which returned to his country.[2]

In the 1830's and early 1840's, when the first Europeans since the Portuguese period entered Showa by way of northern Ethio-

[1] Of the strong attachment of Sahle Selassie to the monks of Debra Libanos, see lament at his death: Guebre Sellassie, Vol. I, p. 77.

[2] See above, pp. 125–6. See also: Harris, Vol. III, p. 191; Isenberg, p. 273; Tubiana, p. 68; F.O., 78/511, Harris, 5.1.1842, para. 19; L.G., 193, No. 2919, Harris, 10.6.1842, paras. 1, 2, 37; F.O., 78/551, Beke, 9.12.1843; Lefebvre, Vol. II, pp. 168, 185; L.F.A., Vol. 28, p. 245, Cruttenden, 31.10.1844; Ibid., Vol. 29, p. 28, Lt. Aden, 17.12.1846.

pia, they were amazed at the contrast between this region and the country they had traversed before. The northern provinces had been completely ravaged by war, were depopulated and extremely poor, and had no law and order to speak of. Their rulers cared little for the welfare of their subjects, and the latter in most cases disliked their masters. Once the travellers reached the borders of Showa, they were confronted with a highly centralized administration which had succeeded in establishing law and order. The Showan countryside through which the traveller passed was dotted with relatively prosperous villages surrounded by cultivated fields of cotton and many varieties of cereals. Alongside them could be seen herds of cattle, sheep and goats grazing and attended in most cases by children.[1] Showans were on the whole happy with their lot and although they feared the iron hand of their government, they still loved their ruler and admired him for his wisdom, benevolence, and justice.[2] The king, for his part, felt a patriarchal responsibility for his subjects. In time of famine he opened the royal granaries to the population. When a plague carried off most of the work-animals of the farmers, he distributed oxen and mules. He kept enormous stores of salt so that his people would not lack this important commodity should the roads to the coast be cut.[3] Hosts of royal pensioners, clergy, veterans, visitors and needy of different sorts were supplied with a daily ration of foodstuffs (the *dirgo* system) from the royal stores in proportion to their position or rank, and on every holiday (Ethiopia does not lack holidays) enormous quantities of meat, cereals and mead were distributed among the poor.[4] New areas were opened by the king for cultivation and bridges were built where torrential rivers had in the past taken

[1] Harris, Vol. III, pp. 27, 213; Johnston, Vol. I, p. 488; Lefebvre, Vol. II, pp. 191–3, 197–9. None could enter or leave the country without the permission of the king. See also: F.O., 78/451, Krapf, 21.6.1841; Isenberg, p. 106; J.R.G.S., Vol. 10, pp. 469, 472, 475; Harris, Vol. II, p. 259; Krapf, p. 42.
[2] Harris, Vol. I, p. 400; Ibid., Vol. II, p. 317; Ibid., Vol. III, p. 241; L.G., 185, No 1440, 20.3.1842; C. & C., Massawa, Degoutin, 13.1.1843; L.G., 175, No. 3970, para. 12, Harris, 8.10.1841; Johnston, Vol. II, p. 185. See also lament after death of Sahle Selassie: Guebre Sellassie, Vol. I, p. 77.
[3] Johnston, Vol. II, pp. 158–9; Cecchi, Vol. I, p. 245; Harris, Vol. III, pp. 21, 25, 33, 343; Guebre Sellassie, Vol. I, pp. 70–1; *Douze ans*, pp. 173–6.
[4] Harris, Vol. II, pp. 61, 245; Ibid., Vol. III, p. 25; Rochet, *Voyage*, p. 286; Beke, *Commerce*, p. 18. See also lament after death of Sahle Selassie: Guebre Sellassie, Vol. I, p. 77.

their toll of the population. The ruler was the patron of industry and crafts, and took a personal interest in the development of foreign trade.[1] All in all, Showa can be considered, in a way, an archaic example of a welfare state.

By the beginning of the 1840's the kingdom of Showa had greatly expanded its size. It resembled a rectangle of about 125 miles (east to west) by 220 miles (north to south) and had a population which was estimated to be between one million and two-and-a-half million people. In the north its boundary reached into the Wollo Galla country, then went nearly as far as the river Bashilo and its confluence with the Abbay, then for a short distance southward along the Abbay and then along the extreme western borders of Marra Biete and Showa Meda. In the south-west it reached the furthest sources of the Awash and in the south it reached the Soddo and Gurage. In the south-east it extended to include the Karayu beyond the river Kasem. In the east Showa touched on the deserts of the Afars and in the north-east it touched on Wollo-Argobba beyond Geddem and Anziokia.[2]

The vast area of Showa was made up of three major blocks: Yifat included the province of Menjar, Fatigar and Bulga in the south, Argobba in the centre, and Geddem and Efrata in the north; parallel to the mountain range of Yifat was the Showa block proper, starting in the Wollo country beyond the river Wonchit and going southwards to include the provinces of Geshe, Menz, Marra Biete, Tegulet, Moret and Showa Meda; the third block comprised newly conquered Galla territories to the south and south-west of Showa, including vast areas as far as the Abbay, both sides of the river Jamma, the sources of the Awash, the Abitchu, the Soddo and a number of other Galla tribes as far as the borders of Gurage.

Most of Yifat had already been conquered by the first rulers

---

[1] L.G., 175, No. 3967, para. 13, 11.9.1841; L.G., 193, No. 2919, para. 26, Harris, 10.6.1842; Combes and Tamisier, Vol. II, pp. 347–9; Ibid., Vol. III, pp. 8–9; Harris, Vol. II, pp. 363–4; Krapf, J.R.G.S., Vol. 10, p. 470; Krapf, pp. 23, 62.

[2] Krapf, p. 35; Rochet, *Voyage*, pp. 264, 269; Harris, Vol. III, p. 28; M. & D., Vol. 13, pp. 280–1; Combes and Tamisier, Vol. III, p. 19; Cecchi, Vol. I, pp. 182–3, 248; Krapf, J.R.G.S., Vol. 10, p. 249; Abbadie, F.N.A. 21303, p. 350, para. 173; Ibid., p. 365, para. 184; Ibid., p. 383, para. 206; Ibid., 21302, pp. 316–17.

of the new Showan dynasty. By the time of Sahle Selassie the authority of the central government was completely established throughout the provinces which comprised Yifat. As most of the Europeans who visited Showa around 1840 were acquainted mainly with the eastern part of the kingdom, they reported that the kingdom of Showa was an absolute monarchy. However, this was completely untrue of most of the Galla block of Showa, and only partially true of Showa proper where many of the provincial dynasties were still in existence although they had very little authority.

From the end of the eighteenth century the rulers of Yifat, as they were called even in the 1840's, did their utmost to amalgamate the Christian provinces in their kingdom through their ties to the Solomonic line (although matrilineal) and the myth connected with it, through dynastic marriages, intrigues[1] and war. However, whereas the process of integration was well on its way in the 1840's, it was not yet complete. Tegulet, the heart of Showa, was completely subjugated, as was Geshe.[2] Marra Biete was on the way to full integration as well, especially after Sahle Selassie married the daughter of the last ruler (Queen Bezabech). The issue of this marriage, Prince Seife Selassie, was appointed in 1842 governor of the province with the title of *Abegaz*.[3] The rulers of Moret were still causing trouble and were finally dealt with in 1842.[4] However, Menz, the largest of the Showan provinces, could still have been considered semi-autonomous. Even though it recognized the overlordship of the king and paid him minimal tribute, it was not required to send an army to the king's military expeditions. It was ruled by Sahle Selassie's mother who was a descendant of one of the ruling families of the province, and the Menzeans recognized no authority but hers. Moreover, Showa Meda, a vast plain south of Moret and west of the capital Ankober, was under hereditary

[1] F.O., 78/343, pp. 288–9, Isenberg, 1838; 'Sahle Selassee, the king of Shoa who claims, in opposition to the Emperor to be the legitimate sovereign of all Abyssinia is also by descent the only monarch of the line of Judah'— F.O., 78/590, Johnston, 8.8.1840. See also: Coulbeaux, *Histoire*, Vol. II, p. 374; Guebre Sellassie, Vol. I, p. 68; Isenberg, p. 315.
[2] Ibid.
[3] F.O., 78/511, para. 19, Harris, 5.1.1842. *Abegaz* literally means war chief.
[4] Isenberg, pp. 290, 300; Combes and Tamisier, Vol. III, p. 222; Ibid., Vol. II, p. 350.

Galla chiefs whose allegiance to the crown was not yet fully established and who had to be coerced from time to time into sending tribute and armies to the annual expeditions of the king. In 1842 the missionary Krapf, who had spent about two years in Showa and who had travelled extensively in the country, summed up the situation as follows: 'Most probably the judicious monarch only waits for an opportunity of doing away with all hereditary governments in the kingdom.'[1]

In the third block the authority of the kings of Showa and Yifat was less effective than in the Showan block. In a succession of bloody battles, the king of Showa managed to subdue the Gallan, Soddo and Abitchu Galla, especially after the latter applied for his help against the Tuloma; after that he succeeded in exerting some authority over the Tuloma and even over the Borana.[2] To preserve this shadow authority in the Galla areas, three annual expeditions were undertaken by the united armies of Showa and Yifat accompanied by contingents of loyal Galla. The aim of the expeditions was to exact tribute when it was not paid and remind all the Galla tribes in the peripheral areas of Showa that the king of Showa considered himself their master.

By the 1840's the Galla in Showa outnumbered the Amhara, and their fierce cavalry was still unmatched. Had it not been for the greater unity of the Amhara and for the foresight of the Showan rulers, especially Sahle Selassie, who acquired firearms whenever and wherever possible, it is doubtful whether the Galla of Showa could ever have been subjugated. As it was, the disunited Galla tribes were no match for the huge armies which the kings of Showa and Yifat were able to put in the field and which annually grew in proportion to the growth of the Showan kingdom.

In the past the Showan kings had initiated the resettlement of the areas previously taken by the Galla to the south and south-west of Tegulet. But Sahle Selassie was well aware of the limited manpower resources of Christian Amhara Showa compared to the heathen Galla and Muslim masses. Moreover, in Showa

---

[1] Isenberg, p. 300.
[2] Beke, F.O.A., Vol. II, p. 172, 15.12.1841. According to Abbadie (F.N.A. 21302, pp. 316–17) all the Tuloma were governed by a *mislenye* (deputy governor) of Sahle Selassie. See also: Plowden, *Travels*, p. 313; Harris, Vol. II, p. 350; Harris, Vol. III, p. 41; Hotten, *Plowden*, p. 203.

more than anywhere else in Ethiopia, the Galla and Amhara were more readily assimilated from a very early stage. Therefore, though earlier rulers of the house of Showa in many cases simply annihilated the Galla and replaced them with Amhara settlers, Sahle Selassie enthusiastically took up the realistic policy of Wossen Segged of complete tolerance to Islam,[1] and of Amharizing, christianizing, and integrating his Galla subjects within the kingdom. Once a Galla tribe was sincerely ready to accept Sahle Selassie's government, and especially when it gave in to the gentle coercion to circumcize and baptize its people, it received the full benefits of Sahle Selassie's government and was considered equal to any of the Amhara subjects in the kingdom. The process of integration and christianization was accelerated and Showa's borders were slowly expanded southwards and south-westwards by the establishment of fortified Amhara villages (*Katama*), royal enclosures, and churches in the midst of the adjacent Galla territories.

On commencing a new city he causes a long trench to be dug around the place where he means to build, then raises a wall, builds several houses of wood, and appoints a governor, under whose command a number of soldiers are placed. By these means he hopes to secure his frontiers against the inroads of the Gallas. Thus had Angollala itself arisen: new settlers came, a church is built by the king, and in a short time a large village springs up.[2]

Another extremely important tool in the consolidation and integration of Showa during the period of Sahle Selassie was marriage. To strengthen his ties with the Christian governors, the Muslim rulers and above all the Galla chiefs, Sahle Selassie took their daughters and sisters as royal concubines. The king was the only person among the Christian nobility allowed a harem. But his Muslim and pagan concubines were all baptized. The many daughters who were the issue of these unions were given in marriage to Christian governors and to baptized Galla chiefs. Thus, the king not only achieved greater loyalty and

[1] Rochet, *Voyage*, pp. 127, 281; of Muslim *sheikhs* receiving *dirgo* see: Johnston, Vol. II, p. 183. See also: Ibid., pp. 88, 250; Harris, Vol. I, p. 343; L.G., 185, No. 1440, Barker, 7.1.1842.

[2] Krapf diary, J.R.G.S., Vol. 10, pp. 471-2; Isenberg, pp. 242-3, 276, 298; Harris, Vol. II, pp. 225, 303; Rochet, *Second voyage*, p. 239; Combes and Tamisier, Vol. II, p. 344; Soleillet, pp. 133, 233; Gobat, p. 341.

unity, but also promoted the spread of Christianity among the Galla aristocracy.[1] Nevertheless, had it not been for the superiority in firearms, supported by the system of fortified military settlements, the Showan kingdom might have been swept away by Galla coalitions which sprang up from time to time to resist the pressure of the continuous Amhara expeditions.

In the more limited sense of Yifat and most of the Christian provinces of Showa proper, the kingdom of Showa could be called an absolute monarchy. The king had complete power over the life and property of his subjects,[2] and although the administration of the country was organized on a system somewhat similar to feudalism, the nobles and the governor of the realm were completely dependent on the will of the king and did not constitute a serious check on his authority. Even in the provinces where the traditional dynasties continued to rule, nearly all of them were completely dependent on Sahle Selassie, and the succession within the ruling families was determined by the Showan king.[3] Rochet d'Héricourt, who visited Showa twice about 1840, wrote after his second visit that:

L'ancienne organisation féodale de l'Abyssinie s'est conservée par la multiplication des dignités et des titres dans le royaume de Choa, mais c'est tout ce qui en est resté: ces dignités ne sont, en effet, l'expression d'aucune force propre et indépendante; elles tiennent uniquement du bon plaisir royal leurs attributions incertaines. Le roi exerce avec jalousie son autorité absolue.[4]

The only check upon the power of the king came from the Church and to a certain degree from the king's mother. Furthermore, to ensure internal stability in Showa, and conforming with the practice in Ethiopia, all the king's male relatives were kept at the state prison in Gonchu under the care of the *Abegaz* Wallasma, the governor of lower Yifat.[5] In Showa the king was

[1] Ferret and Galinier, Vol. II, p. 334; Harris, Vol. III, p. 17. See also: Lefebvre, Vol. II, pp. 198, 213; Harris, Vol. II, pp. 24, 38–9, 312.

[2] Krapf, pp. 35–6; Rochet, *Second voyage*, pp. 247–8; Harris Slave Report, para. 49; L.G., 189, No. 2060G, para. 11, Harris, 1842; Graham, p. 9; Rochet, *Voyage*, p. 284; Lefebvre, Vol. II, p. 191.

[3] Isenberg, pp. 300, 315, 349; Krapf, p. 91; Johnston, Vol. II, p. 7; Cecchi, Vol. I, p. 521.

[4] Rochet, *Second voyage*, p. 247. See also: Rochet, *Voyage*, p. 279; Combes and Tamisier, Vol. II, pp. 344–5.

[5] Isenberg, p. 87; J.R.G.S., Vol. 10, p. 477; L.G., 204, No. 1172, Harris, 31.10.1842.

the *de facto* head of the Church, especially because the *Abuna* never visited Showa and therefore usually exerted very little influence in this area.[1] The king nevertheless respected the power of the Church over the population and was ready to go to great lengths to get its support. He always took the advice of the chiefs of the clergy, and granted special privileges to the Showan ecclesiastics.[2]

As for the king's mother, she was considered after the king the most powerful person in the country. 'She rules in comparative independence nearly half of Shoa in the name of her son.'[3] She appointed her own governors and she was not required to bring her army in time of war like the other nobles. In some cases she even countermanded the orders of the king and in general she had a strong influence on her son.[4]

The king ruled the country through the intricate organization of his court which constituted something similar to a cabinet. About 1840 his closest and most intimate councillor was the eunuch who had been his childhood companion, and was also the guardian of the royal harem. After him in the king's council came the *Dejaj Agafari*(?), the guardian of the door, who arranged appointments, introduced visitors, was master of ceremonies, and was responsible for the court pages. His most important function, however, was to introduce the heir upon the death of the king.[5] *Ato*[6] Kidane Wold, the king's uncle (by marriage) served in his absence as Viceroy and was usually in charge of the

[1] CA/5/016, Krapf Letters, No. 8, Cairo, 3.10.1842; Harris, Vol. III, pp. 133, 141; Rochet, *Second voyage*, pp. 221–2. See also: Coulbeaux (*Histoire*, Vol. II, p. 375) who claims that having quarrelled with Salama, Sahle Selassie invited a Catholic priest to serve as an *Abuna* in Showa.

[2] L.G., 185, No. 1440, para. 34, 20.3.1842; L.G., 159, No. 1486B, Krapf, 1840; Rochet, *Voyage*, pp. 163, 188, 279–80; Isenberg, p. 382; Harris, Vol. III, pp. 25, 134, 141–2, 215; Ibid., Vol. II, pp. 19, 27, 382. A water mill built by an Albanian visitor by request of the king stood idle because the priesthood pronounced it to be the work of the devil. Harris, Vol. II, p. 43; Rochet, *Second voyage*, p. 223.

[3] Krapf, p. 88. See also: Combes and Tamisier, Vol. II, p. 332; Harris, Vol. III, p. 29; Ibid., Vol. II, p. 342.

[4] Harris, Vol. III, p. 29; Isenberg, p. 295; See also: Harris, Vol. II, pp. 341–2; Ibid., Vol. III, p. 191.

[5] L.G., 175, No. 3970, para. 47, Harris, 8.10.1841; Isenberg, p. 87; J.R.G.S., Vol. 10, p. 477; Harris, Vol. III, p. 13; Ferret and Galinier, Vol. II, pp. 333–4.

[6] Nowadays means 'Mister', but in the time of Sahle Selassie had an honorific meaning, and the governor of a district (*negarit*) was called *Ato* X or *Ato* Y. Cecchi, Vol. I, p. 249.

'department' of security and justice.[1] *Ato* Wolde Hana was responsible for the 'department' of the interior and was mayor of the capital. Under him were all the second-class governors, the *mislenye* (deputy) who were directly responsible to the crown and who served as a constant check on the power of the governors.[2] *Ato* Katama Worq was the treasurer and also the governor of the province of Aliyo Amba;[3] thus he was also the commander of the fusiliers who guarded the king's treasuries and residences in Ankober, Har Amba, Debra Berhan, Qundi, Angolalla and other places, and the commander of the bodyguard. The person most frequently mentioned by the European visitors in Showa was *Ato* Serta Wold, who was in a way minister for foreign affairs, because he was responsible for all foreign visitors and had at his command a few hundred *afroch*— royal messengers carrying the royal insignia. The *afroch* were attached to foreign visitors and accompanied them through the kingdom, but their main duty was to carry the king's messages to the governors of the kingdom and to other rulers in Ethiopia.[4]

In the time of Sahle Selassie the country was divided for administrative purposes into five major units.[5] The heart of the kingdom, including the capital Ankober and most of Tegulet, was administered directly by the crown. The Queen Dowager was responsible for the northern and north-western block. The *Abegaz* Wallasma of Yifat was responsible for the eastern and north-eastern block. *Abegaz* Maretch of the Galla was responsible for the southern and south-western block; but there is no evidence as to who was responsible for the western block. The northern and north-western part of the country had eleven districts (*negarit*), the eastern and north-eastern, thirteen, the southern, ten, and the western, seven. The governors of those districts had the title *Abegaz* or *Ato* and were given a silver

[1] Harris, Vol. II, pp. 38–9; L.G., 175, No. 3970, para. 49, Harris, 8.10.1841.

[2] Harris, Vol. III, p. 212; Ibid., Vol. II, pp. 38–9; L.G., 193, No. 2917, para. 2, 7.4.1841; L.G., 175, No. 3970, para. 48, Harris, 8.10.1841.

[3] Harris, Vol. I, pp. 223–4, 387–8; L.G., 175, No. 3970, paras. 52–3, Harris, 8.10.1841.

[4] Isenberg, pp. 77–8, 85–6, 112, 134; L.G., 175, No. 3970, para. 50, Harris, 8.10.1841; Rochet, *Voyage*, p. 217.

[5] Morié, Vol. II, p. 411; Cecchi, Vol. I, p. 248.

sword as a sign of authority.[1] Each district was subdivided into a number of parishes governed by a *Chiqa Shum*.[2] There were altogether about 400 or 500 parishes in Showa.[3] The *Chiqa Shum* was elected by the population of the parish and appointed at their recommendation by the *mislenye* for a payment of twenty *amoleh*. He had the privilege of having his land cultivated by the people of his parish, and in the first two years of his office he was free from taxation. Through the *Amba Ras* he was responsible for the collection of the taxes in the parish, for the execution of the orders of the government, for the recruitment of *corvée* labour for public works and for the cultivation of the estates of the king and of the able-bodied farmers who had to join their governor's unit.[4] Under the *Chiqa Shum* were a number of *Amba Ras*, the heads of the different hamlets or family groups who made up the parish and who were responsible for the execution of the orders of their superiors.[5] The administrative division of Showa in Sahle Selassie's reign was very similar to that introduced by Asfa Wossen. The only difference being that Showa then had forty-one districts instead of the thirty-nine in Asfa Wossen's days.

Although some of the governorships were hereditary in the families of the old dynasties, most of them were given at the king's pleasure and could be repossessed at his whim. There was still a clear distinction between *Gez* (plural, *Gezoch*), an appointed governor, and *Balabat* (plural, *Balabatoch*), a governor with hereditary rights. There was no security even for the hereditary governors, but the position of the appointed governors was even worse, and they were frequently shifted from one position to another or dismissed for the slightest cause.

These frequent changes are designed to counteract collusion and rebellion. . . . The caprice of the despot frequently hurls the possessor from his high station to the deepest ruin and disgrace.

[1] Cecchi, Vol. I, p. 248; Rochet, *Voyage*, pp. 264–5; Harris, Vol. III, pp. 29–30; Ibid., Vol. I, p. 374.
[2] Literally, governor of the soil.
[3] Rochet, *Second voyage*, p. 246; Harris, Vol. III, pp. 29–30; Isenberg, pp. 90, 280–1.
[4] Isenberg, pp. 290–1; Johnston, Vol. II, p. 43; Ibid., Vol. I, p. 486; Lefebvre, Vol. III, p. 192; Borelli, p. 87; Rochet, *Second voyage*, p. 110.
[5] Isenberg, pp. 280–1.

The appointed governor was not even the master of his own property which on his death reverted to the king, together with his horse and arms.[1] Theoretically the governors appointed by the king were supposed to govern their areas, collect the taxes, dispense the law and lead the population of their district in war. The last was the most important duty of each governor. The military system of Showa, wrote Harris,[2] is

entirely feudal, each governor in the realm is required to furnish his contingent of militia in proportion to his landed tenure—the peasantry being at all times ready for foray, and expected to purvey horse, arms, and provisions, without payment from the state.

For performing their duty the governors received a fief which was cultivated by the population, and were allowed a fixed part of the revenue of their district. However, it seems that the real power lay in the hands of the second-class governors, the *mislenye*,[3] as already mentioned, who were directly responsible to the king. They were responsible for the *corvée* labour which each subject was called upon to supply from time to time, they collected the taxes and they appointed the *Chiqa Shum*. In the absence of the governor, who very often accompanied the king when he moved from one residence to another or on the annual war expeditions, the *mislenye* governed the district in the name of the governor.[4]

The fact was, however, that all of the different classes of governors had only limited authority, and in all matters out of the ordinary they found it prudent to consult with the king. The burden of responsibility in the kingdom was carried mainly by the king, who was the head of the administration, the commander-in-chief of the army and the head of the judicial system.[5]

The ruler took a great interest in the dispensation of justice and, when not on a military expedition, spent a few hours every

---

[1] F.O., 78/511, para. 19, Harris, 5.1.1842. Combes and Tamisier, Vol. II, pp. 344–5. See also: L.G., 189, No. 2034, Harris, 12.12.1841; Harris, Vol. III, p. 30; Guebre Sellassie, Vol. I, p. 82, footnote 2.

[2] Harris, Vol. II, pp. 176–7.

[3] Literally, the one who stands for me.

[4] Isenberg, pp. 280–1; Johnston, Vol. II, p. 43; Rochet, *Voyage*, p. 288; Lefebvre, Vol. II, pp. 198, 214; Harris, Vol. III, p. 212.

[5] Krapf (J.R.G.S., Vol. 10, p. 472) says that even a cup of wine could not be given to a stranger without the permission of the king. Rochet, *Voyage*, p. 285; Isenberg, p. 62.

day listening to the debates of the court of appeals, and even interfered in the procedure.[1] But at the lower level it was the governor, or even the *Chiqa Shum*, who dispensed justice in each area according to the importance of the case. The king insisted that the population should follow strictly the law of the country, but he also punished any governor who was found to be unjust or corrupt. Moreover, the population of Showa was further protected from injustice by the right of appeal to a special court of *Womberoch* (the chairs of the kingdom), which was under the direct supervision of the king,[2] and the subject who felt dissatisfied with the decision of the *Womberoch* could still appeal over its head to the king himself.

Although in Showa, as was the case theoretically, at least, in the rest of Ethiopia, the courts relied on the *Fetha Negest*, the Ethiopian code of law, much discretion was left to the judges. In the period of Asfa Wossen and Wossen Segged the *Fetha Negest* and the customary law were closely followed and justice, if it could be called that, was extremely cruel. Death sentences, severance of limbs and branding with hot iron were very common. However, in the period of Sahle Selassie the penal code, especially the customary one, was completely reformed. 'Blood flowing from the veins of a subject found no pleasure in the eyes of the ruler.'[3] Death sentences were passed only in extreme cases of high treason, sacrilege and murder. Even then the death sentences had to be confirmed by the king. Whenever possible, the sentence of death was reduced to life imprisonment and confiscation of property.[4] In the case of proved murder the king was forced by tradition to hand the murderer over to the relations of the victim, but the king usually tried to convince the victim's family to accept blood money instead of killing the culprit.

Corruption within the administration and theft, which had been punished in most cases in the past by severance or branding, were punished during the reign of Sahle Selassie by hard labour in difficult areas and under unpleasant conditions.

[1] Isenberg, p. 62; Rochet, *Second voyage*, p. 251; Harris, Vol. II, pp. 92–3; F.O., 78/508, para. 45, Harris, 24.8.1841.
[2] Harris, Vol. III, p. 317. Even sentences by the queen mother could be appealed before the king. Harris, Vol. III, p. 29; Isenberg, p. 295.
[3] Harris, Vol. II, p. 245.
[4] F.O., 78/508, para. 45, Harris, 24.8.1841; Rochet, *Second voyage*, pp. 251–2; Mondon Vidailhet, pp. 16–17.

Debtors and subjects who could not pay their taxes were sentenced to become bondsmen for a period, until their work was judged to have paid their debt or their taxes.[1]

With law and order strictly enforced by the government, and with the rights of the subject at the same time also strictly observed, Showa became an island within the Ethiopian highlands where travelling was safe to individuals and where property was secure. The farmers of Showa prospered and many merchants were drawn to the country. Consequently, the government's revenues continuously increased.

In Showa there was no distinction between the revenues of the State and those of the king. The king derived his income from four main sources: taxation of the land and on crafts, income from his private domains, receipts from the external and internal trade, and tribute or war booty collected from the Galla tribes.

Showa was an agricultural country. Although each farmer had the right to the use of (and the fruit of) his land, the final master of all the land of the kingdom was the ruler: the farmers were taxed with a certain portion of their produce which they had to deliver to the royal granaries or the royal storehouses in each province.[2] The collection of the taxes in each parish was entrusted to the *Chiqa Shum*, and was imposed upon each village according to the number of the inhabitants and to the land allotted to the village. The non-agricultural population (such as weavers, smiths and potters) were also taxed in kind through the heads (*Alaka*) of the different guilds, who were placed under a certain official in the king's court.[3]

The king had enormous estates all over the country, especially in areas conquered in the time of his forefathers. The cultivation of the royal domains was the responsibility of the parishes of the surrounding areas, and for this purpose the *corvée* labour was organized by the *Chiqa Shum*.[4]

---

[1] Harris, Vol. II, pp. 98, 381; F.O., 78/508, para. 45, Harris, 24.8.1841; Johnston, Vol. II, pp. 159, 190.
[2] Rochet, *Voyage*, p. 284; Rochet, *Second voyage*, p. 248; Harris, Vol. III, pp. 222, 286, 343.; L.G, 189, No. 2034, para. 5, Harris, 2.12.1841.
[3] Rochet, *Voyage*, p. 286; L.G., 175, No. 3970, para. 50, Harris, 8.10.1841; Johnston, Vol. II, p. 168; Harris, Vol. II, p. 97.
[4] Rochet, *Voyage*, p. 286; Rochet, *Second voyage*, p. 248; Isenberg, pp. 280–1; Borelli, p. 87.

Every important market in the kingdom was supervised by the local governor, and the lesser markets by one of his retainers. Those officials collected a tax from any person having a 'stall' in the market, and on every sale which took place.[1]

The produce of the royal domain, together with the taxation in kind received from farmers, from the Galla and from the taxation in the markets, was used to feed the king's court, to supply *dirgo* to the thousands of royal pensioners and for division among the needy population on the occasion of the many Ethiopian holidays.[2] The surplus of non-perishable agricultural produce was stored in the royal storehouses, and used in years of famine.

An important source of foreign-made goods and cash for the kingdom of Showa was the taxation on the import and export trade of the country. The merchants employed in this branch of the trade not only paid customs duties of 10 per cent on all imports and exports including specie, but were also taxed the usual tax in the markets of Showa when they tried to sell the merchandise which was not included in royal monopolies. However, the foreign trade of Showa was mainly a transit trade, because many royal monopolies prevented the population either from acquiring foreign-made fineries or from owning or selling luxury goods such as gold, ivory and musk.[3]

The strict monopolies, the traditional contempt for trade as a profession, the abhorrence of the climate of the coast and the opposition of the bloodthirsty Afar, whose livelihood depended to a great extent on the trade with the highlands, prevented the emergence of a merchant class in Showa. Showan foreign trade depended completely on foreign merchants, northern Ethiopians, Hararis and the Afar.[4]

The foreign merchants were not only a source of revenue; they also provided Sahle Selassie with an outlet for the luxury products which accumulated in his treasury, and supplied him with foreign-made produce and firearms. The northern routes

[1] Johnston, Vol. II, pp. 229–31; Soleillet, p. 97; Lefebvre, Vol. II, p. 198.
[2] Isenberg, p. 77; Beke, *Commerce*, p. 6.
[3] L.G., 184, No. 1099, Harris note, March, 1842; L.G., 189, No. 2060G, Harris, 5.1.1842; L.G., 206, No. 1600, para. 13, Graham, 8.5.1843.
[4] Beke, F.O.A., Vol. I, p. 205; Combes and Tamisier, Vol. IV, p. 102; L.G., 189, No. 2060G, para. 12, Harris, 5.1.1842; M. & D., Vol. 13, Rochet d'Héricourt, p. 230.

being dependent on rulers who in many cases were enemies or potential enemies of Showa, the king took a personal interest in the development and preservation of Showa's outlet to the sea.[1] In preference to his own subjects, foreign merchants were accorded many privileges by Sahle Selassie and they were not bound by the monopolies imposed upon the Showans. Grievances of the merchants against Showans were summarily dealt with, usually to the disadvantage of the Showans. The taxation of foreign merchandise was relatively light, and the tariffs were fixed. Special villages were assigned to different merchant groups while they stayed in Showa, and their representatives were granted a position similar to that of a consul. The foreign merchant communities were given internal autonomy and once a year an audience was granted to the whole foreign merchant community of Showa.[2] With such privileges, with security unknown elsewhere and with more and more of the produce of the interior reaching Showa, many foreign merchants were attracted to the country and consequently the Showan treasury further benefited.

About 1840 the total annual revenue of Sahle Selassie in cash alone was estimated to be between 80,000 and 300,000 thalers.[3] As the revenue of the ruler far surpassed his expenditure, the king's treasuries were bulging with thalers, ivory, gold, musk, cloth and agricultural produce. The provincial treasuries, after the yearly accounting and after deducting local expenditures and salaries, transferred all the surpluses to the central treasuries in some of the royal enclosures such as Doqaqit, Har Amba and Ankober.[4] Many legends circulated in Showa about caves in certain mountains which served to store the king's treasuries. Rochet d'Héricourt claimed that he actually saw such a treasury in a cave near Ankober. He claimed that 300 jars in two rows lined both sides of the cave. Each jar contained blocks of silver

---

[1] Of Showan representatives in Mokha, Zeila and Gondar, see: C.M.R., Vol. 1839, p. 68, Krapf, 28.5.1837; J.R.G.S., Vol. 10, Krapf, pp. 466–7, 473; Combes and Tamisier, Vol. II, p. 351; Ibid., Vol. IV, p. 102.

[2] L.G., 189, No. 2060G, para. 34, Harris, 5.1.1842; Harris, Vol. III, pp. 339–41.

[3] Harris, Vol. III, p. 28; Rochet, *Voyage*, p. 286; Rochet, *Second voyage*, p. 247; M. & D., Vol. 13, Rochet d'Héricourt, p. 286.

[4] Johnston, Vol. II, p. 250; Harris, Vol. II, pp. 359–60; Lefebvre, Vol. II p. 206.

valued at 6,000 thalers. Silver in coin was stored in leather sacks, hanging from a beam.[1] Although Rochet d'Héricourt's story seems to be a fantasy there is little doubt that, as a result of security and prosperity of the population, the continuous flow of booty from the raids against the Galla and the development of trade, the treasuries of Showa continued to grow throughout the second quarter of the nineteenth century.

The king led all military expeditions against the Galla and commanded the army when Showa was threatened by rebellion or by outside enemies. When the king contemplated a military expedition, or when the country was threatened by an enemy, the *Dejaj Agafari* called the people to arms to the sound of the king's *Negarit*. The date and place of assembly were announced but the people were never informed of the target of the approaching expedition. In the case of a major expedition, or when the country was threatened by outside forces, all the able-bodied subjects of the king were commanded to appear at the appointed place with arms and sufficient food for twenty days. The population was warned that whoever failed to comply would be considered an enemy of the king and would forfeit his property for seven years. However, in the case of the less important annual expeditions against the Galla, the people could abstain altogether or indemnify themselves by a payment of eight *amoleh*.[2] Usually most expeditions were short and were planned to fall during seasons when agricultural work was slack. The officers of the different units were the various ranking governors, and the peasants eagerly joined the armies of their governors in the expectation of a good fight and of loot. Thus even for his lesser expeditions the Showan ruler was able to collect armies of about 15,000 to 20,000 volunteers, while for his more important expeditions at least 30,000 to 40,000 could be mustered.[3]

The Showan army consisted mainly of cavalry, as only the poorest did not own a horse.[4] The army was usually divided into three divisions. The first was made up of the Galla of the south

[1] Rochet, *Voyage*, p. 287; M. & D., Vol. 13, Rochet d'Héricourt, p. 286.
[2] Harris, Vol. II, p. 153; L.G., 190, No. 2060G, para. 36, Harris, 14.10.1841; Harris, Vol. III, p. 170.
[3] Rochet, *Voyage*, pp. 285–6; L.G., 175, No. 3970, para. 18, Harris, 8.10.1841.
[4] L.G., 175, No. 3970, para. 18, Harris, 8.10.1841; Rochet, *Voyage*, pp. 385–6; Combes and Tamisier, Vol. III, p. 5.

and south-west who were under their respective chiefs. The Galla cavalry and the armies of the provinces of the south, mainly Bulga and Menjar, were put under the command of *Abegaz* Maretch, the chief of all the Showan Galla.[1] The central division was commanded by the king himself. This division was composed of the royal bodyguard, the royal household, and the armies of Tegulet, Showa Meda, Moret and Marra Biete. The third division was made up of the seven provinces of the north and the command of this division rotated among the respective governors of these provinces.[2]

The only standing army in Showa was the king's bodyguard. It consisted of a few hundred cavalrymen and about 500 matchlockmen who could be distinguished by the white feather they wore, the insignia of the royal fusiliers. Nearly all the matchlockmen were the king's bondmen or ex-slaves who had proved their loyalty and usefulness to him in the past. These soldiers were favoured by the king, were the only ones to receive a small salary, were given special privileges and land and were sometimes even appointed to distinguished positions.[3] Even then the king was not completely free of suspicion of those he entrusted with his precious firearms. After a serious incursion of the Wollo in northern Showa, the handful of Wollo gunmen in the king's service were dismissed. Firearms were issued only to those on duty and even during an expedition the muskets were collected each evening and put under guard.[4]

The first ruler of the dynasty to introduce a few firearms into Showa was Ammehayes, who ruled Showa in the third quarter of the eighteenth century. In succeeding years the handful of firearms smuggled by merchants through the Wollo country or occasionally from the coast became the decisive factor in the battle against the Galla. However, when Sahle Selassie came to power in 1813, the Showan armoury still had only a few score of

---

[1] At least this was so in the late 1830's and early 1840's.
[2] According to Harris, these districts were Geddem, Geshe, Antziokia, Menz, Qawa, Gabriel and Efrata. Harris, Vol. II, p. 319; L.G., 175, No. 3970, paras. 18–22, Harris, 8.10.1841.
[3] Rochet, *Voyage*, p. 283; Harris, Vol. II, pp. 78, 177; Johnston, Vol. II, p. 37.
[4] Harris, Vol. I, p. 371; L.G., 175, No. 3970, para. 22, Harris, 8.10.1841; L.G., 190, No. 2060D, para. 41, Harris, 27.11.1841; L.G., 193, No. 2919, para. 21, Harris, 10.6.1842.

antiquated firearms.[1] But having been convinced of the importance of firearms in achieving his ambitions, Sahle Selassie made
efforts to acquire them, even at great cost, from all possible
sources. By 1840 Sahle Selassie had an arsenal of about 500 firearms of different types, but some were so antiquated that they
required a number of people to load them, set them, aim them
and fire them.[2]

In 1840, having just overcome a series of rebellions, and being
threatened by *Ras* Ali and by a possible civil war in Showa, Sahle
Selassie commissioned the French traveller Rochet d'Héricourt
to acquire a quantity of firearms for him in Europe.[3] Soon afterwards, at the instigation of the missionary Krapf, he applied to
the government of Bombay through its representative, the governor of Aden, for military materials. As a result of these European contacts, the royal armoury was doubled by 1842, boasting
a few small-calibre cannons and 1,000 muskets and matchlocks,
about 500 of which were of comparatively modern make.[4]

Once the arsenal of Sahle Selassie was doubled and modern-
ized, the Showan armies began to penetrate to the south and
south-west deeper than ever before. From 1842 until the death
of Sahle Selassie in 1847,[5] Showan generals led the combined
Amhara and Galla armies of Sahle Selassie even beyond the
Abbay into Borana Galla areas, into Mecha territories nearly as
far as the borders of Enarea, beyond the Soddo areas in the
direction of Botor, and into Gurage and the Sidama lake areas.[6]

Very little is known of the last years of the Showan king other

---

[1] Harris, Vol. III, pp. 7–8; L.G., 193, No. 2917, para. 6, Harris, 7.4.1841;
Combes and Tamisier, Vol. III, p. 24.

[2] L.G., 175, No. 3970, para. 15, Harris, 8.10.1841; F.O., 78/508, para. 39
Harris, 24.8.1841; Harris, Vol. II, pp. 33, 380; Johnston, Vol. II, pp. 399–
400.

[3] See above, pp. 158–9.

[4] Krapf, p. 36; Johnston, Vol. II, pp. 399–400. Isenberg, p. 348; CA/5/013,
Krapf Journals, 30.3.1842, p. 94.

[5] *Nuovi documenti*, p. 394; L.F.A., Vol. 30, p. 143, Cruttenden, 4.4.1848;
L.G., 255, No. 134, Haines, 17.2.1848; Soleillet, pp. 272–3. According to
Cecchi (Vol. I, p. 247) he died in October, 1847.

[6] Harris, Vol. III, pp. 38, 41–2; Lefebvre, Vol. II, p. 235; Rochet, *Second
voyage*, pp. 174–5, 179, 183; Beke, F.O.T.A., Vol. II, p. 140; Abbadie,
F.N.A. 21303, p. 350, para. 173, 1843; Ibid., p. 326, para. 329, Sakka, April,
1846; Ibid., 21302, pp. 316–17; Ibid., p. 112, para. 161; Ibid., p. 141, para.
174; Ibid., p. 350, para. 173; Ibid., 21300, pp. 798–9, according to Ibsa,
April, 1848; L.F.A., Vol. 28, p. 244, Cruttenden, 31.10.1844; Ibid., A letter
from Gordon to Haines, 4.4.1845; Abbadie, *Géographie*, p. 97.

than the fact that he was very sick and tried to abdicate in favour of his son. However, he was prevented from doing so by his closest friends and advisers, who warned him that the result of such an act would be disastrous to the country.[1] Showa's independence from the north was in fact greatly weakened as a result of the Church controversies which had caused disunity and dissatisfaction among the population.[2]

Sahle Selassie had two sons by his legal wife Bezabech, the elder, Beshowarad, better known by his Christian name Haile Melekot, and the younger, Seife Selassie. Although Haile Melekot was the heir-apparent there is little doubt that Seife Selassie was the favourite of his father, and by 1835 it was already rumoured that Sahle Selassie intended to leave the kingdom to his younger son. On one occasion the king, referring to Seife Selassie, told Harris: 'This is the light of mine eyes, and dearer to me than life itself.'[3] However, Sahle Selassie suffered greatly in the last years of his life and was tortured by remorse for having taken the place of his brother and being instrumental in his death. Therefore, in 1847, feeling that his days were numbered, the king gathered his family, his close friends and the nobility of Showa and announced that Haile Melekot should succeed him. On the occasion of this gathering Seife Selassie was made to swear that he would not rise against his brother on the latter's succession, and was sent to Marra Biete where he was governor. Sahle Selassie still feared that, as was the custom in the past, his death might be followed by a general rebellion of his Galla subjects. He therefore ordered his servants to carry him from Ankober to Angolalla, where he called a meeting of all the Galla chiefs of Showa. He called upon the chiefs to remain loyal to his descendants, and tried to convince them that continuous peace

---

[1] Guebre Sellassie, Vol. I, pp. 71–2; Combes and Tamisier, Vol. II, pp. 347–8; Ibid., Vol. III, p. 31.
[2] See opposition to king's policy in the church controversy in some of the old Christian principalities of Showa. L.G., 190, No. 2060F, Harris, 31.12.1841. The queen dowager was herself opposed to her son's policy as were the clergy of Menz. Harris, Vol. III, p. 191. See also the claim of Coulbeaux (*Histoire*, Vol. II, p. 377) that Sahle Selassie's son was betrayed by the supporters of the *Wold Qib*.
[3] L.G., 193, No. 2919, para. 5, Harris, 10.6.1842. See also: L.G., 193, No. 2919, para. 20, Harris, 10.6.1842; Johnston, Vol. II, p. 295; Combes and Tamisier, Vol. III, p. 31; Harris, Vol. I, p. 357; Ibid., Vol. II, p. 243; Ibid., Vol. III, p. 14; Rochet, *Voyage*, pp. 212, 226; Isenberg, p. 87.

and a strong Showa would be beneficial to all. Later on he was carried to Debra Berhan where a few hours before his death he proclaimed Haile Melekot king of Showa.

Haile Melekot came to power when he was about twenty-two years old. On instruction of his father, and departing from the custom of his forefathers, the death of Sahle Selassie was immediately announced.

> It is we who are dead, but it is we who are alive!
> (The king is dead! Long live the king!)
> Our father had said: he who is with us is with our son.[1]

Sahle Selassie's body was carried ceremoniously to Ankober, and the royal *Negarit*s were beaten continuously before the procession.

The death of Sahle Selassie, despite all the precautions taken by the dead monarch, was a signal for a blood bath which surpassed anything that ever occurred in the annals of Showa. The accession to power of the new king was used by many, who had restrained themselves throughout the long reign of Sahle Selassie, to settle private feuds. The Abitchu Galla rose in rebellion and tried to recapture the areas in Tegulet from which they had been dispossessed. They attacked Ankober, and the capital was saved only because of the firearms accumulated by Sahle Selassie and because of the loyalty of some of the Galla chiefs and a few of the generals of the deceased king. After breaking the onslaught of the Abitchu, Haile Melekot called a meeting of the Galla leaders at Angolalla and convinced them that they stood to gain nothing if they persisted in their rebellion.[2] Although the Tuloma, the Soddo and the Karayu were still in rebellion, Haile Melekot succeeded by the beginning of 1848 in securing most of Showa and even organized an expedition against the Arussi, who had been raiding the south-western provinces of the kingdom even in the time of Sahle Selassie.[3]

While he was being threatened by the Galla, Haile Melekot,

---

[1] Cecchi, Vol. I, p. 247; Guebre Sellassie, Vol. I, pp. 76–7.

[2] L.F.A., Vol. 30, pp. 143–4, Cruttenden, 4.4.1848; L.G., 255, No. 134, Haines, 17.2.1848; Guebre Sellassie, Vol. I, p. 77, footnote 3; Ibid., p. 82, footnote 3; Asmye, MS., p. 70.

[3] The expedition failed. See: Cecchi, Vol. I, p. 248; L.G., 255, No. 134, Haines, 17.2.1848; Coulbeaux, *Histoire*, Vol. II, p. 376; Harris, Vol. II, p. 374; Ibid., Vol. III, pp. 253, 258; Abbadie, F.N.A. 21300, pp. 798–9.

who feared an incursion from the north, tried to ingratiate himself with *Ras* Ali by sending him some of the presents which his father had received from the British. Nevertheless, as *Ras* Ali objected to Haile Melekot taking the title *Negus*, relations with the *Ras* in the first two years of his reign were strained. Finally when he threatened to cut all ties with *Ras* Ali, the latter seems to have acquiesced to Haile Melekot proclaiming himself *Negus* of Showa.[1]

In the first half of 1849, after his relations with *Ras* Ali had improved, Haile Melekot decided to follow his father's tactics and further strengthen his position by opening relations with Europeans. He therefore applied to the British for artisans, arms and financial aid.[2] Unfortunately for Haile Melekot, however, the British were not ready to repeat the expensive and unfruitful experiment of the Harris expedition, and thus very little is known of Haile Melekot's reign.

According to an unconfirmed traditional source, *Ras* Ali and two of his generals escaped to the area of the Tuloma Galla after the battle of Ayshal. When *Ras* Ali learned that the Tuloma chief intended handing him over to Kassa-Teodros, he informed Haile Melekot, probably because he thought the Tuloma were Haile Melekot's tributaries. The Showan ruler, for reasons of his own, decided to save *Ras* Ali. But his authority never approached the absolutism of Sahle Selassie's, and his generals refused to march against the Tuloma as they did not wish to bring down Kassa's wrath on Showa. Notwithstanding the arguments of his chiefs, Haile Melekot marched upon the Tuloma with those nobles who agreed to follow him and defeated their chief. The hands of Kassa's ambassadors, who were found in Darra, were cut off and *Ras* Ali and his generals were released and permitted to depart for Yejju, all of which of course did not improve Haile Melekot's relations with Kassa.[3]

After his coronation at Deresge, Teodros returned to Gondar. Then, declaring his intention to check the progress of Islam and after having burnt a mosque built without permission in the town,[4] he immediately began his advance southwards to the

---

[1] Cecchi, Vol. I, p. 248; L.F.A., Vol. 30, p. 144, Cruttenden, 4.4.1848.
[2] F.O., Confidential Print, 1585, No. 81, Cairo, 2.5.1849.
[3] Mondon Vidailhet, p. 88, footnote 13.
[4] CA/5/016, Krapf Letter, No. 113, 4.3.1855.

Wollo country. The Wollo, more than any other Galla tribe, were deeply hated by the Christian population of northern Ethiopia because of the atrocities they had committed during the past centuries and because of their strong anti-Christian attitude.[1] But no less important was the fact that the Wollo country served as a buffer between northern Ethiopia and Showa, and Teodros's main objective was to subjugate this autonomous realm and reunite it with the rest of the empire. This political objective of Teodros was clearly encouraged by *Abuna* Salama because the Showans still adhered to the *Sost Lidet* despite Teodros's decree that all the Christians of Ethiopia should follow the *Wold Qib*, which the *Abuna* supported.[2] Moreover, *Abuna* Salama had not forgiven the Showan dynasty for what it had done to him in 1845 and 1846.

Realizing the approaching threat, Haile Melekot allied himself with the Wollo rulers, and in order to confront Teodros with a united front he marched with the bulk of the Showan army into the Wollo country. But Haile Melekot, as is clear from the limited available sources, was not made of the same stuff his father was, and could not provide the same inspiring leadership which had made Showa strong in the past. Furthermore, the Showan chiefs were deeply divided over the issue of whether to join hands with Muslims against a Christian ruler, or not. In fact, there was a faction within the Showan nobility that had remained supporters of the *Wold Qib* throughout the reign of Sahle Selassie, and which now that Teodros declared for this doctrine, wanted to submit to the Emperor. It seems that under the pressure of this faction, which also claimed that it would be suicidal to attempt to fight Teodros in territory other than Showan, the Showan army left the Wollo rulers to themselves and retreated southwards.[3]

The huge Christian army of Amhara and Tigre, said to have numbered 50,000 soldiers, fired with religious frenzy which was

[1] 'Whenever they take a Christian district they burn the churches and compel the inhabitants to adopt Muhamedanism.' Krapf Journals, CA/5/013, 22.3.1842, p. 74.
[2] See above, p. 141. See also: Mondon Vidailhet, pp. 10, 13; Rassam, Vol. I, pp. 284–5, 287, according to Plowden's report of June, 1855; Dufton, p. 132; Zeneb, p. 16; CA/5/016, Krapf Journals, 19.4.1855, p. 44.
[3] Coulbeaux, *Histoire*, Vol. II, p. 377; Cecchi, Vol. I, pp. 251–2; Guebre Sellassie, Vol. I, pp. 72–3.

strengthened by the presence of the *Abuna* and inspired by the leadership of Teodros, soon crushed the strong but disunited Wollo principalities. Once the Wollo had been defeated, and after having spent the rainy season in their country, Teodros was ready to advance into northern Showa.

Haile Melekot, abandoned by the armies of the west commanded by his brother Seife Selassie, who was dissatisfied with his indecision, retreated from Wollo to Menz and then to Tegulet. The confused and sick ruler did very little during the time afforded him by the rainy season and left the defence of the Showan border completely to the governors of the northern districts. But the army of the latter was of course no match for that of Teodros.[1] The rulers of Geshe and Geddem were defeated and their soldiers dispersed. The governor of Efrata, who had tried from the start to influence the king to come to terms with the Emperor, went over to Teodros's camp together with other supporters of the *Wold Qib* including Sahle Selassie's mother.[2] Haile Melekot's position was hopeless. He was close to death because of his illness, his cause was abandoned by most of the Showan nobility including his brother Seife, and the Galla took advantage of the disorder, rebelled, and burnt Angolalla. After a few pitiful skirmishes with the army of Teodros, Haile Melekot destroyed his food stores and burnt the capital Ankober so that they would not fall into the hands of the enemy. In November, 1855, after the destruction of Ankober, Haile Melekot died, at the age of only thirty years. The handful of the faithful Showan nobles who still hoped to save Showan independence escaped to the southern provinces (Bulga and Menjar) and took with them Haile Melekot's young son Menelik, the future Emperor of Ethiopia. The final battle for Showa was fought between the Showans and Teodros's general *Ras* Ingeda, in Bulga. The Showans were completely defeated and were forced to bring Menelik to Teodros who was fighting the Abitchu Galla.

For the first time in centuries the Christian kingdom of Ethio-

[1] Guebre Sellassie, Vol. I, p. 83; Cecchi, Vol. I, pp. 250–2; Stern, *Falasha*, p. 76.
[2] Mondon Vidailhet, p. 10; Dufton, p. 133; Coulbeaux, *Histoire*, Vol. II, p. 377; Zeneb, pp. 20–1; Guebre Sellassie, Vol. I, pp. 82–3; Cecchi, Vol. I, pp. 251–2.

pia was again united, and the authority of the King of Kings observed from the northern boundaries of the plateau to Gurage and from the eastern escarpments to Damot. Showa lost its independence and became a province of the Empire under *Meridazmatch* Haile Michael, a son of Sahle Selassie from one of his concubines, who was later replaced by Bezabeh, who had been one of Sahle Selassie's retainers.[1]

[1] Guebre Sellassie, Vol. I, pp. 85–7, 92; Zeneb, pp. 21–2; Coulbeaux, *Histoire*, Vol. II, p. 377; Soleillet, pp. 272–3; Cecchi, Vol. I, pp. 254–6; Dufton, p. 133; Mondon Vidailhet, pp. 13–14; F.O., Confidential Print, 1585, No. 469, Plowden, 22.12.1855; Massaia, *I miei*, Vol. X, p. 190.

Conclusion

The coronation of Teodros and the conquest of Showa are considered by most historians of Ethiopia to be the end of the era of the princes and the beginning of modern Ethiopia. Teodros was not satisfied with the doubtful and much-challenged power of a regent but believed himself to be the prophesied Teodros who would bring an end to the Galla predominance and the threat of Islam, and who would revive the Christian Empire. Therefore he did not hesitate to usurp the throne of the Solomonic dynasty. Once Showa was defeated, Teodros felt that the time had come to do away with the old tribal and regional loyalties and to establish a strong modern central government with a standing national army so that his authority would not have to depend on the whims of provincial rulers. However, in conditions such as existed in Ethiopia in the middle of the nineteenth century, the tasks which Teodros took upon himself were far beyond the capability of one man, even one as gifted as Teodros.

Teodros was not willing to share responsibility with anyone, not even with the Church. Disagreement between himself and the *Abuna* over their respective jurisdictions had started as early as 1855 in the Showan campaign. Relations between the two further deteriorated because of Teodros's suspicion that the *Abuna* and the Coptic patriarch of Alexandria were serving the Egyptian cause. But the final alienation of the Church from the King of Kings resulted from his insistence upon a complete reform of the church administration and fiscal organization. This was mainly the consequence of his need for funds to modernize the country and to maintain a large army which would not live off the land, as was the custom in the past, but which would be fed and paid by the government. Teodros could not hope to obtain the tremendous resources which he needed for the implementation of his many plans from the normal sources of revenue available to the regents during the *Zamana Masafint*. The vast pro-

14

perties of the monastries and churches, accumulated throughout the centuries, presented one solution. A reformed system of land and property taxation, that would be carried out by administrators appointed and paid by the central government and responsible only to it, was another solution. But Teodros under-estimated the opposition which his reforms would incur, and although the crisis in his relations with the Church was tempor-arily postponed by his giving up his extreme demands, there was no avoiding the final break between himself and the Church, after Teodros felt compelled in the 1860's to imprison the *Abuna* and confiscate the property of most churches in Begamder and Amhara.

Teodros's uncompromising attitude towards the old system of government had alienated most of the traditional ruling families in the different regions, which in its turn caused Teodros to try and replace them with his own appointees. The ruling families were not fighting then just for extra privileges and more land as they had done during the *Zamana Masafint*, but for their very existence. The declared enmity of Teodros to Islam and to the Galla also drove a good part of the population to the camp of his enemies. But, above all, the masses of Ethiopian farmers, whose hopes Teodros had revived at first, were gradually becoming estranged from him. This estrangement was a result of his attitude to the Church, the influence of the regional nobility, the growing pressure of taxation and Teodros's failure to feed and keep his huge army, which reverted to the old custom of plundering the farmers.

When Teodros was fighting in Showa in 1855–6 a rebellion had already broken out in Gojjam under the leadership of Tedla Gwalu of the nobility of this province. Soon afterwards, Semien and Wolkait were also in rebellion led by Negussie and Tessema, Wube's grandsons by one of his daughters. In 1857 the Yejju and the Wollo Galla rebelled as well, and in 1858 Teodros was faced with a rebellion in Lasta. Although at first Teodros repeatedly defeated the different rebels, the defeats were not decisive, and while Teodros was occupied with putting down a rebellion in one area, another rebellion would break out else-where. By 1865 most of northern Ethiopia between Dembya and Tigre was in the hands of a rebel called Tiso Gobaze. Lasta and parts of Tigre were in the hands of another Gobaze, the hereditary ruler of the province of Wag (called Wag Shum Gobaze). Tedla Gwalu held most of Gojjam, and Bezabeh, Teodros's appointee in Showa, proclaimed his independence. Other rebels were active in other parts of the country and Teodros's empire consisted in fact only of parts of Begamder, Amhara and Wollo.

Incensed with the European powers' attitude towards him, their lack of response to his call for a 'holy war' against Islam and the seeming disrespect shown to his position as King of Kings of Christian Ethiopia, Teodros imprisoned the European missionaries and consuls in his dominions. Having failed to achieve the release of its consul and other political representatives and missionaries, England reluctantly decided in 1867 upon the Napier Expedition. Teodros's last stronghold, the fortress of Maqdala, was stormed on 10th April, 1868, and Teodros, seeing the remnant of his army defeated by the British, committed suicide. However, the Napier Expedition had only brought the inevitable. Teodros's empire and dreams were collapsing around him even before the Expedition was organized, and when he decided to make his last stand at Maqdala he was accompanied only by a few thousand of his staunchest supporters.

After its conquest by Teodros, Showa sank into relative insignificance for more than a decade. However, great as the achievement of Teodros was, his period was but a corridor to the far wider and more lasting political union brought about by Menelik, Sahle Selassie's grandson. Following the policy formulated by his forefathers, and especially after the death of Teodros in 1868, he reunited and expanded Showa to the south and to the west. Finally, in 1889, on the death of King of Kings Yohannes, when Menelik became King of Kings, he made Showa, which was the geographical centre of the new Empire, its political centre as well. For the first time in centuries the north lost its predominant position in Ethiopian history and politics, a fact lamented until today by the northern Amhara and by the Tigreans.

Today Ethiopia is still facing most of the immense problems confronting Teodros at his coronation at the end of the *Zamana Masafint*. Now, however, Ethiopia has at least an intelligentsia which could carry out the reforms envisaged by Teodros a century ago. The future will show whether this intelligentsia is capable of taking up the challenge and following the ideals of its hero, or whether it will let the disuniting factors, which are as strong as ever, throw Ethiopia into a new '*Zamana Masafint*'.

Bibliography

ARCHIVES

*In this book
abbreviated to*

1. India Office: Bombay Secret Proceedings,
   Range Series   Range
2. India Office: Bombay Secret Proceedings,
   Lantern Gallery   L.G.
3. India Office: Bombay Secret Proceedings,   Harris Slave
   Lantern Gallery, Volume 196, No. 3491,   Report
   Harris Slave Report of 20.7.1842
4. India Office: Factory Records, Egypt and   I.O., F.R.,
   Red Sea   Egypt and Red
                                                   Sea
5. India Office: Home Miscellaneous
6. India Office: Marine Miscellaneous
7. India Office: Political and Secret Records,   L.F.A.
   Letters from Aden
8. Public Record Office: Foreign Office,   F.O.,
   Abyssinia   Abyssinia
9. Public Record Office: Foreign Office, 401.1,   F.O.
   Confidential Print, 'Abyssinian Correspondence 1846–1868'
   — Foreign Office, Confidential Print   F.O.
   No. 1585
10. Archives of Church Missionary Society   CA/5/012
    (London)   CA/5/013
                                                   CA/5/016
11. Ministère des Affaires Étrangères (France):   C. & C.,
    Correspondance Commerciale (et Con-   Massawa
    sulaire), Massouah
12. Ministère des Affaires Étrangères (France):   C. & C.,
    Correspondance Commerciale (et Con-   Jedda
    sulaire), Djeddah
13. Ministère des Affaires Étrangères (France):   C. & C.,
    Correspondance Commerciale (et Con-   Mokha
    sulaire), Mokha
14. Ministère des Affaires Étrangères (France):   M. & D.
    Mémoires et Documents, Afrique
15. Ministère des Affaires Étrangères (France):   Corr. Pol., Égy.,
    Correspondance Politique, Égypte, Massouah, Massouah
    1840–1853

16. Ministère des Affaires Étrangères (France):   Corr. Pol., Égy.,
Correspondance Politique, Égypte,   Alexandrie et le
Alexandrie et le Caire   Caire

17. Ministère de la Marine (France): Dossier
Lefebvre, C.C.7, Ancienne Carton No. 1467

18. Ministère de la France d'Outre-Mer
(France): Océan Indien, Carton 22–117,
1846–1852

19. Ministère de la France d'Outre-Mer
(France): Côte Française des Somalis,
Carton 129/3

20. Ministère des Affaires Étrangères   A.E.B.
(Bruxelles): Dossier 2024
—Dossier 2024II
—AF4

MANUSCRIPTS

1. d'Abbadie, Antoine: Bibliotheque   Abbadie, F.N.A.
Nationale, Paris, d'Abbadie Papers,
Catalogue France Nouvelle Acquisition,
Nos. 21300, 21301, 21302, 21303, 21305,
23851

2. Asmye: *Yegalla Tarik* (History of the Galla),   Asmye
unpublished MS. completed in 1907. Library,
Institute of Ethiopian Studies, Addis Ababa

3. Rochet d'Héricourt: *Troisième voyage en
Abyssinie*, MS. in Mémoires et Documents
(M. & D.), Volume 61, France—Ministère
des Affaires Étrangères

4. Yusuf Ahmed: Arabic MS. included in   Yusuf Ahmed
article (see below)   MS.

BOOKS

1. Abba Tekla Haimanot: *Abouna Yacob*,   Tekla
Paris, 1914, translator and editor, Coulbeaux   Haimanot

2. d'Abbadie, Antoine: *Géographie de l'Éthiopia*   Abbadie,
Paris, 1890   *Géographie*

3. d'Abbadie, Arnauld: *Douze ans dans la*   *Douze ans*
Haute Éthiopie, Paris, 1868

4. Abdul Majid Al-Abadin: *Bayna al-Habasha*   *Bayna*
wa'l-Arab, Cairo (no date)   *al-Habasha*

5. Arnold, T. W.: *The Preaching of Islam*,
London, 1913

6. Beckingham, C. F., and Huntingford, G.   Beckingham
W. B.: *Some Records of Ethiopia 1593–1646*,
London, 1954

Bibliography

7. Beke, Dr C. T.: *Letters on the Commerce and Politics of Abyssinia, etc.*, London, 1852 — Beke, *Commerce*

8. Beke, Dr C. T.: *On the Countries South of Abyssinia*, London, 1843 — Beke, Southern Abyssinia

9. Berlioux, F. E.: *La Traité Orientale*, Paris, 1870.

10. Bernatz, J. M.: *Scenes in Ethiopia*, Munich-London, 1852 — Bernatz

11. Bianchi, G.: *Alla terra dei Galla (1879–1880)* — Bianchi

12. Bieber, F. G.: *Kaffa: Ein alt-Kuschitisches Volkstum Inner-Afrika*, Wien, 1923 — Bieber

13. Blanc, H.: *A Narrative of Captivity in Abyssinia*, London, 1868 — Blanc, *A Narrative*

14. Borelli, J.: *Éthiopie Méridionale*, Paris, 1890 — Borelli

15. Bowring, J.: *Report on Egypt and Candia*, London, 1840 — Bowring

16. Bruce, J.: *Travels to Discover the Source of the Nile in Years 1768, 1769, 1770, 1771, 1772, 1773*, Edinburgh, MDCCXC — Bruce

17. Budge, Sir E. A. Wallis: *A History of Ethiopia, Nubia, and Abyssinia*, London, 1928

18. Budge, Sir E. A. Wallis: *The Egyptian Sudan, etc.*, London, 1907

19. Burckhardt, J. L.: *Travels in Arabia*, London, 1829 — Burckhardt, *Arabia*

20. Burton, R. F.: *First Footsteps in East Africa*, London, 1894 — Burton

21. Cadalvene et Breuvey: *L'Égypte et la Turquie 1829–1836*, Paris, 1836

22. Cattaui, R.: *Le règne de Muhammad Ali*, Paris, 1931

23. Cecchi, E.: *Da Zeila alla frontiere del Caffa*, Rome, 1886–1887 — Cecchi

24. Cerulli, E.: *Documenti arabi per la storia dell'Ethiopia*, Rome, 1931.

25. Cerulli, E.: *Ethiopia Occidentale*, Rome, 1933

26. Chihab ed-Din Ahmed Ben Abd el-Qader (Arab. Faqih): *Futuh al-Habasha—Histoire de la conquête l'Abyssinie*, translated and edited by René Basset, Paris, 1897

27. Combes, E.: *Voyage en Égypte et Nubie, etc.*, Paris, 1846 — Combes, *Égypte*

28. Combes, E., and Tamisier, M.: *Voyage en Abyssinie*, Paris, 1838   Combes and Tamisier

29. Coulbeaux, J. B.: *Histoire politique et religieuse d'Éthiopie*, Paris, 1829   Coulbeaux, Histoire

30. Coulboaux, J. B.: *Un martyr abyssin*, Paris, 1902

31. Cruttenden, C. J.: *Memoir of the Western Edour Tribes*, Bombay, 1848   Cruttenden, Edour

32. Deftera Zeneb: *The Chronicle of King Theodor* (*Yeteodros Tarik*), editor Enno Littmann, Princeton, 1902   Zeneb

33. Deherain, H.: *Le Soudan égyptien sous Mehemed Ali*, Paris, 1898   Deherain, Soudan

34. Dimotheos, R. P.: *Deux ans de séjour en Abyssinie*, Jerusalem, 1871   Dimotheos

35. Douin, G.: *Histoire du règne du Khédiv Ismail*, Cairo, 1936

36. Douin, G.: *La mission du Baron Boislecomte dans l'Égypte et la Syrie en 1833*, Cairo, 1827

37. Duchesne, A.: *Le Consul Blondéel en Abyssinie*, Bruxelles, 1953

38. Dufton, H.: *Narrative of a Journey Through Abyssinia in 1862–1863*, London, 1867   Dufton

39. Ferret, P. V. A., and Galinier, J. G.: *Voyage en Abyssinie*, Paris, 1847   Ferret and Galinier

40. Fusella, L.: *La cronaca dell'Emperatore Theodoro II di Ethiopia*, Rome, 1957 (author unknown)   Fusella

41. Gobat, S.: *Journal of a Three Year's Residence in Abyssinia*, London, 1834   Gobat

42. Guebre Sellassie: *Chronique du règne de Menelik II*, 1930, Ed. Coppet   Guebre Sellassie

43. Haberland, E.: *Untersuchungen zum äthiopischen Konigtum*, Wiesbaden, 1965

44. Halls, J. J.: *The Life and Correspondence of Henry Salt*, London, 1834   Halls, *Salt*

45. Hamont, P. N.: *Égypte sous Mehemet Ali*, Paris, 1843

46. Hanotaux, G. A. U.: *Histoire de la nation égyptienne*, Paris, 1931

47. Harris, W. C.: *The Highlands of Aethiopia*, London, 1844   Harris

48. Her Majesty's Stationery Office: *Routes in Abyssinia*, London, 1867

49. Hoskins, G. A.: *Travels in Ethiopia*, London, 1835

50. Hotten, J. C.: *Abyssinia and its People*, London, 1868   Hotten, *Plowden*

51. Huntingford, G. W. B.: *The Glorious Victories of Amda Seyon*, Oxford, 1965

52. Huntingford, G. W. B.: *The Galla of Ethiopia*, London, 1953

53. Isenberg, C. W., and Krapf, L.: *Journals of the Rev. Messrs. Isenberg and Krapf 1839–42*, London, MDCCCXLIII   Isenberg

54. Johnston, C.: *Travels in Southern Abyssinia*, London, 1844   Johnston

55. Kammerer, A.: *La Mer Rouge, l'Abyssinie et l'Arabie depuis l'antiquité*, Cairo, 1929–52

56. Katte, A. Von: *Reise in Abyssinien in Jahre 1836*, Stuttgart, 1838   Katte

57. Krapf, L.: *Travels and Missionary Labour in East Africa*, London, 1860   Krapf

58. Lefebvre, C. T.: *Voyage en Abyssinie executé pendant les années 1839, 1840, 1841, 1842, 1843*, Paris, 1845–51   Lefebvre

59. Lejean, G.: *Voyage en Abyssinie*, Paris, 1868   Lejean, *Voyage*

60. Lejean, G.: *Theodore II*, Paris, 1865   Lejean, *Theodore*

61. Lepsius, R.: *Letters from Egypt, Ethiopia, and the Peninsula of Sinai*, London, 1853

62. Levin, D.: *Wax and Gold*, Chicago, 1965

63. Lewis, H. S.: *A Galla Monarchy*, Wisconsin, 1965   Lewis, H.

64. Lewis, I. M.: *Peoples of the Horn of Africa*, London, 1955

65. Licata, G. B.: *Assab e i Danachili*, Milan, 1885

66. Low, C. R.: *History of the Indian Navy*, London, 1877

67. Madden, R. R.: *Travels in Turkey, Egypt, Nubia, and Palestine in 1824–1827*, London, 1829

68. Massaia, G.: *I miei trentacinque anni di missione nell Alta Ethiopia*, Rome, 1925   Massaia, *I miei*

69. Massaia, G.: *In Abissinia e fra i Galla*, Florence, 1895   Massaia, *In Abissinia*

70. Matteucci, P.: *In Abissinia viaggio di . . .*, Milan, 1880   Matteucci

71. Mengin, F.: *Histoire sommaire d'Égypte, etc.*, Paris, 1838

72. Mondon Vidailhet: *Chronique de Theodros II, Roi des Rois d'Éthiopie*, Paris (no date) — Mondon Vidailhet

73. Morié, L. J.: *Histoire de l'Éthiopie*, Paris, 1904 — Morié

74. Pankhurst, R.: *An Introduction to the Economic History of Ethiopia*, London, 1961 — Pankhurst, *An Introduction*

75. Parkyns, M.: *Life in Abyssinia*, London, 1953 — Parkyns

76. Paulitschke, P.: *Harar*, Leipzig, 1888 — Paulitschke

77. Paulitschke, P.: *Ethnographie Nordost-Afrikas*, Berlin, 1893

78. Pearce, N.: *Life and Adventures of Nathaniel Pearce*, London, 1831, ed. J. J. Halls — Pearce

79. Plowden, W. C.: *Travels in Abyssinia and the Galla Country*, London, 1868 — Plowden, *Travels*

80. Rassam, H.: *Narrative of the British Mission to Theodore King of Abyssinia*, London, 1869 — Rassam

81. Rochet d'Héricourt: *Voyage sur la côte orientale de la Mer Rouge, dans le pays d'Adel et le royaume de Choa*, Paris, 1841 — Rochet, *Voyage*

82. Rochet d'Héricourt: *Second voyage*, Paris, 1846 — Rochet, *Second voyage*

83. Rubenson, S.: *King of Kings Tewodros of Ethiopia*, Addis Ababa, 1966 — Rubenson

84. Ruppell, E.: *Reise in Abyssinien*, Frankfurt am Main, 1838, 1840 — Ruppell

85. Sabri, M.: *L'Empire Égyptien sous Mohamed Ali*, Paris, 1930 — Sabri, *Mohamed Ali*

86. Sabri, M.: *L'Empire Égyptien sous Ismail*, Paris, 1933 — Sabri, *Ismail*

87. Salt, H.: *A Voyage to Abyssinia, etc., in the Years 1809 and 1810*, London, 1814 — Salt

88. Sammarco, A.: *Il viaggio di Mohammed Ali al Sudan*, Cairo, 1929

89. Soleillet, P.: *Voyages en Éthiopie, 1882–1884*, Rouen, 1886 — Soleillet

90. Stern, H. A.: *The Captive Missionary*, London, 1869 — Stern, *Captive*

91. Stern, H. A.: *Wandering Among the Falashas*, London, 1862 — Stern, *Falashas*

92. Sulivan, G. L.: *Dhow Chasing in Zanzibar Waters and on the Eastern Coast of Arabia*, London, 1873

Bibliography

93. T'arikh Muluk al-Sudan: editor Mekki   T'arikh Muluk
    Shibeika, Khartoum, 1947/1347 A.H.

94. Tekle Tsadiq Makuria: *Ye Itiopia Tarik ke*
    Atse Tewodros Iske Qedamawi Haile Selassie,
    Addis Ababa, 4th ed. 1946 (E.C.)

95. Tremaux, P.: *Égypte et Éthiopie*, Paris, 1861

96. Trimingham, J. S.: *Islam in Ethiopia*,   Trimingham
    London, 1952

97. Ullendorff, E.: *The Ethiopians*,
    London, 1965

98. Umar Tusun: *Al-Jaysh al-Misri al-Barri*
    wa'l Bahri, Cairo, 1946

99. Valentia, J. G.: *Voyages and Travels in*   Valentia
    India, Ceylon, the Red Sea, Abyssinia and
    Egypt in the Years 1802, 1803, 1804, 1805,
    and 1806, London, 1809

100. Waddington, G.: *Journal of a Visit to Some*
    Parts of Ethiopia, London, 1822

101. Weld Blondel, H.: ed., *Royal Chronicles*   *Royal Chronicles*
    of Abyssinia, Cambridge, 1922

102. Wellsted, J. R.: *Travels in Arabia*, London,   Wellsted,
    1838   *Arabia*

103. Werne, F.: *African Wanderings*, London,   Werne,
    1852   *Wanderings*

104. Werne, F.: *Expedition to Discover the*   Werne,
    Sources of the White Nile, London, 1849   *Expedition*

PUBLICATIONS (articles and letters)

1. d'Abbadie, Antoine: *Bulletin de la Société*   Abbadie,
   de Géographie, Paris, Vol. 17, 1859   B.S.D.G.

2. d'Abbadie, Antoine: *Athenaeum*, London   Athenaeum
   Literary and Critical Journal, Nos. 1041
   from 1847, 1042 from 1847, 1078 from 1847
   and 1105 from 1848

3. d'Abbadie, Antoine: *Nouvelles annales de*
   voyage 1845, Vol. III

4. Abir, M.: 'Brokers and Brokerage in
   Ethiopia in the First Half of the Nineteenth
   Century', *Journal of Ethiopian Studies*, Vol.
   III, No. 1, 1965

5. Abir, M.: 'The Emergence and Consolidation of the Monarchies of Enarea and Jimma
   in the First Half of the Nineteenth Century',
   Journal of African History, Vol. VI, No. 2,
   1965

6. Abir, M.: 'The Origins of the Ethiopian-Egyptian Border Problem in the Nineteenth Century', *Journal of African History*, Vol. VIII, No. 3, 1967

7. Amin Sami: *Taqwim al-Nil*, Cairo, 1927

8. des Avanchers, L.: (1860) *Bulletin de la Société de Géographie, Paris*, Vol. 12, 1866   B.S.D.G.

9. Barker, W.: *Journal of the Royal Geographical Society*, Vols. 10 and 12   Barker, J.R.G.S.

10. Basset, R.: 'Études sur l'histoire d'Éthiopie', *Journal Asiatique*, Paris, 1882

11. Beke, Dr. C. T.: *The Friend of Africa*, published by the Society for the Extinction of the Slave Trade, Vol. I, II; 1840, 1842   Beke, F.O.A.

12. Beke, Dr C. T.: *Friend of the African*, published by the Society for the Extinction of the Slave Trade, Vol. I, 1843   Beke, F.O.T.A.

13. Beke, Dr C. T.: *Journal of the Royal Geographical Society*, Vol. 14   Beke, J.R.G.S.

14. Cederquist: 'Islam and Christianity in Abyssinia', *Moslem World*, Vol. II, London, 1912

15. Cerulli, E.: 'Gli Emiri di Harar dal secolo XIII alla conquista egiziana', *Rassegna di studi ethiopici*, Anno 2 (1942), Rome

16. *Church Missionary Records*, publication of Church Missionary Society of England, Vols. 1833, 1835, 1839 and 1841   C.M.R.

17. Cumming, D. C.: 'The History of Kassala and the Province of Taka', *Sudan Notes and Records*, Vol. XX

18. Guidi, I.: 'La Chiesa abissinia', *Oriento Moderno* (Rome), 1922

19. Kielmaier: *The Friend of Africa*, published by the Society for the Extinction of the Slave Trade, Vol. I, November, 1840   F.O.A.

20. Kirk, R.: 'Journey from Tajura to Ankober 1841', *Transactions of the Bombay Geographical Society*, Vol. 4   Kirk

21. Moktar, M.: 'Notes sur le pays de Harar', *Bulletin de la Société Khédiviale du Caire*, 1876, Série II, Vol. I   Moktar

22. Pankhurst, R.: 'Primitive Money in Ethiopia', *Journal de la Société des Africanistes*, 1963   Pankhurst, *Primitive Money*

Bibliography

23. Pankhurst, R.: 'The Maria Theresa Thaler in Pre-War Ethiopia', *Journal of Ethiopian Studies*, Vol. I, No. 1

24. Robinson, E. A.: 'Nimr, the Last King of Shendi', *Sudan Notes and Records*, Vol. VIII

    Robinson, Nimr

25. Robinson, E. A.: 'The Tekruri Sheikhs of Gallabat', *Journal of the African Society*, Vol. XXVI, 1926/7

26. Robinson, E. A.: 'The Egyptian-Abyssinian War of 1874–1876', *Journal of the African Society*, Vol. XXVI, 1926/7

27. Roeykens, R. P. A.: 'Les Préoccupations Missionnaires du Consul Belge Éduard Blondéel', *Bulletin de l'Académie Royale des Sciences Coloniales*, Vol. 1959

    Bulletin de l'Académie

28. Rossini, C.: Nuovi documenti per la storia d'Abissinia nel secolo XIX, *Rendiconti dell'Accademia Nazionale dei Lincei*, 1947, Ser. VIII, Vol. II

    Nuovi documenti

29. Speke, J.: *Blackwood's Magazine*, 1860, Vol. 87

30. Tagher, J.: 'Mohamad Ali et les Anglais', *Cahiers des Histoires Égyptiennes*, Vols. I–II, 1948–9.

31. Tubiana, J.: Deux fragments du tome second de 'Douze ans dans la Haute-*Orientalistyzny*, Tom XXV, Zesztt 2

    Tubiana

32. Yusuf Ahmed: 'An Enquiring Into Some Aspects of the Economy of Harar 1825–75', *Ethnological Society, Bulletin No. 10*, July–December, 1960, University College of Addis Ababa (with Arabic MS. included)

    Yusuf Ahmed

OTHER PUBLICATIONS

1. Annales Maritimes, 1er semester, 1853

Index

Index

203

Index